TEN AFRICAN CARDINALS

TEN AFRICAN CARDINALS

Sally Ninham

Connor Court Publishing

Ballarat

Published in 2013 by Connor Court Publishing Pty Ltd

Copyright © Sally Ninham 2013

ALL RIGHTS RESERVED. This book contains material protected under International and Federal Copyright Laws and Treaties. Any unauthorised reprint or use of this material is prohibited. No part of this book may be reproduced or transmitted in any form or by any means, electronic or mechanical, including photocopying, recording, or by any information storage and retrieval system without express written permission from the publisher.

PO Box 224W
Ballarat VIC 3350
sales@connorcourt.com
www.connorcourt.com

ISBN: 9781922168863 (pbk.)

Cover design by M. Giordano

Printed in Australia

Photography by Billy Peters

CONTENTS

Prologue 1

About the interviews 5

Introduction 9

1 South Africa: Wilfred Fox Cardinal Napier, Archbishop of Durban 31

2 Nigeria: Francis Cardinal Arinze, Prefect Emeritus of the Congregation for Divine Worship and the Discipline of the Sacraments 59

3 Uganda: Cardinal Emmanuel Wamala, Archbishop Emeritus, Kampala 101

4 Mozambique: Alexandre Jose Marion Cardinal Dos Santos, Archbishop Emeritus Maputo and Archbishop Jamie Pedro Gonçalves, Beira 133

5 Guinea: Robert Cardinal Sarah, President of the Pontifical Council *Cor Unum* 165

6 Ghana: Peter Kodwo Appiah Cardinal Turkson, Cape Coast, President of the Pontifical Council for Justice and Peace 179

7 Ivory Coast: Bishop Raymond Ahoua, Bishop of Grand-Bassam and Bernard Cardinal Agré, Archbishop Emeritus Abidjan 211

8 Cameroon: Christian Wiyghan Cardinal Tumi, Archbishop Emeritus Douala 269

9 Congo: Interview with Cardinal Monsengwo by journalist Gerard O'Connell 301

Conclusion.. 313

Appendix

1. "Bishops of Africa", Call for the cessation of the war and the respect of the territorial integrity of the DR Congo... 319
2. Gerard O'Connell with Cardinal Arinze........................ 321
3. Gerard O'Connell with Cardinal Turkson..................... 326
4. Gerard O'Connell with Cardinal Polycarp Pengo of Tanzania... 331

Bibliography... 349

Acknowledgements.. 361

Index... 363

...They brought me to a place of wonders, taught me to pay attention, and set me on a path of exploring the great, shifting terrain between righteousness and what's right...[1]

---

[1] Barbara Kingsolver (1998), *The Poisonwood Bible*, Faber and Faber, London, p. x.

Prologue: In the beginning …

A youngish woman at the end of a PhD qualification submits her thesis. Seven years of work negotiated alongside marriage, the birth of five children, her husband's career, the death of her mother, is to be judged worthy by senior men in her field – colleagues some of whom then take her idea and bid for a quarter of a million dollars to publish it as a book. They win the bid of course, and hire a young researcher to repeat every interview she has completed (a researcher who approaches her and asks for copies of her tapes!) on the basis that they think she won't publish, or that she won't be able to publish with so many children, or that she won't want to put the work in required for publication with such a noose around her neck, or perhaps that she won't be able to find a publisher interested in the climate of publishing as it then is. They move forward with their stellar careers, passing comment on politics in local papers, taking sides in popular debate. Her thesis is eventually passed, printed and bound, put on to the shelf in the university library in the basement where theses are stored. The mother is forgotten. The topic appears to be theirs.

But they underestimate her ability to juggle the impossible. She publishes first, and launches her book to a room full of family and friends, people who don't judge her as a mere housewife with a hobby, as the wife of a successful professional who should have known her place as mother and as wife from the start. (These ideas bite chunks out of her courage and her legs shake when she delivers her speech, but then it is over and the book is officially launched and those friends buy copies for themselves and their friends who write and tell her they like it). And she is ever so grateful, grateful in a way that is hard to explain, grateful because the room was empty of the godless, objective, rational and clear thinking academics who made a mark on her upbringing, her adolescence, her motherhood, and her years as a postgraduate according to a set of well researched norms. Grateful because it is over. There are a few promotional talks to give, and a recording with New York Broadcasting Network "New books in History", and here and there she entertains the idea that she could work overseas. But these are small moments. In the main her wrestle with universities and university libraries becomes a thing of the past and she goes home to her five children, feeling a non-academic, half a mother, a grumpy wife wondering if she will write anything more.

It's hard to be motivated to work in isolation, to fit those ideas in around the needs of a young family (without collegial support, without like-minded conversation!). To justify the time it takes her to think them when her small people need her to focus too. New projects become an indulgence, prioritising them becomes an act of abandonment. The house becomes a prison, an endless beach of mess that flows in and out and that she attacks in great bursts of energy, trying to sweep the shore free of sand. Each day she withdraws with her lap top to a cafe after dropping her children at school or day care (at least it is tidy there), but she becomes depressed by her intellectual isolation and by her incompetence at home. Her sex drive disappears (it seems to have eloped with her confidence), she stops cooking (starts assembling), and she begins arguing with people through the car window at traffic lights. She searches for a compromise, a way to both prioritise her family and to write. She will work in blocks, she thinks; escape the family to focus for a week or two a few times a year, then nothing in between. Her husband's uncle suggests the cardinals. "Of course you will have to go to Africa … a week or two here and there. And there is the issue of funding …" of which there is none, bar her husband's continual support that she feels she can no longer justify. She is unsure how to move forward without compromising the people she loves. Her father offers to mind the children and her husband pays the first fare. All of a sudden Africa becomes a reality.

There is only one problem. She is not Catholic. She was born and raised in a godless world, a 1960s hangover that arrived aching and miserable in Australia after a decade of parties in the States. That world turned its back on religion, called it names (as it left holding hands with that rational rogue-Science). Religion was a non-science, a fiction, a band-aid for mortality and for fear. It indoctrinated, it was a panacea, a sell-out for morons: "If God existed he would be a bastard anyway." There have been no Godly rhythms in her life: no religious education at school, no Sunday Mass, no funerals (no-one she knew besides her mother ever died). She has only attended three weddings after reaching her twenties. One of those was her own. Demonstrations of atheism were fashionable in her teenage years. In her twenties she used them to claim the intellectual upper hand. In her thirties she baptised her children to give them the advantages of belonging to her husband's tribe while still clinging tightly to a world of non-believers – the space where she thinks, has been told, imagines she belongs so that in the end she can offer them balance. And she jumps between identities: earth mother, the barrister's wife, the objective academic until suddenly she finds herself wandering, cast adrift by the non-believers she thought were her people.

So the cardinals are a strange fit, perhaps even a non-fit; a sock on a hand, a glove on a foot. This fact does not go unnoticed, does not go without comment, without question. It is the "why you?" of every conversation. Later she will claim that it is a journey that she wanted to take. She will tell you that she wanted to leap blindfolded and directionless into an unknown. With her protective covers in all the wrong places, Africa was the unknown, she will say, and she embraced it and made it recognisable. But when she says that to you she is either not being honest or she is yet to understand what Africa has been to her. She has yet to understand that Africa rejected her embrace and assaulted her senses, made it clear to all and sundry that she had no right to be there, has not the stamina to survive it, but that Africa opened its arms wide and made room for her to sit down amongst its people, nevertheless. Yes, she wanted to walk into Africa, and she wanted to be found wanting ... and she willed the cardinals to unscrew the lid on the godless vacuum that she had always occupied in the vain hope that in so doing there would be room enough for angels to guide her to her next challenge: the proof of her worth. But at this stage in her story there was really only room enough for herself and her ego and possibly a can of worms. Eventually the peelings of arrogance that will also mount up around her will fill any spaces left over.

A beauty salon, on the way to Bamfoussam, Cameroon

About the interviews …

These conversations have attempted to tap into the personal aspects of very public leadership roles. In the West, the public face of Catholicism carries with it many preconceived ideas and prejudices about the kind of people who sit in its senior ranks. Our eagerness to embrace freedom at the expense of the past makes us quick to decry misogyny or hypocrisy when casting an eye across a church that celebrates traditions drawn from long ago. However, stripping that public face away here reveals a firm grip on reality and an extraordinary ability to use lessons of the past as a map for otherwise uncertain, unguided and unpredictable futures. In short, this is humanity at its best. The political ramifications of certain responses the African cardinals make in climates traditionally and currently politically explosive have not held them back from honest and open discussion of the challenges they face both as leaders of the Church in their country and as individuals. A few who have become embroiled in national political conflict were reticent to put themselves at personal risk by discussing politics. Most were open in their condemnation of existing government practice. A couple drew analogies between themselves and John the Baptist in their willingness to hold their leaders publically accountable for unjust and corrupt behaviour.

Establishing trust and rapport is fundamental to conversations in which private revelations are often made. Without such trust, these conversations would have faltered and fallen flat. A formal half-hour appointment often became an enjoyable hour-long discussion. In some cases it was followed up with on-going correspondence, even an exchange of gifts. It was impossible to remain personally unaffected by these meetings. The personal gravitas of the protagonists involved was very moving and my encounters with Africa were a revelation. The cardinals challenged the very Western concepts of individualism, critical thinking and social democracy that had informed all of my thinking, and made interviewing for the book as much a scholarly challenge as a journey of self-discovery and personal growth. As a result, I have endeavoured to create a work that functions at a number of levels. The book offers the interviews as they were recorded, and it tracks the process of finding the cardinals, speaking to them, and the personal impact that experience had on me. (There was a mismatch between my world view and the world of Africa, as much as there was a mismatch between my supposed atheism and the deeply spiritual world of the cardinals). I have also briefly contextualised the space from which the cardinals come and the space in which they now function (in other words millions of other authors' pages!) into a single introduction. As a result the reader may find that chapter dense in the academic sense but I encourage you to read on.

Most of these men speak multiple languages more or less fluently, and in many cases English is not always their first. In those instances where an interview was recorded in English, it was often necessary to substitute some words for others, because otherwise the transcribed interviews would make little grammatical sense for the reader. Great effort has been made to ensure that the final product is an accurate representation of the original conversation. Permission for publication of the interview as recorded at the time was sought at the beginning of each meeting. Furthermore, while I did not always receive a response from the subject, transcribed interviews were always sent to the subject (or an allocated "reader") for correction or approval, and as proof of my intention to record only the exchange that occurred between us when we met.

The original aim of this work was to include an interview with every African cardinal. A number of obstacles put that achievement out of my reach. As a result, three additional interviews have been included in the Appendix. All three were conducted by Gerard O'Connell, Vatican analyst and correspondent for various Catholic news outlets in the English-speaking world and author of *God's Invisible Hand, The Life and Work of Francis Arinze, an interview with Gerard O'Connell*. Gerard very kindly granted me permission to include them in this book to complement the others I completed myself. With these the book is a more complete compendium of discussions with the living African cardinals of the Roman Catholic Church. It is with regret that I was not in a position to include interviews with Cardinal de Nascimento from Angola, Cardinal Zubier from Sudan, Cardinal Sarr of Senegal, Cardinal Okogie from Nigeria, or Cardinal Njue from Kenya. Though I corresponded with all but two, and had appointments to meet three of them, the interviews fell through at the last moment.

Razor wire, South Africa

Already working

Archbishop Samuel Kleda of Douala who kindly offered to speak with me when it seemed as though I had lost Cardinal Tumi

Introduction

The men in this book are still alive, but have perhaps already earned the right to stand alongside such Western heroes as Martin Luther King, Franklin Roosevelt and Abraham Lincoln. Not all of them are here, but many are. Ordained when words like decolonisation, post-colonisation and independence were becoming part of the Western academic vernacular, they stood at the helm of fledgling nations and steered their flocks through turbulent seas. They are men who have committed their lives to justice, to freedom and to humanity without pausing for breath. They are not perfect, they are human. Like the rest of us, ambition, hubris, naivety and bad choices have pulled at their personalities and their careers, and continue to do so as responsibilities make demands on them well into old age.

In this book I describe them as I see them. I am a Westerner, a non-Catholic, a woman and a mother. I tried to look at them sometimes without those labels intact … sometimes with them … At times it was difficult. I have tried to look at them the way that I would see the men in my own life – to take notice of their passions, their frustrations, their masculinity, their strengths and particularly their patience. Above all I have tried not to pander to them as "Princes of the Church". Almost every one of them frightened me, some were kind to me, some were wary of me and what I might do with what they said. In each case I left feeling deeply impressed, hoping to honour the trust they placed in me by allowing me to record our conversations in this book.

Africa is complicated and difficult: a vibrant continent; a vastly diverse array of tribal territories and resource potentials; an endless reserve of material wealth and human trafficking that was pounced upon and exploited from the early 16th century with the arrival of the

Portuguese; a continent then divided across traditional boundaries into "nation-states" by European conquest in the 1800s, and returned to its original owners by the 1960s – in pieces. The march towards functioning societies over the last 50 years has been complicated for many of these new countries. Most replaced white supremacy with black tyranny within the first fifteen years and doomed their peoples to a new kind of misery. Climbing out of that past has been complicated by the tendency amongst some Africans to ascribe blame to exogenous (Western) factors, and a Western tendency to misunderstand, obscure or misrepresent what we see. Our understanding of Africa is laden with "myths, prejudices, exaggerated claims, suspicions, and misconceptions about Africans whom [so many of us] seek to help and yet are so little understood".[1] Both viewpoints, while not helpful, are understandable. Individual African loyalties can be problematical: national, religious, cultural and ethnic sensitivities intermingle and collide across what are easily simplified into obvious polarities: communist/democratic, capitalist/socialist, Christian/Muslim. Ethnic complexities have spurred wars waged across national boundaries and religious identities at the same time. Ethnic-religious loyalties or a combination of the two have often trumped political vision in contests for national leadership. Many honest men and women have died attempting to unite disparate peoples with democratic ideals that make little or no sense within certain cultural contexts. And on-going international greed has infected other leaders with an addiction to power that is encouraged by foreign investment and political intrusion. Potential wealth has disappeared into the pockets of foreigners and of demagogues who flaunted the authority of their traditional leaders once they had power, and left poverty, disease and chaos in their wake.[2]

Our ability to recognise religious leaders as part of the African solution is restricted by the Western ascendency of scientific over

---

1 George B. N, Ayittey (1992), *Africa Betrayed*, St Martin's Press, New York, p. 17.
2 Ibid.

religious beliefs. Historically, Christianity has been painted onto the African canvas as part and parcel of conquest: the first Europeans opened the doors to Africa and early missionaries marched in on their tails, eager to serve in Africa's conversion from the 16th century onwards. Many people outside the continent still view Christianised Africa within the context of those early attempts, a context that pitches "the African native" as "victim" of a relentless series of social, political, and religious impositions spanning the second millennium, impositions that peaked with the frenetic scramble for trading opportunities characterising European behaviours in Africa from the turn of the 17th century.[3]

Certainly there were early and successful attempts at evangelisation that ran alongside foreign conquests. The Congregation of Propaganda Fide, which originated in the second half of the 16th century and was officially founded in 1622, planned a renewed strategy for the evangelisation of the non-Western world in the 1620s, which resulted in the conversion of a number of kings and queens across the continent (Congo, Zimbabwe, Ethiopia, Wairi, Mobasa).[4] All were eager to serve in the conversion of Africa more broadly (with the support of Jesuits and Capuchins) and through that conversion to gain from an

---

3 Pakenham, T. (1991) *The Scramble for Africa*. Abacus, Great Britain.

4 King Pedro of the Congo people in 1620 requested that Jesuit missionaries be sent to him in Luanda after he had been beaten in a war with the Portuguese governor of Angola, João Correia de Sousa. De Sousa, who had invited the Jagas ("a nation of gluttonous cannibals") to be his allies, subsequently allowed them to feed on the Congolese people. Believing that God was willing to punish the kingdom for its crimes, King Pedro convinced himself that only people of the Society of Jesus could placate God for his kingdom. See the chronicle of *Antonio Franco*, translated from Latin and made available on line by John Thornton and Linda Heywood, (http://www.bu.edu/afam/faculty/john-thornton/franco-synopsis/). Queen Njinga of Matamba also converted to Christianity, possibly to strengthen a peace treaty she had recorded with the Portuguese. Upon her death the Portuguese extended their influence into the West African interior and the slave trade expanded. Linda Heywood and John K. Thornton (2007), *Central Africans, Atlantic Creoles, and the Making of the Americas, 1580-1660*, Cambridge.

alliance with the foreign and Christian powers driving cross-Atlantic trade.[5] But the emphatically colonial nature of the religion limited its on-going success. Evangelisation was combined with the slave trade. Converts were baptised en masse on shore before being loaded onto ships bound for sugar plantations in Brazil, "… slaves to the higher God of commodity agriculture".[6] In the 1650s, for example, Luanda (in Angola) was the principal point of embarkation for the Atlantic slave trade (Brazil could never have enough),[7] and the Church of Luanda had the main job of baptising them before they left for other destinations. The trade caused profound social and political dislocation for native Africans, and as both the trade's accomplice and foreigner the Church had no right to claim the moral upper hand. Certainly it was granted very little by tribal kings. Furthermore, and apart from an acute lack of qualified priests on the continent (Portugal was at war with Spain and Rome had sided with the latter), canon law and missionary practices were too rigid for African society. The Church lacked obvious cultural relevance in a space where multiple marriages and multiple children were central to identity and social status; indeed, life circumstances, cultural concerns and a lack of priestly training all mitigated against celibacy.

With time, the Church would develop a fierce and home-grown vitality. It would answer the call for local relevance by printing more books in local vernaculars and by creating a body of often married and local catechists with the power to preach and to baptise. It fired up a continental conversion that was fuelled by African

---

5 Early links between conversion as a path towards economic and military alliances are discussed by Heyward and Thornton in terms of Portugal and Kongo in the 16th century (1518-1600). *Central Africans, Atlantic Creoles, and the Foundation of America*, Cambridge University Press, New York, 2007, pp. 79-80.
6 Kingsolver, Op. Cit., p. 590.
7 Forty per cent of slaves crossing the Atlantic came from Angola-Kongo. Pakenham, Op. Cit. Heyward and Thornton estimate the number at more than double (90%). Heyward, Op. Cit., p. 41.

aspirations for modernity and self-empowerment, and access to European education methods and training at mission schools. Pope Gregory XVI's attack on the slave trade in the 1830s pre-empted a "revolutionary" bent to Catholic missionary work, and the documents of the Second Vatican Council, a hundred years later, would begin to officially pass "ownership" of the Church to its people. But as missionary enthusiasm cooled in Europe at the turn of the 18th century, Africa's first conversion flickered and died. Catholicism became "depressingly lifeless". An archaic and profoundly oppressive co-conspirator in European conquest, it lacked the widely recognised relevance or practical significance necessary for the spiritual, social, or political advancement of the average African whom it would later embrace. Indeed, mission work effectively came to an end and was not reintroduced until the late 19th century. By then, Africa's Christian transformation was fuelled by a very different kind of energy from the one that first drove empires to its shores.[8]

Pope Gregory XVI's encyclical against the Atlantic slave trade (*In Supremo Apostolatus* – 1839*)* foreshadowed a change in Catholic missionary work and the Catholic Church more broadly in Africa that was to continue through the adventures of Livingstone and into the colonial era of the late 1800s, before it was crystallised in the teaching of Vatican II in the 1960s. Gradually, Catholicism (alongside other Christian denominations) became equated with unification, healing and spiritual freedom in Africa.[9] Gifted missionaries like Henri Streicher (in Uganda 1915-1933), Jan van Sambeek (in Tanzania

---

8 Adrian Hastings (1994), *The Church in Africa 1450-1950,* Clarendon Press Oxford, pp.404-405.

9 That was not, perhaps a revolution sought by the Vatican (says Hastings), which continued to favour a model of domestication and subsidisation of Catholic missions by national states such as in West French Africa and Portuguese protectorates. But alongside domestic politics in places like France (the Waldeck-Rousseau government which let loose a new anticlerical campaign in 1899, for example) missionaries were freed to secure closer ties with local Africans (Ibid., pp. 431-433).

between1911-1957) and Pierre Meraud (on the Ivory Coast and still alive in 1945[10]) were able to present the universality of the Christian message in local languages.[11] They made the gospels and the Bible attractive as written expressions of oral traditions that had debated the human condition for millennia. Their work cut across preoccupations with skin colour, racist social theories, and political and economic experiments that were dominating Western conduct at the time (and into the future), and they escaped the censures of Vatican orthodoxy if only through geographical isolation: "... missionaries, with few exceptions, accepted a colonial take-over as both inevitable and desirable, but they wanted it in large part precisely to protect Africans from other aliens – Arab slave traders, Boers, the Portuguese, Cecil Rhodes."[12]

This is not to say that the efforts of the missionaries were (or are) universally applauded. There is a significant body of work pointing out the failings of European missionaries. A number of authors express their misgivings about the links between the mainstream Christian religions and European colonisation, citing a preoccupation with racist ideologies and a paternalistic approach amongst European missionaries to Africans, African intelligence and African culture. It

---

10 See (http://sthweb.bu.edu/stories/cotedivoire/ouandete_louis-marie.html)
11 Generally speaking, this was not a "new" phenomenon. Unlike other missionaries who went to African nations in the 19th century, the Congolese Catholic Church began in the 1600s. Thornton, through his translation of Roboredo's sermon in Kikongo, notes that Bonaventura da Sardegna (or da Nuoro) together with the assistance of Spanish Capuchins (José de Pernambuco and Francisco de Veas) and Roboredo – who was a member of Kongo's spiritual, intellectual, and social elite, and spoke both Latin and Portuguese – had actually compiled a Latin-Spanish-Kikongo Dictionary for missionary use before 1650. Furthermore, a publication of the Kikongo catechism had already been arranged when the Carmelites planned a mission to Kongo in 1556. It was probably the work Cornelio Gomes, Thornton says, a bilingual priest born in Kongo of Portuguese parents, who eventually joined the Jesuit order. See John Thornton on the Roboredo, Kikongo Sermon (http://www.bu.edu/afam/faculty/john-thornton/roboredo-kikongo-sermon/).
12 Hastings (1994), pp. 428-429.

goes without saying that the missionaries were a product of their time. The "science" of eugenics was well and truly in vogue by the 1890s and would reach its peak in the subsequent thirty years. Indeed the Church acknowledged the most abusive of the racist policies it had supported in its very public criticism of the slave trade, just as it recognised the overwhelming need for cultural validation in the decrees of the Second Vatican Council more than a hundred years later. The point is not that these criticisms are valid (which they are), but that individual Catholic missionaries *were* attempting to build bridges between the wrongs of the past and existing and oppressive colonial regimes, and African futures nevertheless, and they *were* sheltering those most victimised by all three where they could despite the insidious and discriminatory culture that pervaded most European activity in Africa at the time. From the viewpoint of the social milieu that had shaped them, these men were breaking new ground and carving a space for the Church that would be occupied by their indigenous heirs.

An unwillingness to commit the vast resources required for a pre-1880 development of Africa limited the early impact of Empires on the continent. But the invention of "… the steam engine, the breach-loading gun, the telegraph, quinine, and a coherent knowledge of Africa put together by explorers, missionaries, and geographical societies…"[13] changed everything. All of a sudden it was possible for Europeans to plan for the future of the entire continent, and Africa became a theatre for demonstrations of political ascendency in Europe just as much as it was a trough for the greedy. Colonialists became tyrannical, they denied common humanity, flouting the "… traditions, land rights, historical polity, and moral norms …" of local Africans, and becoming a vicious force that destroyed entire populations when challenged, which naturally they were – though fighting back

---

13 Ibid., p.398. See also A. Abu Boahen (1987), *African Perspectives on Colonialism*, Johns Hopkins University Press, Maryland, chapter 3.

could equate with obliteration.¹⁴ As the continent was parcelled up into European packages, African life was irrevocably changed; the demands for tax payments, forced labour on roads, and the alienation of land for settlers pushed Africans into a new kind of economy that demanded they be employed, that they follow new rules and, should they wish to have access to anything considered profitable or powerful within Western contexts, that they become literate. The only people in a position to provide access to the requisite Western education were the missionaries who had in most cases been given responsibility for schooling within colonial orders. Most importantly, however, "Africans themselves had been placed in a situation of objective intellectual unsettlement and were thoughtful enough to seek appropriate positive answers of a religious as well as a technical kind to their current dilemmas."¹⁵ The evident continuity between the religions of Africa and Christianity ("... a finally single personal God of creation and providence ...") and the hold that Ethiopia in particular already had on Christianity (along with Sierra Leone and Cape Colony too) made that transition much easier.¹⁶ Well-intended and numerous

---

14 The Herero people and the Nama were virtually exterminated by the Germans in Namibia for example, and the Maji Maji in Tanzania. The Maji Maji rebellion (1905) spread out over 10,000 square miles, involved over twenty different ethnic groups, was a mass movement of peasants against forced labour, taxation, and oppression, and is viewed as "the final effort by Tanganyika's old societies to destroy the colonial order by force." Hastings (1994), pp. 398-401; Boahen, Op. Cit., p. 65; D.K. Fieldhouse (1981), *Colonialism, 1870-1945: An Introduction*, Weidenfeld and Nicolson.

15 Hastings (1994), p. 404.

16 Hastings (1994), p. 405. Christianity in Ethiopia began in the fourth century as an extension of the Egyptian church, and in response to the mission of Frumentius, bishop of Aksum, and was later expanded with the arrival of the 'Nine Saints' (nine monks possibly from Syria) who established a number of enduring monasteries in the fifth century. From the seventh century, however, it became largely isolated, arguably right up until the 15th century. The Red Sea fell under Islamic control, the Church of Alexandria lost much of its power and influence, and the kingdom of Ethiopia withdrew into the highlands. Hastings (1994), p. 5-11.

missionaries were only able to Christianise because of Africans' *desire* for Christianisation.[17]

Between the 1880s and the Second Vatican Council in the early 1960s, the missionary impulse gained a revolutionary momentum that distinguished it from the colonial siege.[18] Some European missionaries and missions had a reputation for sheltering escaped slaves and communities devastated by the trade, and tribal outcasts. Generally, they fell out with colonists over issues like slavery and the political representation of African interests (or lack thereof). Having fought slavery from within Africa well before colonists arrived many were prepared to breach local laws to offer sanctuary to slaves escaping Arab masters, while French, British, and German authorities continued to promote it within Arab contexts for political expediency (even though it had been officially abolished in the United Kingdom in 1833).[19] (The story of Ouandété, a young man from the north-east of what is now Ivory Coast who escaped slavery in the mid-1890s when his village was attacked and pillaged by the forces of the Dioula

---

17 Note too that Islam also had continuity with African religions and had, like Christianity, already established an enormous African presence. Indeed, suggests Hastings, Africans were in a position to choose between the two. Colonial regimes were essentially pluralist, the aim being colonisation not proselytisation. The lack of colonial hostility towards Islamic tribes (in fact their heightened sensitivity to Islamic sensibilities – particularly the British), the view that Islam was a more sensible religious choice for Africans because it was "monotheist, literate, and universalist, while more indigenous and less difficult to understand than Christianity, as well as being unwedded to a seemingly futile attack on polygamy", the fact that the Muslim community presented as apparently more accommodating, pietistic, and other-worldly than the jihadist face it sports today, the fact that German colonialists favoured the movement of people and ideas and Muslims were "among the most mobile of Africans", and above all the need to create and maintain political cooperation with tribes that were already Muslim supported the ongoing spread of Islam across Africa alongside Christianity, and in many cases the creation of a Muslim majority in previously Christian cities. Ibid., pp. 405-408.
18 Boahen, Op. Cit., p. 16.
19 Hastings (1994), Op. Cit., p. 388

conqueror Samory Touré and who was embraced by the Society for African Missions with eleven other refugees is one of many such examples.)

Missions also offered sanctuary to women, their Christian morals impinging directly on issues specific to female existence in Africa. That is not to say that African tradition subordinated woman to man any more than European tradition did. But the missions provided scope for female initiative within the new social circumstances that colonialism had established, even though women remained pretty low in the Catholic hierarchy. "… the missionary church saw itself as a champion of the dignity and education of women…the impact on education, midwifery [and] the psychology of individual expectations …" were considerable.[20] Despite obvious rigidities, missionary work conveyed the message that women were equal, free, and capable of independent responsibility.[21] Women may have been "… escaping cruel husbands, a marriage they did not want, confinement to a chief's harem, punishment for some offence, or even being sacrificed at the death of a king." Onslaughts on polygamy, the payment of bride wealth, clitoridectomy, the killing of twins, or the pursuit of alleged witches, for example, could possibly define missionary Catholics as liberationists for the Western and modern feminist.[22] (Ouandété eventually married Marie Valérie Ama in 1902, a young girl who had been held captive but became aware that her master had destined her

---

20 Hastings (1989),"Were Women a Special Case?", Chapter 3. In *African Catholicism, Essays in Discovery,* SCM Press, London and Trinity Press International, Philadelphia, p. 39

21 Galatians 3.28: "There is neither male nor female." Hastings (1989), p.38.

22 Hastings (1989), pp. 42-43; Nwando Achebe (2011), *The Female King of Colonial Nigeria Ahebi Ugbabe,* Indiana University Press, Bloomington and Indianapolis, p. 253 n113; Ogbu Kalu (1996), *The Embattled Gods; The Christianisation of Igboland 1841-1991*, Minaj Publishers, Lagos, p. 80 (quoted by N. Achebe); Edmund Ilogu (1974), *Christianity and Igbo Culture*, E.J. Brill, Leiden, pp. 56-60 (also quoted by N. Achebe).

to be sacrificed during an upcoming feast. She escaped to the sisters of Dabou before meeting and marrying Ouandété.[23])

In societies traditionally dominated by older men, mission schools also supported the young by giving them a place to stand on their own feet. It released individuals from the burdens of a traditional life, and it gave them access to resources (like wives and money) that the older men had always controlled. In this it facilitated an adolescent rebellion of sorts, and carved a line in the sand between generations. "The elders seemed suddenly poor, and ignorant, and felt that they were despised."[24] The disruption such empowerments made to traditional social dynamics must have been enormous,[25] but no more than the disruption that both slavery and colonialism had caused to African societies more broadly. Many European missionaries saw themselves as providing a bridge between a traditional world under siege, and survival in a new and inevitable composite.

Missions and missionary schools offered the education and skills that were needed if Africans were to merge with and succeed in a Europe-centred world, while the ethnocentrisms and racist preoccupations (that condemned everything African) maintained by many within the established Church fuelled resentment amongst some of the Africans they educated and empowered future independence action that used Western method for social action. New political control meant working within a new system, and literacy, education and a wider sense of possibility made functioning within that system achievable.

From 1927, Catholic missions throughout British Africa were told "to cooperate with all your power ..." with the government's education

---

23 See (http://sthweb.bu.edu/stories/cotedivoire/ouandete_louis-marie.html)
24 E. Isichei (1995), *A History of Christianity in Africa*, Society for Promoting Christian Knowledge, U.K. p. 237.
25 See the classic by Achebe, C. (1994) *Things Fall Apart*, 50th Anniversary edition. Anchor Books, U.S.A

policies, "... and where it is impossible for you to carry on both the immediate task of evangelisation and your educational work, neglect your churches in order to perfect your schools."[26] Missionary societies not only preached, converted to, and translated the Bible, they also promoted agriculture; they taught carpentry, printing, and tailoring skills, and they promoted trade, literacy, and Western education.[27] Along the way, reading and church affiliation became synonymous and the Book of Gospels became the key to the modern world. Through it one learned to read and write, doors opened, power was ascribed and opportunities for advancement in the modern world became real.[28] "... the school served in many ways. It made the children literate, and [gave them access to] political, cultural, economic, and religious [contexts]..." Attendance at mission schools also ensured a regular meal and a roof over one's head; with time, those who chose a religious vocation would enjoy advanced social standing, as well as the practical necessities of daily survival in abundance.

> ... to us education meant reading books, writing and talking English, and doing arithmetic ... we resented all forms of manual work ... at our homes we had done a lot of ploughing, planting, weeding and harvesting ... We knew how to do these things. We

---

26 R. Oliver, *The Missionary Factor in East Africa*, Longmans Green, London, p. 275, also quoted in Hastings (1994), p. 562.

27 Boahen Op. Cit., pp. 16-20. See also Hastings (1994), Op. Cit., pp. 404-405: The emergence of educated African elite would also underpin the development of African religious nationalism (Ethiopianism), the principal object of which was "the establishment of churches which would be controlled by Africans themselves and whose doctrines and rituals would be in tune with African cultures and traditions."

28 Francis Cardinal Arinze (Nigeria). See Gerard O'Connell (2006), *God's Invisible Hand, the Life and Work of Francis Cardinal Arinze*, Ignatius Press, San Francisco, p.17. Similarly James Morris describes the decision to attend schools sponsored by the British colonies: "In most parts of the Empire the British imposed their ways by sheer force of example: the Western culture was so obviously superior, in economic and technical terms, that the subject peoples flocked in self-interest to its schools...", James Morris (1978), *Farewell the Trumpets*, Faber and Faber, U.K., p. 90.

had come to school, not for these, but for those things we did not know. What we knew was not education; education was what we did not know ... We wanted, as we said in Ndebele, to learn the book until it remained in our heads, to speak English until we could speak it through our noses.[29]

In Uganda a class three teacher told his pupils, "Less study, much work, less pay. Much study, less work, more pay". And Kikuyu children sang:

> *Father, mother*
> *Provide me with pen and slate*
> *I want to learn.*
> *Land is gone*
> *Cattle and Sheep are not there*
> *Not there any more*
> *What's left?*
> *Learning, learning*[30]

However, above all else, the founding of elementary schools, training colleges and sometimes secondary schools as well created an educated Christian and African elite who would eventually refute the racist ideologies of the day in print and speeches; the agitation this group precipitated within colonial paradigms added an intellectual layer to the rebellion and revolutionary activity already underway (and for many years) amongst the general populace and across a number of social contexts: "We want educated Fantis not Europeanised natives. We simply want our education to enable us to develop and to improve our native ideas, customs, manners and institutions," said the chronicle *Gold Coast Aborigines* in 1902.[31] It also reinforced

---

29 Quoted in Isichei, Op. Cit., pp. 236-237.
30 Isichei, Op. Cit., p. 256.
31 *Gold Coast Aborigines* was one of the many newspapers founded in Ghana from the 1890s, as an outlet for the criticisms of the existing colonial regime by the educated African elite. Boahen, Op. Cit., p. 68.

African racial consciousness and a post-WWII African identity in the 20th century, and the ideologies of African personality and Pan-Africanism that drove the independence movements (though many of their protagonists became despotic in the end).[32]

The energy with which many missionaries empowered people to "own" the religion and preach it themselves gave Catholicism vigour and a home-grown relevance that grew exponentially in a relatively short time. In the beginning, missionary work was for most Europeans a death sentence. Malaria, yellow fever and other diseases established the view that Europeans could not survive permanently in Africa:[33]

> There arrives at the station a white man from beyond the sea, who brought with him six corpses – bodies of holy men – to be buried here. The white man asking for the agent in charge of this station, I presented myself; he then handed to me a paper on which was written the names of the six holy ones who are to be buried; with my own hand I wrote my name the seventh.[34]

The likelihood of death by disease (within one or two years) drove the creation of a local clergy in the form of catechists who made important connections between traditional cultures and Christianity, who solved problems that were beyond the missionary's capacity to solve, and who created bridges between the old world and the new. Not being bound by priestly expectations of celibacy, their existence overcame early complications associated with a lack of priests; a single foreign priest or bishop could oversee the ministering of a large

---

32 Boahen, Op. Cit., pp. 16-20. For a discussion of the many protagonists who turned despotic see Ayitte, Op. Cit.

33 Niall Ferguson (2011), *Civilization, The Six Killer Apps of Western Power*. Penguin, London. Ferguson notes that on average retired colonial officials expired seventeen years earlier than their counterparts in metropolitan service, p. 168. See also Isichei, Op. Cit., pp. 78-79, and discussion with French Jesuit (anonymous) in Abidjan.

34 *A vision described by Jacob Akiwuli, a Yoruba CMS catechist before his last illness, in 1905.* Taken from E.M. Lijadu, Journal, 10-28 Feb., 1905 and quoted in Isichei, Op. Cit., p. 153.

number of local catechists without having to do the physical work. Thus a consistent and enduring pattern of Church organisation was established, which supported the Church's early indigenous vitality: "... a central mission, surrounded by a vast network of outstations, run by African teacher-catechists, and only occasionally visited by the expatriate missionary, or African priest."[35] Without that vitality the Church would not have survived in Africa and Africans would not have chosen ordination of their own accord. By the 1960s, when the Second Vatican Council was debating official recognition of a cultural fusion between the Church and societies that were embracing its lead, Catholicism (and Christianity generally) in Africa had already been largely Africanised – and by Africans.

Africans who chose a Catholic vocation in the 20th century would be viewed by their own people as men of integrity, their leadership central to negotiating the political and cultural discord that emerged all over the continent after the Second World War. Until then, they were required to define their practice in line with the ascendency of their European counterparts. Nevertheless, their status allowed them to exercise certain styles of leadership that supported and enhanced the personal and social empowerment that repressed Africans were seeking at the time, and which encouraged the on-going popularity and growth of Catholicism across Africa.[36] Ordination invariably involved travel, exposure to other places and the revelation of possibilities that would be realised as more and more Africans chose the priesthood.

---

35 See also R. Oliver (1956) *How Christian is Africa?* Oliver remarks "the village Catechist and teacher is still today the cornerstone of the African Church ..." While interestingly, Isichei, p. 238, notes that despite his or her long standing importance, the training and role of catechists only became a central pastoral preoccupation in the churches from about 1970 on. Of course there exists the probability that teacher-catechists, isolated from the priest and interpreting the gospel in their own dialect, injected a measure of creative interpretation into the exercise as well.
36 Boahan, Op. Cit., pp. 88-89, also ch. 3.

Priests like Joseph Kiwanuka in Uganda (1899-1966; he was the first African bishop of modern times) followed the emancipatory example of the White Fathers who had supported him.[37] He used his influence to guide his people in the ways of progress as a precursor to economic and political empowerment. He encouraged locals to develop coffee plantations and he established schools, first for boys and later for girls. Mentoring young men like Emmanuel Wamala, he exercised great influence over what would later be Wamala's approach to the repressive regimes of Obote and Amin, to the thuggery of the Lord's Resistance Army in Northern Uganda, and to the devastating HIV epidemic of the mid-1980s. Cyprian Michael Tansi played a similar mentoring role for boys like the young Francis Arinze in Nigeria who as newly appointed archbishop shepherded millions through the war in Biafra. Despite the strict parameters of Catholic doctrine as it then stood, these men followed the examples of their Catholic forefathers and attempted to use their religion for the betterment of societies that sought self-definition and stability within new social and political paradigms.

The Second Vatican Council (1962-65), especially through its decree on missionary activity (*Ad Gentes*) and constitution of the Church in the modern world (*Gaudium et Spes*), gave the first African bishops and priests the freedom to incorporate these early intentions into the construction of newly independent nations with vitality and with a view to local needs. The optimism of the Council was in keeping with the optimism of the early independence era in Africa. The cry for self-empowerment, freedom, democracy, and social betterment on the

---

37 The significance of Kiwanuka's consecration, says Hastings, was that it was carried out in St Peter's by Pius XII himself. The White Fathers are a missionary society founded in 1868 by the first Archbishop of Algiers, Cardinal Lavigerie. The society was founded to educate and instruct the large number of Arab orphans left after the famine of 1867, though the conversion of the Arabs and people of central Africa were always the long term aim. They established themselves in areas now considered central to Uganda. Hastings, (1994), p. 565.

lips of Africa's nationalists, rang out just as clearly from the pulpit and the newly engaged congregation at last. Priests appealed to the laity for guidance on local issues, to women who were appointed to key positions on decision-making bodies often for the first time, to communities to re-establish long lost connections. They began to use dialogue to end entrenched conflict, to dismantle the psychological scaffolding underpinning racist ideologies in places like South Africa, for example, and to make the Mass a living breathing embodiment of African cultures everywhere. But just as the Church became more and more culturally and socially relevant, the euphoria of independence regressed into the misery of tyrannical dictatorships. By the late 1970s the continent was once again destabilised but by one-party regimes that starved or shot their opposition into submission, and that failed to develop the traditional sectors that the colonialists had neglected or to maintain the functioning ones they had left in place.[38] An obsession with white injustice led to a deep rooted resentment and mistrust of educated foreigners who were hastily chased away. Totalitarianism and despotism gave many Africans less freedom than they had enjoyed under colonial rule, and many tumbled out of disempowerment and into wretchedness.[39]

As civil war sent learned and experienced foreign priests packing as well, the integrity of the continent's indigenous clergy became all the more relevant; African priests stepped without hesitation into religious leadership roles where guidance and protection in the midst of ethnic and political confusion were not only expected but necessary. Emerging into a modern yet tortured world, these young men made the

---

38 Ayittey, Op. Cit., ch. 5.
39 "It is true God's children in Africa suffer because there is *less* freedom in their countries than during the colonial times. African leaders need to be reminded that there is totalitarianism and despotism nearly everywhere in Africa. When your people are free, you can also walk freely and you will not need huge security people to protect you." – Bishop Desmond Tutu, 1990, quoted by Ayittey, Op. Cit., p. 98 and taken from *Daily Nation,* March 26, 1990.

Church in Africa their own. They combined the Gospel's central tenet – *love* – with the benefits of the foreign educational experiences the Church had made possible (and that broadened their world view), and they applied both to highly challenging circumstances that demanded great vision: War, epidemics, economic collapse, violent dictatorships and corruption had devastating effects on their flocks. The failed promises of the independence movement – education, human rights, social justice, dialogue, spirituality – along with the priesthood itself have been imperative and defining for a ministry that has maintained its credibility as much through political objectivity as through its commitment to on-going cultural representation and a future without tyranny.

Idealism can be powerful. It fails to see obstacles where realism baulks in advance. Facing a landscape littered with mines these priests were hardly armed for combat, yet they have faced religious leadership in Africa fortified with a belief in and a respect for the universal fragility of the human condition and a commitment to showing others how to respect it too.

Christ the King, Nzulezu

The True Size of Africa

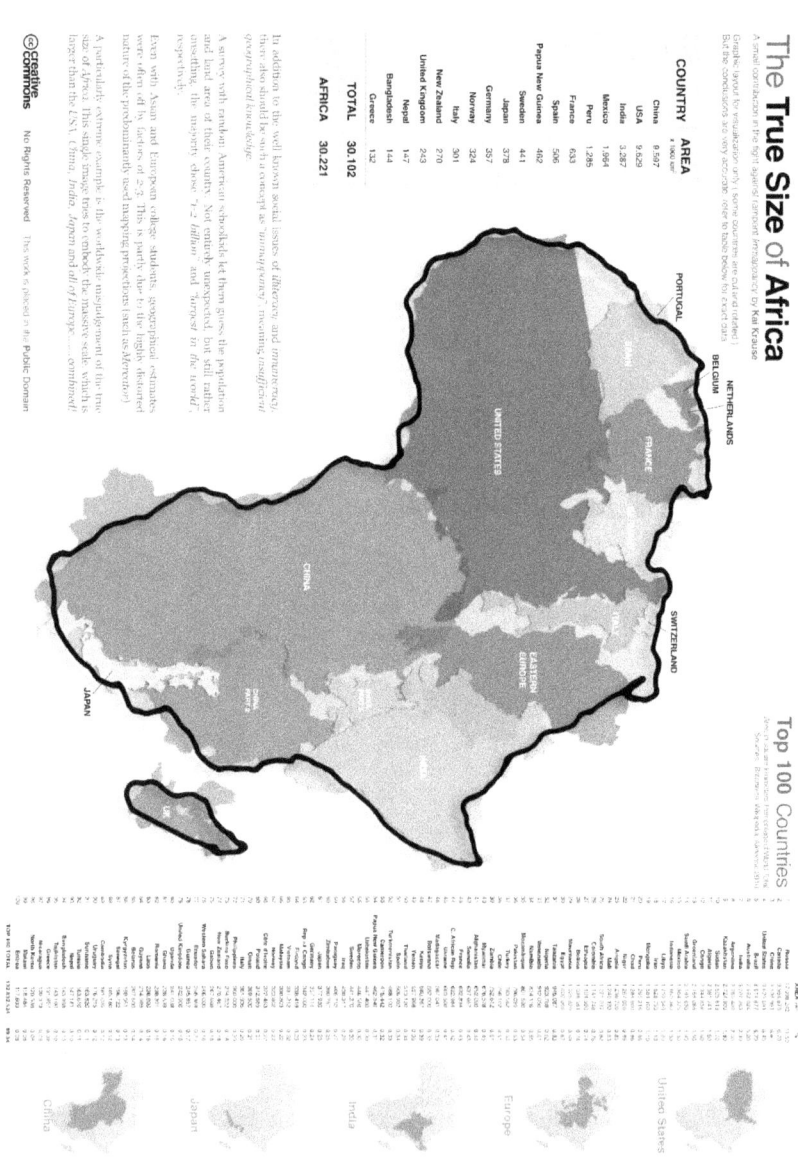

Africa and the Slave Trade

The door of death, Elmina castle, Cape Coast

1 i. SOUTH AFRICA

The Republic of South Africa is a country located at the southern tip of the African continent. It is bordered in the north by Namibia, Botswana and Zimbabwe and to the east by Mozambique and Swaziland. Within its borders Lesotho exists as an enclave surrounded by South African territory. It has a population of just fewer than 50 million people. The people are about 80 per cent African, with ten per cent both "white" and "coloured". The country is approximately 80 per cent Christian (a little over eight per cent Catholic). Fifteen per cent claim no religion, while the other five per cent are either Muslims (about 1.5 per cent) or they practise a traditional religion. Life expectancy is about 50 years. Eighty-five per cent of people over 15 years of age can read and write, and 85 per cent of children finish 13 years of school. On average women have two children (11.6 per cent of children under the age of five years are underweight). In 2010, 5.6 million people over the age of 15 years (17.6 percent of the total population) and 330,000 children were infected with HIV.[40] The unemployment rate sits at 24.4 per cent (2012), with GDP at 408.2

---

40 For discussion of percentage of the world that is Christian see: "Global Christianity, A Report on the Size and Distribution of the World's Christian Population", 19 December, 2011 (http://www.pewforum.org/Christian/Global-Christianty-exec.aspx), accessed 4 August, 2012. For HIV statistics see: "Sub-Saharan Africa HIV and AIDS statistics" (http://www.avert.org/africa-hiv-aids-statistics.htm), accessed 13 March, 2012. Sources for this document are UNAIDS (2010) 'UNAIDS report on the global AIDS epidemic' (http://www,unaids.org/global report/-2010), and UNAIDS (2011) 'UNAIDS World AIDS Day Report 2011" (http://www.unaids.org/en/resources/presscentre/pressreleaseand statementarchive/2011/november/20111121wad20-2011), accessed 13 March 2012.

billion USD (2011), and population density at 41 people for every square kilometer (2010).[41]

Dutch, British, Xhosa and Zulu claims for ascendency in South Africa weave together a fairly complex historical timeline across a number of major events of the 19th and 20th centuries in the area now called South Africa. The Dutch established the Cape of Good Hope in the mid-1600s as a refreshment station along the Cape Sea Route that was used by the Dutch East India Company until it went bankrupt in the mid-1870s. In 1806, the British seized control of the resultant Cape Colony. There were various skirmishes with Xhosa and Zulu kingdoms as Europeans sought to expand the nation towards the east, though ultimately, and despite the abolition of the slave trade by the British in 1833, Africans in the area remained severely marginalised. Europe's scramble for the spoils of the African mineral revolution from the middle of the 1800s, spurred wealth and migration and intensified the subjugation of the local Africans in what was to become, in 1910 (and after two wars waged between the British and the Dutch) a nation ruled by a minority, and white, British/Boer elite who were set on the segregation of the races and maintained a serious aversion to Catholicism.

By that time there were nearly 6,000 Catholic missionaries in Africa, over half of which were nuns. Half of those were in South Africa and most served only the white population.[42] The Catholic Church had been banned in South Africa by the Dutch and then the British until the late 1830's, and very little was done towards establishing missions or for the indigenous people in South Africa for another fifty years. The first significant results came with the Trappists of Marianhill in 1880, who developed innovative missionary methods combining farming, schooling and preaching. But the first

---

41 (http://www.indexmundi.com/facts/south-africa/population-density), accessed 25 May 2013.
42 Hastings (1994), p. 418.

concerted efforts to train a local clergy did not happen until the late 1920s and the first seminary for blacks until the late 1940s. From 1948 and until the late 1970s, when segregation was legalised via apartheid and discrimination against the African majority became entrenched, the Church did little to oppose the government's policy of segregation. Despite having condemned apartheid as "intrinsically evil" in the 1950s, the Church hierarchy adopted a conciliatory stance towards the government "in the hope of maintaining the Church's network of schools, hospitals and welfare institutions" and a defacto discrimination continued to exist within the Church at many levels. "In the 1970s, under the influence of the Vatican Council and spurred by protests from black clergy, catholic opposition to apartheid started to intensify," culminating in a focus on conflict resolution, education, democracy, and development in 1990.[43]

The foundations for apartheid had already been laid at the turn of the 19th century when the British High commissioner, Alfred Milner, advocated segregation and separate locations for blacks on the fringes of cities and towns for the first time.[44] It was not long before white privilege was institutionalised and its protection made murderous via

---

43 (http://www.sacbc.org.za/about-us/history-of-the-catholic-church-in-south-africa/), accessed 14 June 2013.

44 Lord Milner was a German-trained lawyer. He was a consistent believer in white imperial unity and sought to make sense of South Africa by fusing Britons and Boers together under the British crown. While laying the foundations for establishing a union between the Boers and the British, (resettling landless families, building new schools and farms, evolving constitutions for the new Boer colonies, getting Rand mines back to production using imported Chinese labour, starting irrigation schemes, founding municipalities in Boer townships and so on) he underestimated the strength of Boer national feeling. "Embedded in lore and faith, inherited emotions and tribal certainties, it …found expression in political movements, secret societies, religions and cultural chauvinism…" Milner returned to the United Kingdom in 1905, but was publically criticised for his disregard for South African blacks under the new Union. "Their welfare had been the only good reason for fighting the Boer War in the first place." Morris, Op. Cit., pp. 86-93.

the total exclusion of blacks from political life in 1910. From 1948, South Africa became notorious for advocating vicious discrimination against its African citizens. Its efforts mirrored those of the National Socialist Party in Nazi Germany, which from the late 1930s created laws that governed on the basis of race. Black South Africans were removed from their homes, excluded from employment and discriminated against in education. As the African National Congress was embracing the Freedom Charter in the mid-1950s, a document that proposed that blacks and whites be treated equally under law, white police were being empowered to commit acts of violence against those who opposed them. In the 1960s, protests were shut down, demonstrators murdered. Terror, suspicion and divisiveness were encouraged within anti-apartheid organisations by a government bent on protecting its policies at any cost. Those who did protest, including Mandela, Sisulu, Kathrada and Goldberg were labelled communist terrorists and thrown into jail. In 1963 detention without trial for up to 90 days was legislated and hundreds of thousands of people were detained, tortured and killed. From the 1980s through a campaign known as the "Total Strategy" that used political, economic, military and psychological components, the government made a final effort to destroy the resolve of the black consciousness movement that had begun to make headway after forty long years.

The state failed. Mandela was released and apartheid was abolished. Before long, Mandela was elected president. His government was given free rein to define and express a new kind of morality that drew on the need to right so many years of wrong and South Africa now boasts the most democratic constitution in the world. Step-by-step, the country's new leaders are creating initiatives to pull back the entrenched social, legal and political inequalities that for 100 years had ensured the total exclusion of black Africans from decisions determining their futures. Religious leaders inspired a truth and reconciliation commission to free the country's citizens from the bonds of bitterness and the need for revenge. Forgiveness became a catch phrase for peace and a precondition for moral integrity. Oppressors became enlightened about the darker side of their privilege, and the oppressed, endlessly patient and continuing to suffer, became owners of the moral upper hand.[45]

Wilfred Fox Cardinal Napier, OFM was born on 8 March 1941 in Swartberg, South Africa. He studied in Galway and Louvain from 1960 to 1970. He was ordained priest in 1970, bishop of Kokstad in 1981 and elected president of the South African Bishops' conference in 1987. Appointed archbishop of Durban in 1992 and consulter to the Congregation for the Evangelisation of Peoples, he was named Cardinal-Priest in 2001. Having participated in the 2005 papal conclave that selected Pope Benedict XVI, he was appointed a Member of the Pontifical Council for the Pastoral Care of Health Care Workers by Pope Benedict XVI in 2012.

Cardinal Napier visited Melbourne in 2010 to participate in the 25th annual Dom Helder Camara Lecture series hosted at Newman College in Parkville. I interviewed him in offices behind St Patrick's Cathedral, within the Archdiocese of Melbourne.

---

45 For a thorough account of institutionalisation of oppression and murder under apartheid go to Pumla Gobodo-Madikizela (2003), *A Human Being Died That Night*, Authorhouse, London.

ii. Forgiveness

... Mother, you can still hold on but forgive, forgive and give for as long as we both shall live I forgive you, Mother. I shall turn the hearts of the fathers to the children, and the hearts of the children to their fathers. The teeth at your bones are your own, the hunger is yours, and forgiveness is yours. The sins of the fathers belong to you and to the forest and even to the ones in iron bracelets, and here you stand, remembering their songs. Listen. Slide the weight from your shoulders and move forward. You are afraid you might forget, but you never will. You will forgive and remember. Think of the vine that curls from the small square plot that was once my heart. That is the only marker you need. Move on. Walk forward into the light ...[46]

In the beginning it was not about the cardinals. It was about a potential career and another book ...

There was a 40th birthday and a holiday to South Africa, where I slept in a king-sized bed and had access to a swimming pool. I was wrapped in Egyptian cotton, poured wine in Stellenbosch, which I drank with roasted kudu, and I dived with great white sharks off the coast of Gansbaai. I was blinded by beauty and colour and rocks and houses that, perching on cliffs in thick midst, peered out across a turquoise sea. I was awestruck by the Cape of Good Hope and the Atlantic and Indian Oceans smashing tides over sea creatures that had climbed out as monkeys, and by beasts that I stalked from the back of an SUV. But I was uncomfortable.

South Africa's recent past was a fresh disgrace. The politics of segregation still resonated in the location of black townships outside the city. The protection of privilege was still evident in the endless rolls of razor wire across town. The inequalities in education and

---

46 Kingsolver, Op. Cit., p. 614.

health care were clear in the overcrowded classrooms and in rates of infection and disease. The influx of migrants across the northern borders gave away the country's role in foreign conquest, in foreign civil war. There were three-metre high fences and armed guards in the evenings, and laser lights that threw off crooked and haunting shadows into the dark and quiet nights of Constantia, shadows that I felt myself dodging by daytime as well. It was hard to tell where they came from during the day. The brighter the sun shone, the more frequently they were cast and in multi-colours too (black, white, brown); they hung around street corners in the city, or wafted in through windows on the breeze that carried the scent of coffee in the early mornings. They were not menacing, at least not intentionally so, but rather stood and shadowed basic (and comfortable) human interaction as reminders of the endless misunderstandings, the ground swell of confusions, that had washed around the separate islands of humanity that apartheid made non-negotiable in the not so distant past.

Clearly some did not see them … many were happy to share good wines and talk business over plates of extraordinary food. In such cases the nation's past remained unpalatable, the African maid invisible behind the partition that separated kitchen from laundry. "Apartheid", like "Aboriginal" became the "A" word, the first letter in an alphabet of unspoken pain and discomfort that was better left unsaid. But others let their guard down. Drawn into their confidence by the shared colour of skin they showed me the downside of a dead supremacy; confusion about democracy; resentment over the sharing of economic and political control; fear of the potential for "uneducated blacks" to throw the country into a self-destructive spiral. These conversations were conducted in almost whispers, at the table in a French-style bed-and-breakfast in the champagne valley. Another glass of wine and an Afrikaner farmer bemoaned the decline of the rand, the gifting of half his business to a "black" colleague, his fears for his life. Holed up overnight at Heathrow (a separate trip), a formerly Rhodesian business man heading for Australia foreshadowed his view of South Africa's future. He described being hounded out of his homeland at gun point by Mugabe, and cried over the loss of five generations of honest work and the decline of his country, the "loss of his soul".

Here, for the first time, I too became "white": paternalism, entitlement, sophistication and possibility were all apparently revealed by the shade of my skin. I was at once a "friend" to those who looked like me and a "foe" to those who did not. Bridging the gap involved a proof of worth that was impossible in the space of a holiday and I was forced to wear the new title for the duration; to drive, privileged and wealthy, through the mass of workers who left crowded townships before daylight to attend menial and poorly paid jobs; to look my own good fortune square in the eye and to endure the gaze of those less lucky. To bear past complacencies and guilt by association with my racial brethren (who saw something of themselves in me!) without being able to unburden myself – besides bleeding money into the hands of cunning hawkers who sold beaded souvenirs. In the end it was only Andrew, the African maid,[47] who offered me relief by accepting my friendship and the chocolate I bought him. He alone allowed me to be his friend, forgave me the colour of my skin.

And so this book started as a conversation with those shadows. I wanted to understand the psychological nuances and complexities that had sustained that divide among colours, and those that would sustain peaceful democracy in the new republic. How can other people forgive what I as Westerner, non-Catholic, part-time academic, saw as the unforgiveable? How can everyone else face themselves in the mirror? These were the kind of questions that drove my interview with Cardinal Wilfred Fox Napier in Melbourne, Australia later that year. We met in offices of the archdiocese of Melbourne, near St Patrick's Cathedral in the city. I was expecting someone stern, serious and

---

[47] The term "maid" (a predominantly female term in the West) is also used for men who are employed to tend to the house keeping duties in South Africa.

perhaps cautious, judging by the formality of his post, a post that I knew came with fierce demands on his time. So I arrived in my very best suit with a feeling of eternal gratitude, a sense that there was less of me and more of him, a sense that I should choose the smaller seat, that I should take the "burnt chop" (as a "good" wife always does). But his affability caught me off-guard. He was tall, well built, good looking. And informal: just suit trousers, a neatly pressed shirt and clerical collar, an enormous smile that stretched before it opened and questioned my interest in him, obviously pleased in the tilt of the conversation, pleased with the gifted bottle of red wine. Perhaps even pleased by the momentary pause in the religious conversation he had been having with the city of Melbourne, and with its replacement by an interview that swirled around his past, his work for South Africans pre-democracy, around the implications of apartheid for a coloured priest in the 1970s, 80s, and 90s. An interview that questioned how and why people justify avoiding the eyes of privilege and carry on. How can we view the beneficiaries of apartheid in terms of human frailty? How can we grow? Certainly he expressed nothing less than pleasure, amiability, indeed gratitude for my making time for him, and I felt nothing less than elevated to the position of equal sitting there beside him.

At the end of that previous holiday, in a crowded restaurant in Constantia, I had asked the African waiter how he coped with his country's past, how he saw a future growing out of such pain. He answered me solemnly: "After the rain falls madam, the sun will always shine." Looking back, he could have been the cardinal serving my wine.

iii. **Wilfred Fox Cardinal Napier, Archbishop of Durban, South Africa**

(April 2010)

"Are you alone?"

"Yes I am alone."

"Can you speak?"

"Yes I can speak."

"Well I just wanted to tell you that the Pope has appointed you cardinal."

And I got such a shock. I said,

"WHAT?!" And he said,

"Yes." He said, "Look come around some evening and I'll tell you what it's all about."

Can you tell me about your studies overseas and what you felt they did to you and what they did for you? You were in Ireland and then Belgium, is that right?

Yes I was.

It must have been extraordinary for you at that time.

It was extremely so for two reasons:

The first was that I am from what was called the "coloured" group in South Africa and therefore slotted in, I suppose (in the scale of rights and privileges) just below the whites. Indians and coloureds were more or less on a par; Africans were on the bottom rung of the ladder. So going to Ireland for me was a challenge because I wasn't sure how I was going to fit in, living with white people for the first time. It was also a completely different culture and country, and I was worried that I would not measure up. You see, we (from South Africa) understood that because apartheid had made serious inroads by 1948 and people's rights had been defined much more rigidly by the apartheid philosophy, then white people, Europeans, would have a higher standard of education. I was concerned that the education that I had received as a member of the coloured group would not be up to the standard required by a university in another country.

To my surprise I found that apart from things like the sciences, physics, and chemistry and so on, my education was almost on a par with that in Ireland. (In fact in some areas it was possible that our standard of education was a little more rigorous, more demanding!) In Ireland, for example, I don't remember them doing subjects like the ontology of poems and of poetry. We just had extracts from poems here and there, whereas in South Africa we had a whole set of books on the whole ontology of poetry. In some ways I was quite surprised to find that.

When I actually started to study at the University in Galway I found that it wasn't as difficult as I had imagined it might be (and in fact I did very well!), and I became used to the idea of being a foreigner among people who were foreign to me. Going to Louvain (after Galway) "spread" that experience because there were many more nationalities at the University of Louvain than in Galway. Galway was part of the University of Ireland but it had a particular focus on the Gaelic language. (In normal circumstances applicants would have been required to have had Gaelic as one of their subjects in order to qualify for admission in that college. But because I was a foreign student, they gave me an exemption).

When I got to Louvain I discovered a much broader spectrum of people. There were lots of people from the Congo, from Nigeria, from America, from South America and so on – it was a much more international community. And again, the thing that I was most concerned about was, "How am I going to measure up against these different kinds of people and standards of people?" The big challenge in Louvain was also that the studies were taught through the medium of French. I had done a little French during the holidays in Ireland but I hadn't grasped it by any means. The six of us who went over to Louvain to do philosophy did a good intensive language course over the Christmas holidays and by the end of that year we passed the exams without too much difficulty and carried on there for another five years.

And how do you think that foreign experience impacted on you when you returned to South Africa?
I returned home permanently after 1970, after ten years. But I had been back for one short period. I came home for a holiday after 1965, for a period of six weeks I think.

Was that a shock?
Oh it was quite a culture shock when I got back! Having had the experience of apartheid all my life until then, and then having those five years completely free of any kind of restrictions, in fact having been made a celebrity, if anything, because I was the only dark-skinned fella around the place (everyone else was full of admiration, they wanted to know who I was and so on) ... to come back in that frame of mind and to then find myself back in the thick of apartheid, in what was possibly a worse state than before I left ... it was a huge shock. The country had become a republic while I was away [1961], and the leaders believed that the British were here, or the English speakers were here, by sufferance more than by right. Anyone who stayed had to conform to the philosophy and the thinking of the Afrikaners. But once I was home, I was in among my family and that compensated for the shock.

But there is an experience that I would like to relate to you because it has some significance for later on. When I got over there and I was asking myself, "How am I going to fit in? How am I going to make it? and so on, I reached a point where it suddenly struck me that the people there were not superior, and I was not inferior. They were different but they were also the same. And therefore I realised that I had to deal with them just as people: equal to equal. Until then I had always thought of myself as inferior to white people. I had always thought that the whites were higher, the whites were superior, and that I mustn't let down my side. But once I began thinking that they're just different, and I am different, and they have just got to accept my differences because I am accepting their differences from me ... that made a big change in my thinking and my self-confidence. It removed the imprinted deference that I had carried with me until then – where you look up to somebody as if by nature they have to be superior to you.

When I came back in 1970, I was ordained and I spent a couple of months learning the Corsa language. I had known smatterings of it before I went but with that long absence (and especially having learned another language in the meantime) it had just disappeared, so I started from scratch. My first parish appointment was to a rural parish in South Africa where there was a very small segment of white people (one or two families), about twenty coloured families, and the rest blacks. I was well received by everybody there but the thing that touched me most was the time when I went out to one of the communities and in introducing me and welcoming me, one of the local black women said, "How happy we are now we have one of our own sons as our priest."

And you know that actually twisted me on my head! Here was I thinking that I did not belong to these people. In fact I had been thinking that I was above them because I was a coloured man, not a black man! And here is this woman saying, "This man is like my son". It made such a difference to me to have to recognise that these people were not inferior to me, just as I was not inferior to the whites. They were just the same. Yes, they were different (of course they've got their differences!), but basically we are the same and on one level. Until then I had expected deference from below. Blacks would never call me by my name. They always had to add something like "master so and so". That South African thought structure makes you relate to people in a very particular way.

So this was what I like to call "the two great graces" in my life: I was put into a position where I was dealing with people on an equal footing. It had a huge impact on me personally and professionally, especially when I was involved in the Bishops' Conference as vice-president, after I had been elected bishop. That appointment tossed me right into the maelstroms of political negotiations and mediations that were going on in Southern Africa at the time. And because of those two flashes of inspiration, I found myself not necessarily feeling that when I am talking to blacks I can talk down to them or when I am taking to whites I have to talk up to them, but that here we are all equal and that we all have to share in the same human rights. I think that was one of the great discoveries and great graces that I was given by God. To a large extent that inspiration came from having gone overseas. If I had remained in South Africa I probably would have continued to hate and feel antagonistic towards whites, whilst maintaining a sense of superiority over blacks. Exposure to a completely different setting where people accepted you as a human being without any racial categories or grading philosophies … you know … I think that was one of the great lights of my life.

How was it that you were created a cardinal of the Catholic Church?

Becoming a priest was turned into a reality for me by the priests from my parish. There were five boys in my family and they were constantly saying, "It would be very nice if one of you would become a priest."

In fact, in my final year at school, my eldest brother – who had been working in a Nestle factory, making cheese and chocolate and condensed milk and things like that, but who hadn't decided what he was actually going to do – got very friendly with one of the Irish priests, one of the Franciscans. It was during that time, I think, that he decided he might give the priesthood a try. But he wanted to be a brother. Sometime before he had spent a short spell working with the brothers when they were building a hospital in a place called Bizana, and he really came to admire the way they worked. So he thought he might go and try to be a brother. But the parish priest said to him, "You've got your matric, you've got all your academic qualifications, why don't you go and try to be a priest?"

So he went over to Ireland and spent six months in a seminary and he decided that it was not for him. I think the reason why he did not really persevere was that he wasn't the studying type. I am not very much either, but he was worse than me! And doing this year he realised he would be much happier doing things with his hands. When he got to the seminary he loved the life that it offered, being with the guys and all that, but it just wasn't his vocation. So he came home then and he related to me, "Ah, it's just like boarding school! You've got guys you're going to like, and some that you're not going to get on with, but there is a spirit of fraternity and the Irish are very welcoming and very hospitable." And that encouraged me during the last six months at school to really make up my mind as to what I was going to do.

Making the grade, doing well in my studies, going overseas, getting on well in the Franciscan life, getting to know the friars very well and becoming a member of their community meant that becoming a priest wasn't such a big deal, if I may put it like that. But that's what I expected my life to be like for the rest of my working life in the parish. I was as contented as anything working in the parish; especially as I had become part of a crowd of priest who were trying new things while I was an assistant priest. The after-effects of the Second Vatican Council were being applied very unevenly in different parts of the world and even in our diocese. One part was doing very well and other parts were not doing very well. I got in with a crowd of very vigorous and engaged younger priests who wanted to make Vatican II a reality in our lives, and that shaped my ideas as to how I would lead the rest of my life.

But then I was transferred to another parish. I was there on my own for about five years and then one afternoon (I remember it so well) there was an old tree stump just outside in the yard and I was busy digging it out (getting some exercise) and the next thing that happens is that the phone rings and it's the bishop in Coxford and he says to me, "Can you please come in tomorrow? There is something I want to talk to you about." And I said, "Sure!" And I headed in and when I got there he says to me, "Ah, I've had this note from the apostolic delegate and they want to appoint you the administrator of the diocese." And I said, "Gee! What does that mean?" (They said they want to appoint me, but they had already appointed me. He was just giving me the information). And he said, "I will be here for another month; so come in and I will show you all that you need to do."

So I went home and the first thing I had to do was go to the Code of Canon Law and find out what this was all about. And the new code had not even come out; so there wasn't even an explanation as to what "administrator" meant! Anyway, I went in for the next week. I stayed in Coxford and he showed me where the different documents were; where this was, and that was, and if you want to find something look here … One of the handiest things that he showed me was a book of templates for appointments; for giving people appointments and for writing official letters and so on. It was very handy because if someone came and said, "Can I have this?" I could go to the book and I could find it in there. And then two weeks later he calls me and says, "Come in tomorrow. I wanted to see you for something." And I get in there and he tells me, "I'm leaving tomorrow." So I was literally left to my own devices to run the diocese! So I got together the guys who had been his counsellors and advisors and so on (his college of consulters) and I said, "This is what I am faced with here. Can you help me whatever way you can?" Then I got in touch with the canon lawyer at the seminary to find out from him if he could give me a description of the rights and the obligations of an administrator. And then I walked straight into a whole lot of financial and contractual problems that were rather testing. I thought the best thing I can do is head over to Ireland to try to sort everything out. You see because the friars (the Franciscans) who had been in the diocese were under the Irish province, certain things came directly under the Franciscan province and others were through the bishop. They had to work through the bishop. One of them would be the grants for the missions – they had to run the missions – the Irish province was actually supplying [money to build buildings, run schools, etc.] but they went through the bishop. So I said, "Let me go back to Ireland and meet with the provincial there and meet with the old bishop (who had retired) and one of the priests who had been involved in these contracts and also taken extended leave in Ireland."

So I was going to go and see him. On the way back I went through Rome as well. The friars had advised me to go to the general house in Rome. They told me that there was a guy there who was excellent in canon law. He had taught canon law all his life. So they told me that he would help me if I went to him. And that was the best advice I got. I went and I sat with this guy and he went through the documents with me. He got out every document that he could find.

So when I came back I was a bit of an expert on what an apostolic administrator could and couldn't do! And once I was in that position, and once I was attending Bishops' Conference meetings and so on, I guess it was natural that I be considered a possibility as the next bishop of Coxford. That happened two-and-a half years later in February, 1981. At the time I thought there were a number of other guys in the various dioceses who could have done the job better than I, but you know when I had got that far I think the fountain of grace just carried me along. Certain things do just seem to carry you along – the support of your brother bishops and so on.

In '83 I was elected vice-president of IMBESA (that's a regional conference that includes Mozambique, Zimbabwe and Angola and all the countries to the south of that, nine countries altogether) – how that came about I will never know! Then the next year I was elected vice-president of our Bishops' Conference in Southern Africa itself. And between those two functions I was tossed into the whole operation of what was going on in Southern Africa.

Did that mean that you became involved in decision making and politics?
At the regional level it was not so much decision making as sharing ideas and problems, and showing solidarity to one another. For instance, at that time South Africa was waging a war with Angola using Namibia (it was still called South West Africa at that time) as their front. Both countries were using surrogate countries to fight their wars of communism and apartheid, and Namibia was going through a particularly difficult time as a result. As the Bishops' Conference, we found ourselves going there to investigate the situation, so that we could make public the atrocities and irregularities being committed by the South African government.

So as part of the Bishops' Conference, and particularly as vice-president of the conference, I was thrown into interaction with prominent politicians, civil leaders and church leaders. Intermingling and interacting with other church leaders was a very, very important role because we had to develop a common vision and a common set of objectives that would make a powerful impact on the way the situation in places like Angola was developing.

Were you ever in any position where you could have been forced into exile by the South African government?
No, we were protected by the fact that we were a very strong Bishops' Conference and [there was] a great unity in that conference as well. It

would have been much easier for them to expel a foreign-born bishop than to expel or force one of their own citizens into exile. Withdrawing a resident's permit would have been much, much easier than forcing somebody to leave the country.

The next step, becoming cardinal, was out of my mind completely. I never, never, never would have dreamt of that. In fact I knew at the stage just before I was appointed there was talk about the possibility because Cardinal McCann (the first South African cardinal) had survived [as cardinal] after he had retired and I think the practice in the Vatican (there are no clear outlines) is that if a bishop was a cardinal and he has retired, but still living, then he will not be replaced until he dies.

So there is a limit to the number of cardinals?
I don't know if that was the limit or whether in a country like South Africa you wouldn't replace the cardinal while he was still alive ... You know, Cardinal McCann was the first and I am the second. So while he was still alive, would you put another cardinal in? When he died, people started talking about when South Africa would have another cardinal. And by that stage, yes, I had moved up the ladder into IMBESA and then around about '89 one of the really dynamic bishops in South Africa (Archbishop Steven Nyado) took ill and died from a heart condition. He was a very good theologian and also a very good speaker, and he had been appointed by Pope John Paul II as one of the members of the council that was chosen to prepare the African synod. I had been with him to the Vatican for the synod on two occasions previously; I went to the synod on parents and reconciliation in '84, and then the synod on laity in '87 and we got along very well (… and we looked alike as well. So maybe they all thought they were putting the other guy in as cardinal except he was in the grave by that stage ...). When he took ill and couldn't continue, they appointed me in his place. I suppose that was because I had had exposure to the life

of the Vatican through the synod. But when he died and everyone was speculating about the appointment of the next cardinal, I did not think we would get another cardinal and I told people that we should just wait and see.

And then the names came out. Just that January we were actually in a plenary session of the Bishops' Conference … The first list of 37 names came out and I was like, "Thank goodness. I wasn't one of them, and you guys were just speculating." But a week later while I was still at the conference I got a phone call from the nuncio and this is how he phrased it: "Are you alone?" "Yes I am alone." "Can you speak?" "Yes I can speak." "Well I just wanted to tell you that the Pope has appointed you cardinal." And I got such a shock. I said, "WHAT!" And he said, "Yes," he said, "look, come around some evening and I'll tell you what it's all about."

Sounds very much like being the administrator again.

It's very much the same story. We had a custom every Saturday during our plenary session where we would go down to the nuncio's place for dinner and that whole night I kept as far from him as possible in case he had just had a bad dream and he had called me and made a mistake. Eventually he took me aside and said, "Please, we need to talk." And he told me what I needed to do, and gave me my instructions from Rome, and told me that I had to do this and this and get in touch with so and so and whatever. So I phoned Rome, gave them my directions as to my sizes for a soutane and all of those kinds of things and then I got ready. That was on the 20th of January or thereabouts, and the Consistory was going to be on the 21st of February. There was very little time to do anything.

Then there was so much excitement. All of the family wanted to come and they all had to get visas and get tickets and so on…oh it was a remarkable period, a remarkable event!

Can you tell me how you have translated St Francis the poor man who lived in solidarity with the homeless into your life professionally and personally both pre- and post-apartheid?

There are two things that I would say; one would be that being a Franciscan and having gone through the training I did in Ireland, was very significant. It gave me a real understanding of how human the church is and yet how divinely inspired it is. Because of a renewal that had gone on in Ireland in the early part of the 1900s (1920s or thereabouts), I found that when I arrived in Ireland the Irish province had been completely re-established in the strictest observance of the rule. Previously, British persecution had earmarked friars who were considered enemies of the British crown because they were so close to the people. Their proximity to education and to daily life meant that they could ask questions and influence people in their thinking [in ways] that other clergy couldn't do quite as easily. As a result, the friars had made themselves hardly distinguishable as diocesan priests. They did not wear the habit (it was proscribed to wear the habit) and they dressed as ordinary people, while still living a version of community life.

Then, in the 1920s, Rome decided, "No! We're going to bring our friars back into line with the rule." Every so often Franciscans go through a little spring cleaning that leads them back to the original observance of the rule. And so one of the things that they did in Ireland was return Franciscan life back to its very strictest forms: There was no handling of money, for example. You did not collect money. You went and you asked, you requested, you begged for the things that you needed and the brothers used to go out and do that on a regular basis. In Killarney that quest was systematised. It was still done but it was the Killarney novitiate houses that were doing that. A brother would go out with a pony and trap to the local dairy and as the farmers came there he would ask them if they could help the friary out with the means to live, and each one would put down a certain amount of milk or the value of the milk and that would be translated into supplies for the friary for the next year.

So when I went in, I joined in. My first experience of friars in Ireland was being picked up at Dublin airport. There were two friars in the car and a young fellow who was going into the novitiate with me. On our way into Dublin we stopped the car to fill up with petrol. One friar took some money out of his own pocket, handed it to the young fella, and he paid when it came to paying time. I was wondering, "What the heck is going on here?" When I got to the novitiate we were told that the rule of the friars was to be read every Friday as St Francis wrote it. And then during the week we would have chapter after chapter being explained to us on the use of money. And the constitution was explained as well, including what exceptions could be made with regards to the use of money and so on. But the system then was that if people came to the door and wanted to make an offering for mass or make a donation or something, a layman would normally be the financial administrator of the friary who did all the money transactions, and the superior of the house would work through him in paying bills. So we never handled money.

That was the first big shock to me. On the missions, they couldn't exist if they did not handle the money. So I realised then that this Franciscan ... this poverty is really something that has been taken very seriously! In the relations that the local friars had with the community you could see it as well. The people who frequented the friary churches were generally the poorer people. So there was a direct link up with the poor. So living the life of St Francis and experiencing it in Ireland, in that friary situation, was for me quite an exposure as to how life was supposed to be lived in the 20th century.

Going to Louvain was somewhat different. Belgium was a more secular society, even though it is very Catholic. But it had different customs [from those] I experienced in the friary. The consulate had come in the meantime and as a result there was a loosening up of certain restrictions, which had been there before. I remember the student master said, "The best way to help people to be responsible in the use of money is to give them the use of money".

So we used to get a little allowance every week or every month, and we could do with that allowance what we wished. Those who were smokers knew exactly what they needed to do – buy cigarettes! The rest of us got a certain amount that (if we let it accumulate!) meant that we could go buy what we wanted after making sure we had provided for ourselves. We learnt that that is how you looked after your money. So that was a good introduction.

When I got back on the mission area in South Africa there was a bursar of the diocese and if you needed something for your mission work you would go to him and say, "I need repairs to my car, or I need this, or the other", and he would pay for that or he would give you the money to pay for that. But for your personal and Franciscan needs you had to go to the Franciscan Superior and at that stage they had already instituted a similar kind of thing where you got a certain allowance every month and you worked on that. If you needed more, for something else, you went to him and you asked for it. So that was a good way of doing it and as I mentioned to you earlier, I got into that group of younger priests who were very, very good at being among the people. Their lives were about serving the people, and I was into the same kind of lifestyle myself. So translating Franciscan life wasn't really an issue. It was just living. And living it in the parish situation was just as I had lived it in the friary situation.

Someone once told me that South Africans who left the country during or post-apartheid would claim that they left out of fear for the safety of their families, but that in truth they were racists who could not survive in a democratic South Africa. Can you comment?

Well the first thing I would say is that it is very dangerous to put things too much in black and white. You know? To say that basically the people were racist who left the country after 1994; I think it is much more nuanced than that; much, much more. Pre-94, [there were probably] a lot of people leaving because they did not want to get involved in the black-white conflict that was foreseen, you know. There were times where people said "no, we've got to get out of here because things are going to go up like Congo or some other place [where social cohesion dissolved into outright conflict]."

I know that prior to '94 they were expecting an uprising, and after '94 as well. I think it's also dangerous to put a black-white complexion on the issues because there are so many different reasons why people have left: Certainly some have left because they have feared for their lives. Others felt that there was absolutely no chance of them getting advancement in their jobs. A third category would be those who said [they] are doing it for their children, having calculated for affirmative action. That means that if any job is being offered a black must be given preference whether they are qualified or have an equal qualification or not, and secondly, they would have calculated for black economic empowerment. That means that everything which a white owns in a business sense has to have some black people involved in it in its administration and control.

Now, how do you do that when you don't even know who these people are and you have nothing in common with them? The assumption was that because somebody is black then they would have been excluded. But many people who were white were also being excluded. Whites excluded other whites whose principles and way of life they wouldn't have approved of and they wouldn't have formed common companies with them either. So I think that many people have done it on the basis that black economic empowerment, especially the wealthier ones, the ones who are running companies or businesses would have said, "This is government impinging on my turf" and unjustifiably so! There would certainly be people who would say, "South Africa is going the same way as many other countries.

Look at Zimbabwe! We are getting out!" Of course, many, many white South Africans would have been influenced by white Zimbabweans who came down to South Africa with horror stories to tell. So I think it is much more nuanced than, "They are racists." And one reason why I say that is that many of those you would expect to have been "dyed in the wool" racists – once they were exposed to the new South Africa they became different people. They were just as much trapped by apartheid as the blacks had been.

Let me explain: If you were sitting here talking to me like this, you could be sure a white person passing by (one of your friends) would say, "Oh, there must be something going on there. She's not to be trusted." And you would be ostracised. In order to escape that ostracism, you would rather stay clear of me. So, for example, no white person went into the black township. So it is true ... they could say, "We didn't know what was going on in the black townships."

Secondly, the propaganda machinery was excellent. It was just like Nazi Germany's propaganda machinery, and many white people would believe everything they were told. They were told it wasn't apartheid, it wasn't discrimination, it was separate development, and what the whites have in their towns, we are going to put in the townships for the blacks. Of course they had a few samples, "model" towns. And they tried to create independent black states within South Africa. They created one out of one of the homelands. So they could say, "Look, there is a black president, and a black government." And for a period there was progress, and there was something to show for the idea that blacks could do what whites could do (but they need our little hand of control over them!)

So you know, that story "we didn't know what was going on" – it is quite believable. You would never mix together with people [from other racial groupings] except as master/servant. So you wouldn't sit down and talk to somebody and say, "And by the way how are your children doing at school? And, what are their visions? And, how does it feel when your child wants to be a doctor and they can't do that?" You wouldn't have had the opportunity to talk about it [and so you wouldn't have understood]. I will give you an example. I remember one day, I think I was at a Catholic Women's League meeting or something of that kind; I used to go into these meetings from time to time when they invited me, and one of the ladies as the meeting was closing said, "Woops, I'd better take my maid back to the township!" And one of them said, "What do you mean? You can't go in there! You're not allowed to go in there!" And the first one said, "What are you talking about? I've been going in there for the last five years. I take her home every afternoon." And the other lady said, "Oh It's so dangerous!" And then the first lady said, "Well I've been in there and nothing's ever happened to me."

So, the impression was that because they are out there, we are not allowed to go in there. It was not a case of having asked and having been forbidden. But we just assumed that was the case. So you see, some truth can be found in the statements that would have been made by whites [who claimed that they] did not know what was going on. And I think it would certainly be true that they wouldn't have known [about the actions of] the leaders of the ANC or the operations movements, about PR Sapo, who were identified as troublemakers but [not known] about how they really were. As they said, I don't think they would have known that. As for Nelson Mandela, the state machinery tried to keep everything quiet about Mandela. He was portrayed as a mere terrorist. They never would have actually said what he did or did not do, or what he was put in prison for. As far as the people were concerned, he was a terrorist. As far as I know, while Nelson Mandela was leader of the ANC section overseas and they were planning sabotage attacks, Nelson Mandela himself never triggered or instructed anybody to commit acts of terror. Oh, but the government would have said that Nelson Mandela was a terrorist. That was what the publicity machinery was saying. And it was the same for all of the guys who were in prison. They were portrayed as communists and anyone fighting against the apartheid system was a communist. Even the Catholic Church was accused of being communist and their leaders as communist sympathisers, or [it was implied] that we were too ignorant to realise that we were being used by the communists!

The other thing I would say is that concerns about job opportunities for their children would certainly have got a lot of people leaving South Africa. If it was only racism and people were racists ... Lots of coloured people have left before 1994, and many more have left since then. Many who left in the '80s, possibly into the '90s, would have left because of concerns over job opportunities for their children and because of concerns about the potential for the breakdown of Apartheid turning into conflict.

The other reason that has possibly been left out pre-'94 was the expectation of military service for boys and what that did to them. They were absolutely brainwashed. Somehow they knew that before they entered that military service by the time they left they would be expected to serve the philosophy of the apartheid regime. Once a white boy reached the age of eighteen and left school, he had to go and do his two years military service. And that meant that during those two years you were doing what the Afrikaner government told you to do. Thereafter you would probably be bound by certain secrecies about certain actions that had taken place and that you had participated in.

So, you know, the reasons for leaving post-apartheid would be varied and very different ... I bumped into somebody the other day who said one of his good friends who ... has been here in Australia for two or three years now and one of his reasons for leaving was just [that] there is just no future for him as a business man with all the corruption that is going on among members of the government. Now that's not because they are black. It's because they are corrupt.

So, I would say for every one that you find ... who has left for racist reasons; another nine would have very different reasons for doing so.

You know talking about the Franciscan angle – when I was informed that I was going to be the bishop of Coxford (I got the appointment in December and started making arrangements for things that needed to be made, rings and a cross and so on) one of my [confreres] came to me and said, "By the way have you decided on your coat of arms, your crest?"

This is the picture?
Yes, that's the one and I said, "No." And he says well you've got to choose a motto as well and I said that I'd forgotten about that. So I was busy tossing around what motto I was going to take, and something just lit up like a light and he said, "Why don't you take the one of St Francis? It might sound a little presumptuous, but you are a Franciscan after all."

So I took *pax et bonum* which was the greeting that Francis used whenever he went preaching around the different villages in Italy (*pax et bonum* – peace and goodwill).

For me that was just fulfilling the convention, that every bishop has a crest and a motto. Only some years later I realised that *pax et bonum*, peace and goodwill, was like a challenge that was being placed before me, to work for peace and goodwill from within the people in South Africa. It was when I was [with] our bishops (my Archbishop Hurley, who was president of our conference for example, or one of the other bishops who were busy mediating disagreements between political parties); it just struck me – "Gee! That was a commitment that I was asked to make. It wasn't just a convention I was fulfilling!" It made me realise that sometimes when you make these decisions to do something, you think it's on the spur of the moment, but in fact it's a flash of grace that God has given you and He's got a nice little job attached to it for you to do as well. And when we were in the midst of some of these very difficult negotiations, I'd say to myself, "Gosh, this is what God was telling me when He said *pax et bonum* was your motto."

2 i. NIGERIA

Nigeria is one of Africa's leviathans. Made up of around 240 different ethnic groups, it is Africa's most populous nation. It is bordered by Benin, Chad, Cameroon, and Niger. On its coast in the south are the Gulf of Guinea and the Atlantic Ocean. The average Nigerian will live 52 years. Around 60 per cent of people over the age of 15 can read and write, and most children will spend nine years school. Women will give birth to approximately five children (26 per cent of children under the age of five are underweight). In 2010, 3.3 million people over the age of 15 (3.6 per cent of the population and 360,000 children) were infected with HIV.[48] GDP sits at 244 billion USD (2011), and population density at 174 people for every square kilometre (2010).[49]

British influence and control grew throughout the 19th century in the area now known as Nigeria, beginning with the abolition of the British slave trade (1807) and British determination (after the Napoleonic Wars) to halt the international trade in slaves by stopping trading boats leaving the African coastline and (sometimes) returning the captured to their colony in Sierra Leone. From 1885 the British claim to a sphere of influence in Western Africa was recognised by other European powers, and in 1901 Nigeria became a protectorate and member of the British Empire. For a long time after establishing themselves in the area, however, the British were hesitant to enter the Niger hinterland. Tribal federations (like the Ibos and Yoruba), northern Muslims, numerous and warring tribes, and the sweltering

---
48 See footnote 40.
49 (http://www.indexmundi.com), accessed 25 May 2013; (http://www.tradingeconomics.com), accessed 25 May 2013.

and hostile rain-forest were unnerving for the British who only were only tempted to venture in (and then timidly) by the stimulus of trade.[50] They eventually established protectorates over the whole area (as much to keep the Germans and the French out) and converted those into a unified Crown colony in 1914.

The formal unification of ethnically diverse areas in the north and south continues to be problematic for Nigeria. Early and continuous interaction with Europeans through the coastal economy in the South modernised the South more rapidly than the north. It also established an on-going exchange of ideas which lead to the adaption of Western education, for example. (Many of Nigeria's elite sons were sent to the United Kingdom for education.) Early political life also demonstrated regional differences, with northern Nigeria not outlawing slavery until the middle of the 1930s, for example. Since achieving independence in 1960 and becoming a republic and a federally constituted state in 1963 differences and rivalries have remained. The republic has been swamped by decades of dictatorships.[51] From 1966 the country was embroiled in back-to-back coups and in 1967 a declaration of independence by the Igbo people of the eastern regions led to the Nigerian Civil War. It lasted 30 months and killed one million people.

From a distance the north/south divisions appear to motivated by clear-cut religious differences (Muslim/Christian) but they are more accurately described as political, financial and resource oriented (oil) rivalries, which are now waged as much by Western multi-national corporations as they are by resourceful militia-like Nigerian gangsters. The current government continues to face the daunting task of reforming a petroleum-based economy (oil provides 95 per cent of foreign exchange earnings and about 80 per cent of budgetary revenues) whose profits have been squandered through corruption and

---

50 Of the 48 Europeans of the first Niger trading expedition, 39 never came back. p. 322, Morris, Op. Cit.
51 Jonathon Hill, (2012) *Nigeria Since Independence*, Palgrave McMillan, London.

mismanagement, and institutionalising democracy. And the country continues to experience ethnic and religious tensions that thwart attempts at economic and political unity.[52] Both the 2003 and the 2007 presidential elections were marred by significant irregularities and violence, the latter marking the first civilian-to-civilian transfer of power in the country's history. Nigeria has been lamented as a "theatre of fraud", "a country of marvellous scammers", and the trigger point for Africa-as-pistol.[53] It has also been described as "too big, too wild, too many", the armpit of the continent, and a source of laughably unsophisticated internet fraud and periodic extreme violence.[54] No wonder some continue to see the country as a "monument to humanity's ability to function in the most forbidding circumstances".[55]

Francis Cardinal Arinze was born on 1 November 1931, in Eziowelle, Anambra State, Nigeria. He was baptised on his ninth birthday by Father Michael Tansi[56], who was beatified by John Paul II in 1998. Between 1950 and 1965 he earned a philosophy degree from All Hallows Seminary of Onitsha, taught at All Hallows, studied theology at the Pontifical Urban University in Rome, was ordained a priest in 1958, awarded a master's degree and then a doctorate in theology, was a professor of liturgy, logic and basic philosophy at Bigard Memorial Seminary, regional secretary for Catholic education for the eastern part of Nigeria and graduated from the Institute of Education in London. In 1965, aged 32, he became the youngest Roman Catholic bishop in the world. He was appointed titular bishop of Fissiana and named coadjutor to the Archbishop of Onitsha, Nigeria. He attended the final

---

52 (https://www.cia.gov/library/publications/the-world-factbook/geos/ni.html), accessed 16 May 2013.
53 Colin Powell quoted in Peel, Op. Cit.
54 Ibid., p. xx
55 Ibid., p. 76, (https://en.wikipedia.org/wiki/Nigeria, https://www.cia.gov/library/publications/the-world-factbook/geos/ni.html), accessed October 2011
56 See (www.catholicculture.org/culture/library/view.cfm?recnum=323), accessed June 2011

session of the Second Vatican Council (along with the 45-year-old Archbishop of Krakow, Karol Wojtyla, the future Pope John Paul II). He was appointed the first native African Archbishop of Onitsha in 1967.

Made Archbishop of Onitsha one week before the outbreak of the civil war (1967-1970), Arinze fled with fellow refugees to Adazi and Amichi where he worked tirelessly for the displaced and supervised what has been described as "one of the most effective and efficient distributions of relief materials" in history. After the deportation of foreign clergy and the confiscation of Catholic schools he built the Church into a truly Nigerian space that promises political objectivity and ethical solidity within a country ruled by chaos.

Between 1979 and 1996 Arinze was a member of the Vatican's secretariat for non-Christians, later renamed the Pontifical Council for Interreligious Dialogue, President of the Nigerian Bishops' Conference, and created cardinal in 1985. Named prefect of the Congregation for Divine Worship and the Discipline of the Sacraments in 2002, he participated in the 2005 papal conclave that elected Pope Benedict XVI who made him Cardinal-Bishop of Velletri-Segni, which had been vacated by Benedict's election as pope.

I interviewed Cardinal Arinze twice in Rome, in September 2011 and April 2012.

ii. Arrogance?

... For I am afraid that when I come I may not find you as I want you to be, and you may not find me as you want me to be. I fear that there may be quarreling, jealousy, outbursts of anger, factions, slander, gossip, arrogance and disorder ...[57]

The first time I met Cardinal Arinze was at the top of a four-storey building that flanks St Peter's Square outside the Vatican. It is an impressive address. He lives in a penthouse, surrounded by a balcony with views across Rome on one side, and almost within touching distance of St Peter's Basilica on the other. Since I was a small child, I have never felt comfortable in places like St Peter's. The marble and the sculpture are astonishing, but while the various depictions of Christ on the cross and of Mary, (the Pieta by Michelangelo in particular) are no doubt artistic works of genius, they had not until then resonated very deeply with me. Wandering through St Peter's with my history headset the day before the interview, I heard that Michelangelo was aiming for a "religious vision of abandonment" in the Pietà, but I thought that Mary's composure seemed out of keeping with her predicament. Her chiselled serenity and resignation made her seem insipid and tame. *Perhaps he was aiming for the Renaissance woman with which he was familiar*, I wrote in my journal that evening; *an era when women were generally denied their independence, and their power and agency noticeably declined?*[58] Certainly at the time Mary did not look to me as a leader for the mothers who honour her today. *I do want to identify with her,* I wrote, *and particularly with the love that she undoubtedly expressed for her son, but if I'm going to, then I need to be able to*

---
57 Corinthians 12:20
58 Kelly, J. (1984), *Women, History & Theory, The Essays of Joan Kelly*, The University of Chicago Press, Chicago, pp. 19–50.

"feel her pain": *With my own son dead and stretched out across my knees, I think I would be doubled over and screeching with grief!* My generation of Western women were raised watching the status of motherhood decline. Feminism in the 1960s delivered choices to our mothers. Now it delivers them the "cult of everything". Those who embrace motherhood as a vocation live in fear of the cult's judgement. We often rationalise our choice with vociferous and sometimes angry expressions of love. Perhaps Michelangelo's Mary would have felt more real to me at the time (more like me), if Michelangelo had portrayed her in a more aggressive and protective defence of Jesus.

Inside St Peter's and surrounding those key figures there was a darkness to art forms that I wrote as *preoccupied with suffering, death, and retribution*. That feeling increased and then peaked as I moved to Bernini's ponderous and onerous Baldachino over the papal altar that sits above the ancient tomb of St Peter. The mood lifted as my eyes moved skyward, across Giuseppe Cesari's mosaics of popes, cherubs, and angels and towards the final cupola and a brilliant depiction of heaven that provided relief (and light) from the suffering and sinful humanity (and the dimly lit interior) depicted below. But I still found it difficult to relate to the message as it unfolded. My belief in social democracy, in protection of the underdog, made the juxtaposition of wealth and power (and in the case of Pope Urban VIII – nepotism as well!) problematic. *It presents as a gross demonstration of hypocrisy; an unfathomable indulgence in self-congratulation that sits badly with the over-riding Christian message of love that I assume Jesus intended, at least in part, for the poor of his time.*

That said, as I rounded the corner and Piazza St Pietro came into view that morning, my "objective" scrutiny began to wither. The realisation that I was meeting one of the four most powerful Catholics in the world hit me fairly suddenly. I felt dwarfed by the outstretched arms of Bernini's colonnade and stared down by the saints who stand along its top. I felt both utterly insignificant and hopelessly conspicuous at the same time and my confidence slipped away. The idea that I, a non-Catholic and left-wing woman of the new modern era, should be standing at this powerful man's stairwell in a possibly too-short skirt was all of a sudden ridiculous and intimidating. I instantly became defensive.

Arinze is a relatively short man, good-looking, with an enormous white smile and surprisingly small hands. He was wearing a black cassock when he first opened his door and while he motioned for me to come into his home, he was hesitant about shaking my hand. After I entered he attempted to usher me into a small chapel that he had within his apartment but it confused me. Not being a Catholic I did not understand his expectation. Was the meeting between them to occur there? I felt completely inadequate at that moment, unsure of what to do and then fundamentally aware that I had failed his first test. "Ah," he said thoughtfully, "So you are *not* a Catholic." He took some water, crossed his heart and ushered me into a second room, a lounge room, where I sat on a couch with a view of a huge painting of another dark-skinned priest with a halo. It was *Cyprian Michael Tansi,* the man who had inspired him to enter the Church, he explained, now beatified by a long and complicated process that he said proved his presence in heaven. "Of course everyone is in heaven", he said, "But this man we know for sure!"

Prior to the meeting I had hurriedly forwarded my interests to him to give him some ideas about my questions. My intention, I explained, was to write a group biography about the African cardinals, about the Africanisation of the gospels, about possible collegialities that might exist across the continent and between those who were appointed to the most senior positions inside the Catholic Church by John Paul II. I wanted to know if John Paul II had foreseen a vast expansion of the Church throughout Africa via the appointment of African men to such senior positions, and whether or not he considered such men better shepherds for African flocks amidst the turbulence of the 20th century than their European counterparts. The number of Catholics on the continent of Africa has trebled in the last 30 years. Surely that has something to do with leadership; more particularly it must have something to do with the choice of African leaders? Should we be celebrating the rise of black men to positions of leadership within the Church, and the vast expansion of the Church across that continent, as the genius of John Paul II?

In truth, I was quite unprepared, having landed the interview while on holiday with my family. Many of the ideas contained in the questions were perhaps beyond my comprehension at that time. What I really wanted was to get to know the man under the red hat. I wanted to believe that beneath the somewhat harsh and public face of the Roman Curia that he wore, there was a human being with a kindly soul that ached and loved and cringed and laughed, just as I did. I wanted to believe in the power of forgiveness and above all in the power of love. Quite simply, I wanted to believe that human nature is a universal truth transcending racial origin, skin colour, time, culture and religion. But trying to appear "learned" actually left me feeling stupid. In those first few minutes Arinze turned my thinking upside down with an impressive, albeit haughty, kind of grace. He depicted my emphasis on the significance of racial origin as skewed and painted my preoccupation with skin colour as trite. Discussing skin colour was a dead end, he said. Within the Church, he suggested, (and no doubt elsewhere too) skin colour is irrelevant. People identify with one another through mutual worship of the same God, not by the colour of their skin![59] I had assumed that in a country created by a white man's indiscriminate demarcation of geographical borders that took little notice of pre-existing ethnic divisions, ethnic groups

---

59 Discussions about the relevance of skin colour are many and current. See "Ending Insurgencies, building peace", *'Just World News' with Helena Cobban*, 2 February 2006 (http://justworldnews.org/archives/001707.html), accessed 13 March 2012. Blogging about peace building in Mozambique a discussion ensues about the relevance of mentioning skin colour in describing Cardinal Dos Santos of Mozambique.

would be drawn to one another by a sense of injustice and that they would recognise and identify with other victims of that injustice by the colour of skin.

I had been schooled through my conversation with Cardinal Napier and a vague comprehension of the black consciousness movement. In South Africa, delineations based on skin colour *have* caused different racial groups to either suffer or to prosper. Indeed, the apartheid regime institutionalised a heightened sensitivity to the colour of skin. Cardinal Napier told me that a black priest was naturally identified as "one of us" by his black parishioners, as opposed to "one of them"; and that the colour of his own skin had drawn parishioners to seek him out. But Arinze swept Napier's observations aside: "What South Africa does is a matter for them", he said. Nigeria was created by the combination of more than 200 various ethnic groupings that may or may not have had any interest in one another to start with, he told me. Ethnicity or religions are what link people together across the geographical boundaries that defined what the English called Nigeria. *When everyone has black skin, is colour no longer relevant?*

The argument with skin colour apparently over, Arinze went on to defeat further ideas I was exploring about oppression, injustice, even indoctrination: Educational opportunities offered by the missionaries (and supported by the British colonising authority) were not oppressive, but liberating. "The missionaries were a great instrument of development", he told me. "Once people learnt about the rest of the world [through education] they began to realise their political and economic rights ... The missionaries did not impose their religion. If a young man wanted to go to the Catholic school but did not want baptism, it was not forced. It was free." Catholic missionaries offered children like him an education that was otherwise unavailable and he chose it.⁶⁰ Arinze took possession of his decision to enter the seminary with hindsight, emphasising the notion of choice in baptism a number of times. By describing that choice he seemed very effectively to sidestep the whole question of Catholic indoctrination, to justify what could be perceived as a painful and disloyal rejection of his family by describing the educational experience as "enlightened", and to put modern theories about adolescence to bed.

The discussion reminded me of a book by Paul Dinter (a priest) who talks about the attraction of the Church to young adolescent men in 1950s America, *The Other Side of the Altar.* It was loaned to me by a former Mormon who had rejected the family faith and found herself hounded by priestly elders for some time subsequently. Dinter focuses largely on priestly struggles with celibacy and power, but he also takes the time to depict the priesthood as a safe haven for the growth of a boy's individual identity, particularly if a boy's father was emotionally distant and severe.

> In the idealised male world of the aspirant priest, a boy's identity was defined not by how you stood vis-à-vis young women or even how other guys accepted you, but by feeling included in a circle of men who stood apart from the crowd ... being made to feel special – it was not the style our fathers had followed with us – could help a young man jump through a lot of hoops in the course of his growing up.⁶¹

Dinter's book made me see Arinze's experience in the seminary as part and parcel of a quite natural and normal emotional development, and strangely enough reasserted my belief in the significance of skin

---

60 See footnote number 27. "Often African children came from cultures that encouraged obedience and conformity in the young. In Burundi, a boy who became a priest and an outstanding writer remembered later, 'I contented myself by learning what I was taught "to get marks" and pass for a docile child. But internally I was against anything which opposed my conviction'." Isichei (1995), Op. Cit., p. 236.
61 P. Dinter (2003), *The Other Side of the Altar, One Man's Life in the Catholic Priesthood*, Douglas and McIntyre Ltd, Canada, p. 11.

colour in John Paul II's most senior appointments within Africa. First, I could not help wondering if, as priest and teacher, Tansi had provided the positive role model that Arinze-the-boy was looking for. And that the Christian nature of Tansi's message had become entwined with the lasting impression that he made on Arinze-the-man. (Hence the immediate reference to his portrait as I arrived.) Second, I believed that given the opportunity to choose between a European mentor and Tansi, Arinze would have been drawn to Tansi because he identified with him as a man of African origin, a male mentor who suited, supported and encouraged his self-development into a different adolescent experience that ultimately felt comfortable. "I wanted to be like him!", he said. *Is it possible that Tansi and the priestly mystique of the Catholic seminary was a safe space for Arinze the adolescent; that it made the necessary but painful separation from his father and his family bearable, and that it made him feel special?* I wondered if the Church offered Arinze something that he wanted and that as a young and impressionable boy he grabbed it with both hands and ran as hard as he could.[62]

These questions are the kind that someone like me ponders when confronted by someone like Arinze for the first time. My scepticism had been nurtured by an age of reason, by an unquestioned belief in science, in rational enquiry, in the unwavering belief that a human being should be able to define and shape the journey that he takes. And I continued the interview in that mindset. I discussed the important events in his life (that may have contributed to him moving forward within the hierarchy of the Church) in terms of deliberate steps on his part towards a predefined goal. But he discussed them as acts of obedience to a higher will, as a willing servant just doing his job, and he dismissed the notion of ambition among the clergy with a flip of his wrist, a pursing of lips, and a deep and patronising laugh: "A priest who aims to be a cardinal would be a ridiculous figure!" he said

---

62 Ibid.

theatrically. "He would be funny!" Should he have remained a priest teaching in the seminary, he would have been quite satisfied. He said: "I felt fulfilled."

I left this first meeting believing that Arinze was in denial. He had struck me as arrogant, his first test at the door to his tiny chapel having rattled me from the moment I walked in. He was not interested in conceding the possibility of an alternative position on any subject I introduced. In all things, Catholic doctrine prevailed and more importantly, and to my great disappointment, the man remained firmly concealed behind the priest. Certainly, he expanded the discussion to include personal reflections on the strongest influences in his life; the milestones that he felt may have contributed to his creation as cardinal, and his hopes for Nigeria. But with hindsight I realised that he had failed to mention Vatican II or the war in Biafra, both of which were foundational events, and focused instead on giving answers that highlighted the limits of my interrogatory skills. He was not warm, despite his wicked sense of humour (which I enjoyed) and – unlike Napier – he did not enter into discussions about life outside of the church. Indeed, it seemed non-existent. I left convinced that he had at least subconsciously nurtured ambition, and probably from a young age, and sure that John Paul II's creation of the first African cardinals was a calculated move to draw people across the continent into the Church by creating leaders with whom they could identify on a very fundamental level; as Arinze had with Tansi. I was convinced that I was right.

Arinze has no doubt met people like me many times before and he gave me the impression that we are a tiresome bunch, famous for our belief in "nothing" bar the numbers and theories that, once mastered, have the potential to make the world a very predictable place. Once the tape had stopped running and I was leaving he stopped me momentarily and said: "Just remember, if you publish anything without letting me read it first, I have a whole team of lawyers to tear you apart."

He smiled then, almost threateningly, and laughed, and I did my best to laugh along with him, but I was disturbed. I came out of the meeting with Arinze mistakenly convinced that I had him pinned as a chauvinistic, highly ambitious, patronising, right-wing Vatican apparatchik, yet strangely unsettled by the notion that something significant may have passed me by.

II.

I did not read the transcript of that interview until early the following year. My lack of preparation and the unsettling feeling that I had missed an opportunity to interview him professionally left me feeling sick at the thought of it for some time. I had transcribed it but then put it away in a drawer until I thought I could face reliving it. By then I had contacted other cardinals and had positive responses. I had travelled to Kampala, Uganda and interviewed Cardinal Wamala, and I had almost made it to Luanda in Angola, only a miscommunication between me and Cardinal de Nascimento saw him leaving for Rome on the day I was due to arrive.

My subsequent interview with Wamala was important because seeing it typed gave me the confidence to pull Arinze's interview back out of the drawer. Wamala was a man of great warmth, whose daily burdens were appalling if not catastrophic. Wamala *exuded* love. Meeting with him in Kampala had exposed me to just one African reality that not only laid the deeply painful nature of others bare, but also led me to revisit some of the widespread and public criticisms of the Catholic Church with which I, as Westerner and non-believer, was always familiar. I had begun to sense a divide between the Roman Curia and the African context. Dinner party conversation with well-educated friends always touched on the Church's objection to condom use and its connection with both the proliferation of HIV infection and women's relative disempowerment:

... A number of my friends raise what they call issues of morality with me during coffee mornings. They discuss how difficult it will be for me to objectively present views in the book that "obviously" contradict modern medical science; the Church's refusal to approve the use of condoms in the war against HIV infection, for example, or supporting contraception for women who want to be empowered with choice ...

Dropping kids at school I had been taken on over high-profile allegations of paedophilia in the Church, one going so far as to cast "my" cardinals as potentially sexually frustrated and predatory men:

... outside primary school this morning one woman, a lapsed Catholic, asked if I was going to ask the cardinals about allegations of paedophilia. "I hope you're going to make them answer for that!"

Accusations of chauvinism and hypocrisy from female friends arose in discussions about the exercise of control by the Church hierarchy (particularly the pope and the Roman Curia), about the unquestioned acceptance of dogma, and about the need for Church relevance to modern-day concerns relating to subjects like pregnancy, sexually transmitted infection and homosexuality:

Until now, inherent hypocrisies in the Church have undermined the legitimacy of the claim to leadership and influence that it makes across the globe and attempts to make on me. I met with an ex-priest last night who talked about widespread violations of the vow of celibacy, and who characterised the priesthood as a "safe space" for homosexual men. Today I attended a quiet mass at St Maria Trastevere where a gay man replete with cap and diamond earrings took communion alongside a pregnant teenager who, concealed by her black hoody, was holding the hand of a nun ... When the time came we all shook hands in mutual recognition and absolute acceptance, but how conditional was that acceptance on conformity and silence ...?

I began to wonder if perhaps Vatican etiquette, the grandeur of

Rome, and a steady stream of discussion focussing on these so-called Western concerns before I left for that first interview had blurred my ability to seek out Arinze-the-man the first time around, to appreciate that Africa's experience of Catholicism, or Catholicism's experience of Africa, where the Second Vatican Council particularly was something very different to the experience of it in the West. While pregnancy, sexually transmitted infections and homosexuality are front-running concerns in the West, perhaps they are only some of a number of far more pressing problems in Africa, which Westerners simply cannot appreciate from their positions of relative privilege? One diary entry during this second trip to Rome says:

... the sense of profound love and devotion I have gleaned from my visits to cardinals in Africa is being overshadowed by another impression of absolute power here at the Vatican.

Had I wandered around St Peter's the first time with all of that Western baggage in tow? Emailing the edited version for his approval I included an apology:

I wanted to write firstly to apologise for taking your time over questions that were hurriedly constructed. Coming, as our meeting did, so early in my research and so suddenly, I was ill-prepared for our discussion and did not do myself, you, or your position justice ... perhaps we could meet one more time ...?

An email arrived soon after, offering a brusque list of corrections to the transcript. At the end he had added an extra sentence: "*only the 24*th of April is possible. You pick: 10 or 11am." The date that he suggested coincided with a potential interview that I had already arranged with Cardinal Turkson from Ghana, by then the Head of the Pontifical Council for Justice and Peace and located just around the corner from Arinze in Rome. I could hardly believe that Arinze had agreed to meet me a second time.

I arrived in Rome to the chill of early spring. The airlines had left my luggage behind in Sydney and my first few hours (after 24 hours on planes) were spent shopping for clean clothes (and a toothbrush) to wear in meetings with, first, a journalist and personal acquaintance of Arinze that evening, and then with Arinze himself the following day. We drank coffee together and talked a lot about "my" cardinals and what I could ask them that I had not already considered. Out of season the city was quieter than it had been in the summer the previous year, and priests, religious brothers and sisters seemed to be everywhere. The cafes surrounding the Vatican were full of busy clergy, grabbing excellent coffee from very cool cafes in the early mornings on their way to daily duties near Sta. Maria in Trastevere, or enjoying lunch with pretty young women in between the demands of rigorous study timetables near St Peter's Square. Together these flirtatious gatherings challenged my idea that priests are denied a right to sexual attraction, that the vow of celibacy had "separated" them from one of the most basic human interactions. I began to wonder where that view had originated.

Meeting Arinze again was far less stressful this time for a number of reasons. First, I was better prepared. I had been to Africa a couple of times, conducted a few more interviews and was beginning to understand some of the issues I had not known when I started. Second, he was in a good mood that morning, despite being mildly rattled; having forgotten the option he gave me to meet at eleven o'clock, he expected me at ten and had arranged to meet someone else at eleven thirty. He realised that he had inconvenienced me, so he had to be nice. "Let us work productively and make the most of our time." He smiled.

This time I structured the interview around the most significant milestones in his life. I asked him about his attendance at Vatican II (the fourth session) as a young bishop; his involvement in the war with Biafra; his attitude to women and to the West; his ideas about forgiveness and about his regrets. I had been strongly counselled by my journalist friend to avoid questions about condoms, homosexuality and paedophilia (though I would not have asked them anyway), but I did want some answers to some of those complaints about chauvinism and hypocrisy, and I was trying to understand how the Church was maintaining and extending its relevance in Africa, while its relevance seemed to be dwindling in the West.

This time, Arinze was more forthcoming with personal impressions. He seemed more comfortable with my line of questioning than in our previous encounter. His presence at the Second Vatican Council was relevant to his entire future within the Church, he said. He did not participate, except to listen and learn, but he picked up the optimism of the experience and injected it into his later work as bishop in Onitsha. His responsibilities during the war with Biafra were vast. He talked about the logistics of mobilising the priesthood to support the relief effort in cooperation with nations from Europe, the relevance of the Church to society during war, its role in post-war reconciliation and reconstruction, and his success in rebuilding the Church subsequently. Before the civil war there had been 80 priests in Onitsha. Once the war began, only 33 remained and of those, all were very young. Arinze described it as "… a challenge … which the people embraced!" He reflected on the generosity of families, who encouraged their sons to be trained as priests despite their centrality to family growth and prosperity, indicating the level of status inherent in a religious life as a vocation in Nigeria, and noted that after ten years, the same area has been divided into three dioceses, two with over 300 priests, one with over 450.

Arinze was effusive about the place of women in the Church, the importance of their contribution to decision making at all levels. He acknowledged their inability to enter the priesthood, claiming it was dogma and unreformable, but described their potential to shape leadership and decision making as real and powerful. Women are liberated through Catholicism from the binds of patriarchal social systems found in tribal religions and cultural practices, and in Islam. Women, he said, function at the source. Being responsible for the on-going wellbeing of their families and shaping the thinking of subsequent generations gives them unique insight into the day-to-day consequences of decision making at the highest levels. Senior men, like himself, were reliant on their community connectedness and ignored their advice at their own peril. Working in highly organised and efficient groupings with sophisticated leadership structures, women are able to affect specific outcomes by communicating the needs and the views of their community to their spiritual leaders. Arinze had experienced a lack of receptiveness on the part of some of his priests to the input of women, but as archbishop, he had insisted on the centrality of their contribution to the health of the Church. Should the bishop be ineffectual in dealing with political leaders, he added, women also have clout at election polls, denying their vote to politicians whose policies may impact on the on-going well-being of the communities that they represent.

Forgiveness and suffering also became central in the conversation, particularly in the context of post-war reconstruction where "confession" and its partner, "forgiveness", became a healing and strengthening act that comfort the sinner but also give him or her grace not to do it again. In the context of unstable societies or outright war, where gross human rights violations are a daily occurrence, where people seek strength to get through each day, surely the need for confession and forgiveness is much more urgent? Links between personal reformation and the building of stable and democratic societies gain a vitality that may not be so obvious from the West. The creation of truth and reconciliation commissions in many African nations recovering from civil war seems to be a pre-requisite for the establishment of a potentially peaceful future. As Wamala and others say in subsequent chapters, we must forgive to move forward. If people stop trying to improve with a view to our mistakes of the past, does that mean we will move backwards? *Non progredi est retrogredi* (not to advance is to fall back)? We ended the conversation talking about his regrets (which largely concern modern interpretations of Vatican II), and the election of an African pope.

Arinze surprised me by being simpatico, which I had not seen the first time we met, and then even more with a gutsy grit that applauded those "made of sterner stuff", that portrayed priests as tough guys patrolling the world's moral frontier, and women as humankind's engine. All at once I was able to redefine the patronising aggression I had misread in our first meeting as a kind of bold masculinity. He became just the kind of gracious, polished and virile leader that I felt a man in his position should be, albeit with a temper one might care to avoid provoking. I still maintained that he is ambitious, that his status in the Roman Curia gives him a certain personal satisfaction, and that his respect for and admiration of Cyprian Tansi were linked with normal adolescent development. I left feeling impressed by him as a man, not as a black African cardinal of the Roman Catholic Church.

Once the tape had stopped running and I was heading for the door he stopped me momentarily just like he had the last time: "Just remember, if you publish anything without letting me read it first …" But I interrupted him. "I know", I said, smiling my widest smile because at last I felt like I had him sorted well and truly. "You have a whole team of lawyers to tear me apart?"

I like to imagine that the way that he was smiling at that moment said that he was a little impressed too. Perhaps I was no longer a naïve, non-Catholic, Western academic, but a woman and a mother (in a slightly longer skirt). It's a long shot, but perhaps I had begun to demonstrate a small measure of the dignity and composure Michelangelo carved into Mary for his *Pietà* ? When he emailed the transcript back the second time he wrote:

Well done Sally, you did a good job.

iii. Francis Cardinal Arinze, Nigeria, Prefect Emeritus of the Congregation for Divine Worship and the Discipline of the Sacraments
(September 2010)

"... When I reach 80 (if I reach 80) I can stay here and die if I want to die in Rome. The problem is that it is very expensive to fly a corpse back to the home country. You know a coffin costs a lot more than a live passenger flying business class? Yes, it is very expensive for a corpse to fly on a plane, even though that person doesn't eat in the business class, even though he is in the baggage area! ..."

Tell me about the relevance of skin colour to the creation of a cardinal. Do you think that skin colour was relevant in the creation of African cardinals by Pope John Paul II?
Should the cardinals be distinguished because of the colour of their skin, is there no other way to distinguish them? You do not say pink cardinals, you do not say coffee-brown cardinals, there are no white cardinals and I never see a white person. So it is better to distinguish cardinals geographically: West African cardinals, European cardinals, United States cardinals, Latin American cardinals, Indian cardinals, and Asian cardinals. That's geographically exact. I do not think that skin colour is the most important thing for a human being. There are other things that are much more important. In Nigeria, our concern is not the colour of the skin at all.

Is there a collegiality amongst African cardinals West African and East Africa?
You are using a theological word "collegiality". I am not sure that "collegiality" would mean to you what it means to me.

What does it mean for you?
Catholic theology understands "collegiality" to mean the pope and the bishops forming a college, to whom Christ entrusted his church, and to work within that college as a team with the pope as their leader. That's the meaning of collegiality.

And is that college able to work together for the benefit of nations within Africa?
Africa has 53 countries, the number of bishops I cannot tell, but it would be anything like 300 or 400, in countries that are very diverse – from Algeria and Libya in the north, right down to the Republic of South Africa in the south, from Senegal in the west to Tanzania in the east. There is great variety and one has to go carefully.

When a bishop is appointed bishop, it is normal for him to be assigned a diocese. There are a few bishops working within offices of the Church – offices in the Vatican or big offices like [that of] the representative to the United Nations, but those are very few. Most bishops are engaged with their people in their diocese. That's the immediate assignment of the bishop. Then, the bishops in one country form a national Bishops' Conference because there are many problems and challenges that are best faced together in a country. That's normal and it is also common sense.

When you go beyond one country you can touch a region like West Africa. In Eastern Africa, for example, you have the Association of Episcopal Conferences of Eastern Africa, which includes seven countries or so: Tanzania, Uganda, Kenya, Ethiopia, Zambia and Malawi … Each of those countries has a national Bishops Conference of their own and together they also form a regional conference. At one time in West Africa we had English-speaking West African countries and French speaking-West African countries forming their own separate regional conferences. Now they form one regional conference. Altogether there are about nine regional Bishops' Conferences in Africa.

At the level of the whole continent we have one organic organisation called "SECAM": The Symposium of Episcopal Conferences of Africa and Madagascar. Obviously at the continental level there is a limit to how much you can do together. But there are some things that we can achieve; so we have an executive meeting maybe once in three or four years. In all those ways, we work together.

Can you tell me, how did you become a cardinal?
A young person doesn't wake up from sleep and become a cardinal. The usual thing is a young person wants to be a priest. And he goes to the seminary – you see here this big picture? [Arinze pointed to a large, painted portrait of a priest named Cyprian Michael Tansi, hanging on the wall behind him.] That's the priest who was in my parish, he baptised me, heard my first confession, gave me my first communion, and I was his "mass server" – his assistant at the altar. So he was the first priest I ever knew. And he was a remarkable person. Now he has been beatified by the pope – that means his is declared to be in heaven. He is the only Nigerian who has been beatified … It doesn't mean that the others are not in heaven, but the church has not gone through the very demanding ceremonies and investigations [incumbent] on it to declare the person in heaven. We don't control who is in heaven, God controls that. But the officers control who is declared to be in heaven and propose who is going to be a model for the people.

When I was a boy in elementary school, he was very inspiring and I wanted to be like him. To be a priest! That's the normal thing for those who want to be priests. Then they go to seminary secondary school, then if everything goes well they go on to what we call major seminary philosophy (that's for three or four years), then they do theology for another four years minimum. Then, if everything goes well, the person is ordained a priest. That's how I was ordained a priest in Rome. I did the philosophy in Nigeria and my archbishop sent me to Rome in 1955 to complete theology, and then I was ordained a priest in 1958. That's what I was looking for: to be a priest.

I came back to my country in December 1960, I was not appointed to a parish, as most priests are. In my case I was sent to the seminary where we trained the students who will become priests in Nigeria. I was there for two years. For me that was my joy. And I felt fulfilled. I was not aiming to be "cardinal." A priest who is aiming to be a cardinal would be a ridiculous figure, he would be funny!

But while I was a priest, the bishop sent me to London to do a diploma in education at the Institute of Education, London University. After that, I was put in charge of schools, Catholic schools, as the link person between schools and the government in eastern Nigeria until 1965. Then the pope made me a bishop ... I was rather young, 32 years old, and I was assistant to the archbishop in Onitsha.

After two years the archbishop died and I took over the archdiocese of Onitsha in 1967. I worked then as archbishop for 16 years. I was happy just doing that work. Then in 1984, which meant I had been archbishop for almost 20 years, the pope said, "Ah, please come now to Rome, to the Vatican." He was not an army officer commanding what I should or shouldn't do. He would make a proposal and if I did not want to go, I was expected to give him good reasons as to why I should not come. If I said, "The climate will kill me inside two weeks!" he might say, "Oh okay, if you will die within two weeks you had better stay in your country." But I did not say that, and it was clear that he wanted me to come here and work. So I said, "If you want me to work I will do it." So he said, "Okay, so you come to Rome."

So for 18 years I was president of the Pontifical Council for Interreligious Dialogue. That is the office of the Church in the Vatican for contact with all the other religions in the world except Christians and Jews; therefore: Buddhists, Muslims, Hindus, African traditional religions, Australian Aboriginals, native religions in India and Native Americans ... any religion in the world. I was in that work for eighteen years – from 1984 until 2002. In 1985 when I had been working there for one year I was created cardinal. That was ... 27 years ago. But that was then all normal. If the pope calls an archbishop who is already 20 years a bishop and he's heading one of the organisations in the Vatican, if he is made a cardinal, nobody is surprised. It is a natural progression.

He must have been very happy with you.
You can draw the conclusion that if he was very unhappy with me, I don't think he would make me a cardinal! After 18 years in that office, I was sent to another office in the Vatican called "Congregation for Divine Worship and Discipline of the Sacraments". In simple language it means Church worship. It is the office of the Church for prayer, the prayer life of the Catholic Church worldwide – I was there for six years.

Now our law says that when your reach 75 years of age you can write to the pope and say, "According to Canon Law 401 I am now 75 so I should retire." Then the pope can say, "Ok, I got your letter, I will tell you when to go." And he will tell you, within five years, generally (laughs). He can say immediately or next month or next year that you are free to retire. But you can't remain in that position beyond 80. If a man is already 75 years, it's better not to keep him for too long, you don't want him to die in office. So one year later I was relieved [of] that office and another cardinal was appointed in my place.

But here at the Vatican we still have men serving until they are 80 years old – as members of several congregations and within offices in the Vatican. That means meetings and reading documents and contributing without being in charge. There is less work, but there is still work. Once a person is 80 years old, if he is still alive, then he is free.

If he wants to die in Rome he can stay here. When I reach 80 (if I reach 80) I can stay here and die if I want to die in Rome. The problem is that it is very expensive to fly a corpse back to their home country.

You know a coffin costs a lot more than a live passenger flying business class? Yes, it is very expensive for a corpse to fly on a plane. Even though that person doesn't eat in the business class, even though he is in the baggage area! But if a cardinal does prefer to die in his country, he can discuss it with the Pope and he can go back there to his country and die there. It's cheaper to fly there first you see. That's the stage I am coming dangerously near. I have to make a decision but I am not in a hurry.

Can you tell me the strongest influences in your personal and professional progression?
Firstly, Father Cyprian Michael Tansi, the priest who inspired me and whom I mentioned earlier. When he became a monk in England he took the name Cyprian and then his family name is Tansi. He is a priest from my area. From his home to my home was about twenty miles. He was made priest in 1937. I was made priest in 1958 so there were about 21 years between us. He was the first influence in my life. God's grace attracted me to be a priest through him.

Then another one of the major moments in my life (apart from the actual seminary) was when I was sent to Rome as a young person to study theology – so the last four years, well indeed five, that I was studying here in Rome. That was a major event in my life because here I was, a young person living with other young people in the Pontifical Seminary: people from about 30 countries all over the world including Australia and New Zealand, India, Vietnam, Japan, countries in Africa ... That particular seminary is called Propaganda Fide. It is still in Rome for countries that are of recent evangelisation. Those are called "mission countries". That means they were evangelised in the last 100 or 200 years, which for the church is recent. It's a very different situation for countries like Italy and France that have been Christian for 2,000 years. Those countries have their own seminary in Rome. There is a French college, a North American college, the Italians have many colleges of course, and there is a German college and so on. But there is no Nigerian college here or South African college for example. If you wanted a South African college you would have to pay for its construction. It is not enough to say you want it. So there is one big seminary for countries that don't have their own college here in Rome. That ensures that they have the Roman experience. That experience is important because they meet people from many parts of the world. They are trained in the university, where there are people from many parts of the world and that emphasises the universality of the church. That was very important in my life.

The third influence would be my exposure to the British educational system when I worked in London. When I was a priest, the bishops put me into the seminary to teach, and then later they put me in charge of the Catholic schools and coordinating Catholic school education with the government.

The last influence in my life was being made a bishop. Twenty years as a bishop in Nigeria taught me a lot about life and often brought me to Rome to fulfil my duties as a member of several offices here. That was good for my country, and it was good for me as an individual.

Did any of your ideas change from those experiences?

If a person is a normal human being the person will grow. If the person is willing to listen to others, if the person is willing to observe, if the person is willing to ask questions, the person will learn.

And how did you grow? How did your ideas change from those you held as a young adult in Nigeria to those you hold now?

I developed a greater awareness of the universal church, a greater awareness of the world as a big family. I developed a greater awareness and understanding of difference: An Australian is not an Indian, a New Zealander is not an American, a Mexican is very different from a Nigerian, and an Irishman is very different from a Canadian. Living with such people taught me that if I was willing to observe and listen and to ask questions, that I would learn a lot. It also made me aware of how much I didn't know. A person comes into the world with a capacity to learn but has nothing yet, everything is yet to be learned. A young person thinks he knows a lot, you know? He doesn't. But if he is willing to learn, you know, he will learn.

So you grew up through that experience?
Yes through all those experiences. They were gifts from God.

What are your aspirations for your country from now?
… Development, harmony between the 240 ethnic groups that have as many languages; promotion of the economic good of the people; honesty in public life, so that the petrol money will be used for the people; the whole of it and nobody taking part of it illegally. Then religion and its influence in life: Religion is not only a matter of Sunday mornings … It should influence our lives on Monday, Tuesday … every day, so that there is much more justice, peace and respect for the rights of others.

There is another peace, the peace of the cemetery, the peace between those killed and those who kill them. There is perfect peace in that matter. But we don't want that kind of peace. We want peace for those who are alive, those whose rights should be respected and those who should have the opportunity to develop themselves. People should have the freedom to say what they think, the possibility to work – especially the young people if they have studied, or if they have no work, or if they are in trouble. And there should be good relations between people of many religions. It would be nice if all of us were one religion but you cannot use force in religious matters. So, if another person has another religious conviction, then we should at least respect one another.

And are people with different religious convictions able to cooperate in Nigeria?

Yes – sometimes more, sometimes less. But the challenge is there and the more we cooperate the happier we shall be. Nigeria was not always a nation with that name. The name was coined by the British who colonised us in 1916. They didn't know what to call us. They were interested in trade. First they were interested in buying us as slaves, then they realised that that was not good, so they thought, "Oh, let's buy their products, the palm oil and the palm kernel and the ground nuts and the cocoa." That was preferable for them. So for the British, our area was a big market. Later they got the idea, "Why don't we put together all these areas where we trade and have them as a colony instead." They said, "That's a good idea, yes! What should we call the colony?" And the wife of the British governor said, "Look, there is this river Niger. So let's call them 'Nigerians.'" And the governor said, "Oh yeah, that's a good idea!", and they called us Nigeria in 1916.[63] Before that we were not a political unit. We lived happily where we were. We were not a country. But we were happy. Those from the south didn't even know that those of the north existed; except a few who travelled. So the colonising authority brought us together. The colonising authority did well. Not everything was negative. Of course there were those who had their own interests …

Catholicism came to the area in the 16th century … to parts of Benin city and Warri, in the south-west. But it didn't last. The Catholicism

---

[63] Sir Frederick Lugard was the governor of Nigeria. He is famous for saying, "Give me a man with a straight bat and a good third against a chap with a first anytime." His wife, Lady Flora Lugard (nee Shaw) was formerly Colonial Correspondent of *The Times*. Considered special for her independent presence on the frontiers of Africa, Flora Lugard is described as exceptionally intelligent, a confidante if not fellow conspirator of Rhodes and Jameson, a maverick, a rebel and a visionary. See Morris, (1978), pp. 253, 325, 336-337.

we know now came in the last 150 years, in 1861. That's very recent. Various Protestant families also came around that time. The Protestant missionaries who sought to colonise us were from England. The Catholics were generally from Ireland. In the beginning there were a few from France (Alsace) but most Catholic missionaries who were in Nigeria were from Ireland.

I am interested in how Catholicism merges with the great variety of ethnicities in Nigeria and the degree to which Catholicism was an act of European colonisation exercised through education as much as through the state.

The British colonising authority did not impose any religion. Understandably they brought their own Anglicanism with them. But it was the missionaries that generally promoted the school. Not the government, not the colonising authority.

Mind you, the colonising authority was happy that the missionaries promoted the school. And the school became the instrument of development. Once people went to school, they learnt about the rest of the world, and they began to realise their political and economic rights. In that way the missionaries were great instruments of development. But the missionaries did not impose their religion. If a young man wanted to go to the Catholic school but did not want baptism, it was not forced. It was free.

Can you tell me about your family's experience of Catholicism?

There were seven in our family: Four boys and three girls, and our parents sent all of us to school. When my father was small, nobody ever saw a priest in our village. The African traditional religion was predominant in his day. Later on, the missionaries came and they understood that it was easier and was wiser to bring their religion to the children first. The parents appreciated the value of the Christian religion later and they converted.

And your parents were happy for you to go to the school? Was that only because it provided you with education?
Yes.

And outside of the school did you share their traditional African religion?
Well, no. When we went to the Catholic school, we eventually became Christians. My father liked it. He didn't oppose it except on Sundays when we didn't go to work on the farm with him. He would say, "Today we go to farm work." And I would say, "No, we Christians do not do farm work on Sundays." He asked me, "Do you Christians eat on Sundays?" I said, "We eat on Sundays." He said, "Ah, you eat on Sundays but you don't work on Sundays!" But he said it was good and gradually the older people became Christians. When they themselves saw that their children were benefitting from being Christian and from attending the church school they came to feel that it was good for them too. So they were converted but not by force.

So you grew up on a property, a farmland?
Yes, my parents never went to school; it was just a humble village setting. My father didn't even know how to write his name. But he was very wise; he taught me many things and so also did my mother. They saw the value of the church school and he sent me there to learn, not to be a priest. Indeed, when I declared that I wanted to be a priest he was not very happy at all. It was understandable – but because he loved me he didn't oppose it. When he saw that I insisted he said, "OK". Then when I came home on holidays from the seminary he said, "Ah, I was told that I would never see you again … so now I realised they were deceiving me!" Then he said, "If it is God's will you will succeed."

You were present at Vatican II. You were in the fourth session. Can you tell me a little bit about what that was like? It must have been very exciting?

Exciting, yes. I was made bishop, just two weeks before the last session. That was the 29 August 1965. The last session began 11 September of the same year, so I was very happy to be there. It was fascinating. I was aware that I was just a newcomer; I was only 32 years old. So my main work was to listen, admire and pray. It was illuminating to see bishops from all around the world having their say. Think of 2,000 or more bishops!

Did it leave you with a sense of optimism for the Church in your country?

Yes. The general impression was of a new freshness within the Church and a new level of encouragement. The Church made it clear that it was not afraid of the world of today. Not that the Church thinks everything is perfect. Certainly not! But the general attitude was one of openness and readiness to meet, to listen, to dialogue, and to give and receive.

You were appointed archbishop immediately prior to the onset of the civil war?

Yes that is true. I had been assistant bishop for two years prior to the onset of war. Then the archbishop I was assisting died in February 1967. In July 1967 I was made the archbishop and the war began in the same week.

For many of us in Australia, conflict on that level is a very foreign experience. Can you tell me what it was like to be in the midst of civil war?

Unpleasant. Not what I would wish on anybody…

Nigeria is a big country. Today we have a population of 150,000,000. It takes time for such a conglomeration of peoples to have the sense of being one nation and one country. The only common language is English. It is not a surprise that after some time tension between the various groups began to develop and eventually to escalate into violence. For bishops (and I was just a young bishop) it was a very sad thing to see your people at war. My side of Nigeria was on the receiving end of the war, because in the six months prior to war there was a killing of the Igbos who came from my area but who had begun to live in other parts of the country. Those who were still alive came back to my area, and then the area declared itself a separate republic. They said, "If the rest of the country doesn't want us, very good, we are going to be a separate state!" The rest of the country said, "No, we will not let you be a separate republic!" And that's how the war began. Now that is to put it in very simple terms. Of course, every war has many causes.

For the bishops who are the spiritual fathers of people who are suffering, people who have lost their dear ones, there were certain responsibilities, not the least of which was supporting those people who were now expected to proffer their sons for the war front. It was not pleasant. The bishops needed to look after those who were sick, those who had been displaced within their own country; who could not stay within their own homes because there was fighting in their area so they had to move out … Where do they stay? Where do they live? What do they eat? So we had to learn to manage and grapple with all of those issues.

At the time, many of those missionary priests who were getting on in age were rather worried, so I arranged for their return to Ireland if they wished. It was very edifying to see the courage of those who had the stamina to stay with us, to risk being displaced in their parish, and there were quite a number. So we went on for almost three years.

It must be an incredible effort to sustain your people in the midst of that suffering. How do you encourage them to continue to forgive?

If Christianity does not teach people to forgive, who will teach it? Then we would not be good Christians. Christ not only taught us with words, but by example. From the cross he forgave those who were killing him. He prayed for them, he even excused them. St Stephen was the first martyr to do the same. We have to teach forgiveness. We have to teach reconciliation. We have to teach coming together again – not as a political formula, but as a demand of the gospel.

As a bishop I have no competence to speak of the unity of a federation, or of the dividing of a federation, or of the making of a separate republic. As a bishop, I have no mandate from Christ on those points. But, as a bishop I am concerned when people are persecuted, discriminated against, when they are forced to leave their homes. When they are hungry, sick, when they are poor, when their schools are disturbed, when the students don't know where to go. Without those concerns the Church would become irrelevant.

Indeed, those years of war taught us many things. War brings out the best in some of us; heroism, seeing people devoted to the good of others. I was in admiration of the universal Church. I sent an Irish priest who was in charge of social services in Nigeria to the Vatican to inform them of the situation in Nigeria in the first year of the war. He was very capable. (He is still alive, getting on in age.) And he so convinced them that Caritas Internationalis (the office of the Church for relief in emergencies worldwide) got into action. So at the height of relief operations, Caritas and the Diakonischeswerk (the World Council of Churches' counterpart in Germany) would send in anything like 30 aeroplane loads of relief supplies every night into the area called Biafra. That means that they organised charitable people in Germany especially, in Ireland, in England, in Italy and so on, and they donated food, medicine, clothes, that sort of thing.

So you were working at that time at coordinating that sort of relief work?
Not I personally, obviously all the bishops work alongside the capable religious priests. I remember one sister (she is getting on in age) who I put in charge of everything medical in the diocese. I said, "You are in charge of everything medical!" With all the temptations that exist for some people to take too much, I got a priest whom I could trust to be in charge of everything about relief supplies, then … it was wonderful. We also had to arrange for priests to minister to soldiers and to refugees, to give them spiritual assistance. It was a fascinating time.

And how do you encourage people to continue to forgive, particularly if their faith ever wanes in the face of terrible loss?
Yes, suffering can shake a person's faith. Very much. Suffering can make a person say, "Oh my God have you forgotten me? Where are you now? See what I am suffering?" Even Christ on the cross said, "My God, my God, why have you forsaken me?" (Yet Psalm 22 is a long Psalm and later on it says "You are always with us," and then "Your people will come to you to rejoice in you,") you do find those people. So it isn't a cry of despair but a cry that demonstrates intense human suffering. People have to be taught (and bishops like myself have to help them) to accept that suffering is a reality in human life. We don't choose it, we don't want it but sometimes, it comes: sickness, oppression by relatives, ingratitude, ungrateful children, when husband and wife quarrel fiercely instead of being happy together. These challenges are very painful. Christianity has to teach people reconciliation and peace. What are some of the considerations?

First, God is especially with us. He does not decide to kill us or even to wipe us out so that nobody will see our corpse. That is one. God himself forgave. When Christ was on earth, he forgave. He not only forgave those who were killing him, but when one woman was caught (by the Jews) in sin and they brought her to him and said to him, "Moses asked us to stone such a person; what do you say?" They thought that he would say, "Oh yes stone her." But he said to them, "Any of you without sin, throw the stone first." And they went away beginning with the eldest leaving the woman behind. And Christ said to her, "Go, but don't sin anymore."

So he was merciful. He was not approving sin, but he was merciful to the sinner. And we have many other examples. Christianity has to have that element of forgiveness. People have to have the heart to forgive also knowing that none of us are perfect. We all offend God and he continues to forgive us. Christ included in "Our Father" the prayer: "Forgive us our trespasses as we forgive those who trespass against us…", which means that anytime a person who refuses to forgive says their "Our Father", that person is condemning themselves. They are practically saying; "Since I do not forgive those who have offended me, don't forgive me." It is a very important consideration. Obviously we must ask the person who offended to accept guilt and ask for pardon. If the person who offended refuses to accept guilt and refuses to ask for forgiveness, it makes reconciliation more difficult.

Did you face that issue after the war ended?
Yes, the government did what it could. The federal government said, "No victor, no vanquished," and talked of reconciliation and reconstruction. So it could have been worse than it was. The federal government made an effort. But the Church of course was in a stronger position for that.

You took part in that process?
Yes I did. I promoted reconciliation. The bishops came from the many parts where their people were quarrelling to have meetings and open communication. The people saw that effort and it was good for them. We worked together with religious sisters who were from many ethnic groups, working in all parts of the country. That gave a

strong message. Without preaching they showed that peoples of very different backgrounds can live together.

I want to ask you about rebuilding the Church in Nigeria after the war.

Yes, of course the country of Nigeria is very big, very vast. Some parts were not affected by the war at all. So there was no fighting there and the priests and religious were already there, so they had nothing to reconstruct. But in some areas it was very much the opposite. Where I was, for example, it was the opposite. The city in which I was bishop at the time was one of the most badly affected by the war. There was a great deal of fighting; so we needed a lot of courage and optimism. We also received financial assistance from outside of the country, and medical equipment (especially from the Germans who were very generous). In our area, the eastern part of Nigeria, where most of the fighting was, the federal government sent the missionaries away, mostly to Ireland. So we were left with fewer priests than before. Where I was archbishop of (Onitsha) we had 80 priests before the civil war, but after the missionaries were sent away I had only 33 local priests, and those who were there were very young and very few. A challenge … which the people embraced!

And I gather that you had to bring a lot of people in and educate them.

Yes. We had to encourage the young men to be trained to be priests. The people were also very generous. Those families with many children would not refuse to let their son go into the seminary if the boy wanted. Nobody was forced, mainly because you couldn't force anybody to be a priest, he would run away! You could not tie him up (laughing). So it worked. In the long run, after another ten years, we received the fruits of our labour and there were plenty of priests. That area where I told you there were 33 priests has now been divided into three dioceses. In one of them I have about 300 priests; in another one I have about 450. And in another I have maybe about 300.

Suffering is like a school, we don't want it, but those who have suffered are generally of stronger stuff. Those who have not suffered are generally weaker, less ready to make sacrifice. And if a priest is to succeed in his vocation he must be ready for sacrifice. If he is "allergic" to sacrifice he cannot be a priest. Indeed, if he becomes a priest he will not be a good one. The same thing for sisters or brothers. So in that area where people suffered much, there was also a greater readiness for religion. It is very interesting.

Where I come from, suffering to that degree has in many cases gone from many lives and in many ways, and perhaps as a result some people appear to be moving away from or becoming cynical about the relevance of spirituality to daily life.

That is true. When the human being has all the creature comforts desirable, there is a tendency to forget God. But when a human being is without some desirable creature comforts, it helps the person to think of God. There's the origin of religion. You think of God, you accept there is a God. The one who has all the nice things tends to think, "I don't need God, I have everything".

The Church is often portrayed, the Catholic Church particularly, as being highly patriarchal. However I read in some conversations that you shared with Gerry O'Connell for the writing of his biography of you, God's Invisible Hand, that you felt that Catholicism actually offered women options that hadn't necessarily been available to them in their traditional religions. I wondered if you could talk a little more about that subject and about how Catholicism has been a liberating experience for Nigerian women.

Many African traditional religions and Islam don't take women as seriously as Christianity does. In Nigerian traditional religions and the cultures in which they evolved, daughters, for example, have no share in the family property. Only the sons divide the whole property – whether money or houses and so on – because the daughters are expected to marry and to go to their husbands and stay there. That's number one. Number two: ordinary rights between husband and wife are not equal at all. The man says, "This is my house. You are a woman whom I married and for whom I paid money; so when I talk you don't talk!" That mentality is not good. In Islam it is clear! A woman's evidence in court is worth 50 per cent of that of a man, if at all she is admitted in court. You know what happens in some Muslim countries. I am not going into that. I am focusing on Nigeria.

Christianity for our Nigerian women is a liberating force. Firstly, because Christianity regards the marriage partners as equal. They are two persons and their rights are equal. Equal rights are a revolutionary idea for African traditional religions. Christianity does not enter into property arrangements; I mean in terms of a daughter receiving a share. But if Christianity influences people's mentalities sufficiently, they will see that.

Secondly, Christianity gives women the opportunity for leadership. Granted that in our traditional religion women also had leadership, but generally that leadership only existed in women's circles amongst the women in the village. Those women from the village who married elsewhere would have an association elsewhere. Yes, they would have their leaders amongst themselves, but those women would have no authority over men.

With the Church it is not the case. For example, when I was archbishop I had a council, a committee, to look after the seminary, to advise on the quality of seminarians and so on. And I appointed some women among the members of the seminary committee. These women were married with children and they had educated them well. I also appointed one or two sisters, and of course priests. Some of the priests said to me, "What businesses have women on the seminary committee?" I said, "They have a business because they are members of the Church, and when we ordain a priest we assign him to a parish and these women will know a good priest within two weeks." Some priests did not consider that it is for them that he is ordained; but they couldn't stop the women's participation.

Looking back I am very happy it was done. It helped these women to see that they were taken seriously within the Church, that they had a voice in the training of their priests for the future. The woman is not ordained a priest because for us that is a matter of dogma, which even the Pope cannot change. But the woman is a member of the Church and her contribution is valid. So I had a diocesan and a general council; priests, men, women and people who were appointed by election from their parishes; men or women. In each parish we worked out a constitution where people elect their parish council, but the parish priest is the chairman. But the next person to him is elected by the people, not by him. They are not appointed. It could be a man, it could be a woman. Then of course, we have Catholic men's organisations and Catholic women's organisations. The Catholic women's organisation is more dynamic. They are more disciplined, they attend meetings, and they are active in social and political matters. For example, when the government took over Church schools, and said, "nationalise them" (not the whole country, we have 36 states), it was the Catholic Women's Organisation that got into war with the political parties. That organisation said, "Why did you take our schools? You give us back our schools; otherwise you can't expect our votes at the next election!"

Now that's a language that every politician understands. If it is just the bishops making a big declaration, and the politician thinks that the people are behind the bishop, then the politician might be worried. But if that politician thinks that the people will not listen to the bishop, they will just laugh and say, "Bishop, you made a big statement, very good. But I collect the votes." But what the politician understands very well is, "Can I get these people's votes in the next election?" The Catholic women are very good at that and because they are disciplined. The politician knows that if they decide not to vote for him, then he will not get their votes.

But not just that, these women were not only involved in politics, they are also very positive in Church affairs. For instance, if we had seminarians for the priesthood and if, in their view, that seminarian should not be ordained, then they would send one or two of their leaders to say to the priest in their area, "Please tell Archbishop Arinze to look again at this particular seminarian." Just that! And they saved us from ordaining some candidates that were not suitable. How could I know (as archbishop) what a seminarian is like on his holidays if he is always on his best behaviour when he saw me? But these women could tell you, "This is a good type, this one will make it, but this one will not make it."

If they see there is a problem, of course they don't come and disgrace anybody in public. No, no! They would come and let me know in a wise and quiet way that was very effective. They also have their priest. If their priest is doing very well, then they know how to encourage him. If he is not doing very well, then they can also send one or two of their leaders to say a few words to him. This may produce more results than a bishop firing in all directions! The bishop will still speak. But every priest wants to be well received by his people. If his people tell him, "Father, if you are of this kind we will not receive you well", that will shake any priest. So that's behaving as grown-up members in the Church.

So, women rise to their responsibilities and they take part in Church events. Not because they are women, but if they can deliver the goods then they are there … Some of them also have received appointments as members of Roman Offices – the Pontifical Council for Culture, the Pontifical Council for Family, and then they go to international meetings. And that's good. That's the sort of thing we want. So if the bishop sees clearly, he will share such a vision with his priests. It's a woman's right as a Christian to be involved in such a way. Men of course should also be involved; I am not saying that all the attention is on women. But I should add that the key to the family is the mother. The father is important, but the mother is the key. She holds the children in her hands. If the woman is doing her job well, then there is hope. In our culture if the man doesn't do well, the people say, "His mother did not do a good job." They don't blame the father. They will say, "Your mother did not do a good job." And if the person is doing well they praise the mother not the father. We never say "father tongue", but rather "mother tongue."

So after all these years at the Vatican, do you have any regrets?

Some people misinterpreted some elements of Vatican II. Some people don't distinguish what they would like and what Vatican II actually said. So in interpreting it, they move beyond what the Council said into what they would like. Some people want Vatican III! So they will say all the things that they wanted the Church to say. Also in Vatican II there were some parts that weren't presented as "dogma". Rather people were encouraged to analyse situations. So some people, in interpreting and carrying out their duties and their interpretations, went beyond what Vatican II perhaps expected. Let us say for example, liturgy, church worship. Vatican II said, "Vernacular language can be useful you know. So it can be introduced." What happened after? More vernacular, more and more, and Latin finished up in the ecclesiastical refrigerator. Vatican II didn't say, "No more Latin!" But in many parishes that is what is happening. So they have gone beyond what the Council said. We cannot blame the Council for that. It is like whatever problem people have, they blame it on the government; If it's the rainforest, they say it's the government is guilty. Some people say that Vatican II was rather optimistic about the world today. Well, do you want the Church to be pessimistic? You can assess the world of today after 50 years of Vatican II, but I think that Vatican II took a good position at the time. And I don't regret any of the things it said. But I do regret some of the interpretations.

Do you think that Africa or the global south is adequately represented at the Vatican, in senior positions?

At the time of the Second Vatican Council there were not many representing the global south, now there would be more. At that time in Africa south of Sahara, most of the bishops were Europeans or Americans. That is not so today. So change is normal to growth, because the Church has only recently evangelised areas of Africa south of Sahara in the last 200 years (except some presence in Congo, Cabinda, Angola). It had to be so. If we were today to have Vatican II, Asia would have a greater voice. At that time those in the global south didn't have such a voice. For example, ceremonies we would have been far more colourful ceremonies. (In Europe, they get a bit tired of ceremonies …)

Can you see any problems being evoked with the election of an African Pope?

I don't know why people would fix on an African pope. What of a North American pope? What of a pope from another nation? What of an Australian pope? (Laughing)

I only ask you because you are from Africa.

Ah I see. Any cardinal who gets the two-thirds votes plus one becomes pope. But I think the most important thing is to have strong Christianity; the rest in God's good time.

You've met the pope. Do you really tell him what you think and if you think his decisions won't go well?

You want to know all my personal discussions with the pope? You're going a bit far!

No I just wondered if you have a good rapport with him.

Yes a good rapport with him, yes. But I would not go further than that.

3 i. UGANDA

Uganda sits on the Eastern side of the African continent, and is bordered by Kenya and the Democratic Republic of Congo. It is approximately 40 per cent Catholic, 40 per cent Protestant, and 12 per cent Muslim. On average a person will live until they are 54 years of age in Uganda. Sixty-six per cent of the population over the age of 15 can read and write. Most children will finish 11 years of schooling.[64] A woman will give birth to six children (15 per cent of children under the age of five are underweight). In 2010, 6.5 per cent of the adult population (1.2 million people) were infected with HIV, and 150,000 children.[65] Eighty per cent of the workforce is employed in agriculture with coffee accounting for the bulk of exports. GDP sits at 19.3 billion USD (2011), and population density at 167 people per square kilometre (2010).[66]

Early explorers (Speke, Grant, Stanley, and Baker) trudged into the interior of Uganda in the middle of the 1800s, searching for the source

---

64 Note that in 2011, the state aim was to achieve a student-teacher ratio of 56:1 in all government schools. *Uganda Joint Christian Council Parliamentary Bulletin*, May-August 2011, p. 14.
65 (https://www.cia.gov/library/publications/the-world-factbook/geos/ug.html), accessed 16 May, 2013. For HIV statistics see footnote 38.
66 (http://www.indexmundi.com), accessed 25 May 2013; (http://www.tradingeconomics.com), accessed 25 May 2013.

of the Nile River.[67] A remarkable level of organised structure within the existing African Kingdoms made later colonisation complicated. Rival chiefdoms flexed their muscles over guns, ivory and slaves and battled for the advantage with the help of alliances formed both with Arabs from Egypt in the north and later the Europeans. Vulnerability to eastern chiefdoms led the powerful southern and Bugandan king, Mutesa, to try out both camps as a security measure. In the process he converted first to Islam and then later to Christianity when he sought an alliance with the British under the guidance of John Stanley. Mutesa wrote a letter inviting British missionaries to his Kingdom, and paved the way for the creation of modern day Uganda. Ultimately the ascendancy of the Southern Bugandan was swept aside with colonisation, and a number of different ethnic groups with different political systems and cultures were grouped together to form a British protectorate in the late 1800s.[68]

The country's inability to form a working political community after independence (1962) has been attributed to those differences.[69] From the 1960s until 1986, the country was subjected to a series of violent and devastating dictatorships that systematically incorporated military rule and mass murder into their modus operandi and left the

---

67 John Speke (1827-1864) went to East Africa in the middle of the 1850s in an attempt to find the source of the Nile. He found both Lake Tanganyika and Lake Victoria, which he named. He did most of his exploration with Burton and Grant. James Grant (1827-1892) travelled with Speke to solve problems associated with identifying the source of the Nile. Henry Stanley (1841-1904) was a Welsh American journalist who travelled in to central Africa in 1875 and is famous for his rescue of the Scottish missionary and explorer David Livingstone. His work included establishing the lack of connection between the Nile and Lake Tanganyika. Samuel Baker (1821-1893) was an explorer, abolitionist, and big game hunter. In Uganda he is known for his discovery of Lake Albert, and his exploration of the Nile and the African interior.
68 (http://humanistuganda.wordpress.com/2012/03/13/coming-to-africa-explorers-find-a-not-so-dark-continent/), accessed 6 June, 2013.
69 (https://www.cia.gov/library/publications/the-world-factbook/geos/ug.html), accessed 16 May 2013

economy in ruins. Since the end of the Amin[70] (1971-79) and Obote[71] (1980-85) regimes, who between them murdered half a million people, and the overthrow of Okellos (six months between 1985-86), the National Resistance Movement led by Yoweri Museveni has begun to revive hope by establishing relative stability and economic growth. Inching towards constitutionalism and democracy despite the country's "exhaustion, impoverishment, and demoralisation", the current government has fought wars inside and outside national borders. The nation has suffered under the Lord's Resistance Army in the north,[72] which has been guilty of numerous crimes against humanity including child slavery and mass murder, and it has battled one of the worst HIV epidemics in Africa with great success. Despite apparently humanitarian motivations and democratic aspirations, some still question Museveni methods, and Cardinal Wamala himself has suggested that the leader is now addicted to power, much like his predecessors, having altered the constitution to allow him to serve unlimited terms. (Corruption, alongside power costs, and inadequate transportation infrastructure, continues to inhibit investor confidence.)[73] Nevertheless, Cardinal Wamala remains one of Museveni's closest advisors and has provided guidance and support to Ugandans through every dictatorship since independence.

---

70 Idi Amin (1925-2003) was president of Uganda from 1971-1979. He rose through the military from 1940 to 1970, taking over the country in 1971 and becoming a brutal dictator. He lived a lavish lifestyle and is attributed with the collapse of Uganda's economy.

71 Obote (1925-2005) was Ugandan statesmen, prime minister (1962) and the nation's first president (1966) after he overthrew King Mutesa II and declared Uganda a republic. After Amin was deposed in 1979 he was re-elected President (1981) but was then ousted again after a bloody civil war and coup led by Brigadier Okello (1985).

72 Alex Perry/Obo, "The Warlord vs. the Hipsters. How a group of American filmmakers and 100 special-operations troops are pursuing Africa's most-wanted war criminal." *Time,* 26 March 2012, pp. 18-23.

73 See Phares Mutibwa, (1992), *Uganda Since Independence, a story of unfulfilled hope,* Africa World Press, Inc., New Jersey; Olive Kobusingye,(2010), *The Correct Line? Uganda under Museveni,* AuthorHouse, London.

Emmanuel Cardinal Wamala was born on 15 December 1926 in the Kamaggwa parish of Lwaggulwe Masaka district, Uganda. He was ordained priest in Rome in 1957. Between 1957 and 1981 he completed further studies in Rome, Uganda and the United States, maintained a pastoral ministry in the diocese of Masaka, served as inspector of diocesan schools and faculty member of the Minor Seminary of Bukalasa, and as chaplain and faculty member and rector of the University of Makerere. He served as vicar-general of the diocese of Masaka from 1974 to 1981. In 1977, he was created chaplain of His Holiness and was appointed Cardinal-Priest of Sant'Ugo in 2004. In 2005 he participated in the 2005 papal conclave, but has since lost the right to participate in any future conclave as a result of passing his eightieth birthday. He remains patron of the African Prisons' Project, an international non-governmental organisation with a mission to bring dignity and hope to men, women and children in African prisons through health, education, justice and reintegration.

I interviewed Cardinal Wamala in Mengo-Kampala in October 2011.

Village cathedral, Bamfoussam, Cameroon (see pages 273ff)

ii. Hope

... who is going to harm you if you are eager to do good? Even if you suffer for what is right you are blessed. Do not fear what they fear. Do not be frightened ...[74]

I.

Five stars; five armed and dangerous soldiers waiting at the door, five stops between here and the airport in Entebbe, five senior politicians lodged upstairs, and five days away from my five children. Last night there were five people staffing the front desk and five footmen carrying bags. This morning there are five white tourists sitting having breakfast and five Ugandan waitresses watching every move we make. They have said exactly five words to me, "Can I take your order?" before wandering away to gather five cups of bad coffee, and returning later to utter five more – "Would you like your bill?" and then, despite my smile and attempts to engage them, "Please pay at the desk."

They were reserved, perhaps distant, detached, or even tired. It took me a day or two to catch them out laughing and they whispered a lot. I tried to engage with the young women in the hotel restaurant the following morning, but they were unwilling and refused to meet my gaze. I could not read the social cues (*are they angry or depressed?*) and I found it hard to gain the attention of staff. There was some relief in the hotel bar (*a kind of international refuge*) where I sat and worked once the interview was over and where I talked to a young waitress when the cook burnt my pizza. She offered me an apology in the form of pleasant conversation and there was even some smiling – a facial expression I thought I could read, and one that joined us together (one younger, one older) across cultural lines. In the morning (4am) there was more smiling and even momentary joviality. William, at the

---

74 1 Peter 3:13-14

service desk, turned on the internet so I could email my husband to say when I was coming home. *A crack appeared on an otherwise bleak horizon*, I wrote.

At breakfast the hotel restaurant was peopled by huge, well-dressed men who looked like Forest Whitaker did as Idi Amin in *The Last King of Scotland*. I ate eggs and beans and drank some kind of juice (*maybe mango?*), and then black coffee. I was anxious about the interview, and perhaps too about actually finding the cardinal that morning. It was the first time that I had met a cardinal in his home country. Finding him in person was potentially as difficult as making first contact from Australia. De Nascimento, the Angolan cardinal and archbishop of Luanda, had hinted at divine intervention when he told me where he would be. "You come to Luanda and you ask for the cardinal. They will bring you to me!" Clearly I had to trust in the cardinal's confidence.

My driver, Joseph, arrived in the morning. He spoke briefly with the hotel butler who told him where to take me before Joseph motioned brusquely for me to get into his car. *There was no smile. He treated me with disdain.* Like the others, he was reserved and spoke to me only to indicate that he knew where to go. "Of course", he said softly, eyes focussed on the road in front of him, "everyone knows the cardinal. He is Kampala's old lion." *Indeed*, I would write in my journal later that evening, *Uganda's very own Aslan*. I locked my passenger side door and felt ashamed when Joseph blinked at the sound of it.

Finding Cardinal Wamala had been difficult. I had sent him a letter but then heard nothing back, and without understanding the idea of "African time" had quickly become frustrated with the pace of communications. As the weeks passed, I began to appreciate that in sub-Saharan Africa, bar some parts of the Republic of South Africa, there was very limited internet access, no fax machines and no landlines. People relied on mobile phones (and perhaps word of mouth) but finding mobile numbers was difficult. By the time I found the cardinal, I had made almost 50 phone calls, all at two o'clock in the morning. Each time I was given a new number by an "assistant", posing as the cardinal's PA. It was not until I had convinced people at the other end of the line that I would not give in until I had found him that I found someone who was willing to help me. Even then we had trouble understanding one another. He would have to ask another priest for the cardinal's private number, he told me, "Call back in another hour madam."

My publisher was similarly perplexed by the communication problems. "Can't you do these interviews on Skype?" he kept asking. "Skype? I can't get through on the telephone, let alone hook up on Skype!" I would say. "Then meet them in Rome", he told me. "The African synod is in Rome in October. You could interview them all at once and it would be a lot safer." Certainly it all *sounded* a lot easier that way. And later without success I would rely on that supposed convenience of the synod to gather final interviews. But in this earlier stage I tried to use my publisher's connections to religious bodies in Sydney to get in contact with priests working in Africa who might approach the cardinals about my meeting them in Rome, but no-one seemed to appreciate how hard it was to make contact. "Why don't you just call them, or send them a letter?" referring me to contact details listed in the Big Red Book.[75] One drew my attention to a website handling diocesan information, not realising that I already knew that none of it was up-to-date. Sometimes male clergy dismissed me entirely. They could tell I was not Catholic; what's more, I was a woman. They spoke to me through my intermediary, the other man in the room and smiled at me generously, suggesting that I try baptism. I went away feeling angry, frustrated, and stupid. At times like that it was hard to keep going. What structure the book had gained crumbled

---

75 The *Annario Pontificio* – the Papal Year book or "Big Red Book" is kept by all the Cardinals and contains contact details for every member of the Church operating at a senior level.

into my sleepless nights. My stomach churned a lot and I cooked cakes for my children, and their lunch boxes became daily works of art. Finally a letter arrived from Uganda and I was myself again. I told my publisher that I was booking flights. "I have to meet each cardinal in his own context," I told him, "I need to find *unknown unknowns*." But he, like everyone else, held "grave" concerns for my safety.

Later, I would wave off comments about safety. What my naivety called "dangerous" my intellect labelled "complex". Danger evolved into an intellectual challenge that I wanted to unpack and I welcomed it. But my friends' and publisher's concerns made me uneasy. Discussion about the book had a tendency to attract negative energy. Dinner table conversation would spiral into excited demonstrations of African know-how: disease, infection, car-jacking and internet fraud would steadily take up more of the conversation through the meal. By the second coffee, they were talking rape. By the time the bill arrived, they were on to fatalities: "Photocopy your passports, pack antibiotics, keep your bags out of reach of the windows, lock the door when you sleep, never use your credit card … don't let anyone know you're an American …" One tipsy friend suggested that I swallow my cash. Before I left for Uganda my publisher topped the lot by asking me to sign a disclaimer that released him and his company from responsibility for my death.

The judgements that my planned trip inspired became irritating. A class teacher pointed out how many children I had, hinting that my leaving was self-indulgent, a cavalier act of abandonment: "It would be a shame to leave them without a mother," she said. After a few months the book became a white elephant anyway. It was just *too* hard to explain the "why?" or "why you?" just as it was too hard to justify taking on more than I already had on my plate. Plagued with self-doubt I imagined that it was my energy alone that had spurred my publisher's commitment and that I had been seduced by the opportunity to write another book rather than the topic that would drive it. It did feel self-indulgent to say that I was going to go to Africa because I was drowning in the relentlessness of a parenting routine that I had *chosen all by myself*, and enormously ungrateful to express my frustration at having to subordinate my own priorities to the demands of my husband's career when that career had provided a "river to his people".[76] Furthermore it was a betrayal to attack the privileged school community that was shaping my children (and to which *they all belonged*), or to describe it as prejudiced and paranoid when so many of their friends relied upon its undeniable worth as an affirmation of identity and their own self-esteem. Yet such ideas surrounded and hounded me and I remained *driven* though I could not articulate why.

Somewhere between finishing the PhD I had written and the first interview in Rome, the meaning of my life had become intellectualised. Ideals and ideas had replaced the earthy significance and personal satisfaction of practical tasks. "Career" had trumped "motherhood" in a list of priorities that had emerged from the feminist movement of the past, and women like me were strangled by options as doors opened across the Western world to careers previously reserved for men. Of course it had to be that way and women deserved access to those spaces too. The issue was not one of what should or should not be, but of how to manage the complexities of a life that expected involvement and excellence in clashing domains. There was always a sense of inadequacy, of being unable to apply oneself fully both to motherhood or a career, and as a result, failing in both. Choosing career over motherhood was seen as "selfish", motherhood over career as letting the team down. Yet those like me who chose both and who

---

[76] The first of seven advices of Mevlana (1207-1273) a 13th century Muslim saint, Anatolian mystic and founder of the whirling dervish sect of Muslims. Mevlana's doctrine advocated unlimited tolerance, positive reasoning, goodness, charity and awareness through love. In 1958, Pope John XXIII wrote a special message saying: "In the name of the Catholic World, I bow with respect before the memory of Rumi." (http://www.mevlana.net/), accessed 11 June 2013.

approached them with gusto were afraid that they might be judged as "greedy". I made my arrangements silently, in between loads of washing and dishes and while the children were busy at school, and learned to live with the continuing isolation.

My letters made it to Uganda and the cardinal wrote back to me via the archbishop of Melbourne. "Tell Dr Sally that I will meet her any time," he said. But there was no email or telephone contact. When I was finally given his direct number (a fortnight before my plane flew), it was as if he was waiting for my call. I imagined his hand cast deep in the pocket of his cassock holding his phone while he waited for it to ring. When he picked up, I could hear the cars splashing through wet season mud in the background.

"Hello?" I said. "I'm looking for his eminence Cardinal Wamala. Do I have the right number?"

"Yes", he said back. "This *is* Wamala."

"Your eminence," I stumbled, momentarily shocked, "this is Sally from Australia …", but he spoke over me quickly, saying, "It is wonderful to finally hear your voice."

II.

Cardinal Wamala was waiting for me under the arched entrance to Kampala's Catholic residence, deep in the heartland of Mengo-Kampala, a desperate slum. I felt its ache when I drove into the district. Later I remembered that I had heard it groan: *Perhaps it was the sound of my own voice?* Beyond the car windows the streets were busy. People were going about their business amidst the chaos of traffic and soldiers who milled together on street corners. Here and there, an open sewer flowed along the edge of dusty and then (once the rain came) muddy streets, along with rubbish. Open front doors drew my eyes into dark, one-room shacks that sheltered women washing clothes and preparing food, surrounded by small children barely visible as they scuttled around the women's knees. Idle young men wandered in groups, and young women walked alone carrying heavy loads, picking their way through chunks of broken concrete.

After my first interview experience of Arinze in Rome, I had been anxious about what I would find in Uganda. The formality of Rome had been difficult to negotiate. The strict Roman Catholic culture that defined Arinze had added to the incomprehensible cloud that Catholicism had always seemed to me. In Italy I had felt out of my depth because the Vatican spoke a language that was foreign to me, and because the sheer masculinity and opulent surroundings were intimidating. But Italy was not unfamiliar territory. At least it was Western, which made it culturally accessible in part.

Uganda was a different story. I walked onto the plane with my mind's eye closed. My experience of Africa as a continent had ended at the South African border, a different experiment in European conquest. I had no image or idea of Uganda to draw upon except the notorious regimes the country had suffered under Idi Amin and Obote in the past, and the thugs of Joseph Koney's Lord's Resistance Army that maintained a vicious grip on the north of the country in the present. My assumption was that the Church in Uganda sat within the context of the country's colonial history. I expected cathedrals and clean cassocks, and a measure of Catholic opulence; an image intertwined both with histories written about Speke, Grant, Stanley or Livingstone, some of the protagonists of British high culture who had first trudged the way into Africa's tribal heart, and with the mooted groundnut scheme of the early 1950s.[77] My thinking still placed Africans as victims of conversion and the Ugandan cardinal

---

77 In 1946, Frank Samuel (head of the United Africa Company) came up with an idea to cultivate groundnuts in the British colonies for the production of vegetable oil for the shortage of oil in Britain and the economic problems of the British Colonies, and using servicemen returned from the Second World War. It was a monumental disaster. The crop was destroyed by heavy drought, cost 49 million pounds, and was abandoned after a year. See Alan Wood (1950), *The Groundnut Affair*, Bodley Head.

(like Arinze) as a successful aspirant to higher honours on European (and Catholic) turf. And so my intention was probably to record an interview that supported that mind-set, an interview that I expected would unpack yet another example of Western arrogance, justify my idealistic stance and feed my First World guilt.

But Wamala was not Arinze and Kampala was not Rome. The place was so utterly foreign to me that it threw me even before the plane touched down. Before landing in Entebbe[78] we crossed Lake Victoria, a vast, rich and fertile inland sea; the end of the great Nile River; so massive that its waters could have swallowed my entire home state. *No wonder they called it Africa's pearl* ... The main road from the airport to Kampala was a river of dust; lined with shabby towns that were joined, one to another, by wonky shops and piles of rubbish. Young men walked together under rows of blinking and faulty street lamps, shocking me with their sex appeal; a physical presence, an athleticism intensified by the colour of their skin. Later that night I would label the same young men as "predatory" (... *young men who wandered in packs* ...) unaware that the label reflected my own confusion about the way their looks made me feel. There were traffic jams everywhere: vans, police cars, corrugated tin roofs waving at me in the night air atop shacks that lined the endless dirt. Motorbikes revved beside concrete buildings that crumbled. Families walked quickly through a dark night with small children; sacks with babies on mother's backs, below more sacks on heads. Bikes, girlfriends riding side-saddle, and energetic youths hastened past the van as we waited for the cars in front to move on. Then Christianity appeared through the darkness, rushing by on billboards (Holy Trinity, Mother Mary and the Holy Rosary ...), on posters (for Christian gatherings, support services, health centres) that were stuck

---

78 The site of the Palestinian hostage crisis of 1976. "1976: Israelis rescue Entebbe hostages", *On This Day,* BBC, 4 July 2005, (http://news.bbc.co.uk/onthisday/hi/dates/stories/july/4/newsid_2786000/2786967.stm), accessed 22 May 2013.

to lampposts or that hovered, unstuck, at intersections – they rose and fell, slipped sideways or floated; lingering just centimetres above the carriage way on diesel fumes that gathered in clouds beneath the wheels of the traffic.

Maybe Jesus came from a place like this? This idea came to mind time and time again. I imagined him, 2,000 years earlier, nurturing souls harangued by the same kind of guards (but Roman) that I met at the hotel gate; now they wore army greens and carried machine guns. They went through my bags, the boot of the car and peered through the window demanding I wind down the glass. *They were weedy and menacing ... lacked stiff discipline ... seemed unpredictable.* I felt exposed and vulnerable, and then bewildered by yet another set of security checks at the hotel doorway that x-rayed me and my baggage for weaponry, *as if I were a possible threat.*

This was a woman who was used to a certain degree of protection: the rule of law, health policies, educational advantages and even social etiquette had provided me with a stable, safe and civilised existence. Feeling unsafe caught me off-guard. I became suddenly sensitive to my lack of "rights". It seemed impossible to read the social cues. And I was intimidated by the native language that scuttled ahead of me in conversations between hotel staff about the arrangements that had been made for my stay. Words like *target* and *cagey* began to appear in my journal. What I would later describe as *under confident* was initially recorded as *menacing. There was an unwillingness to meet my gaze*, I wrote, *or to engage in casual conversation.* Despite my determination, everything that I had been warned about at home began to appear and I quickly misjudged offers of assistance as badly intended and felt uneasy. The following morning when I mentioned my concerns about travel in Khartoum (where conflict had recently erupted) Wamala said to me, "there is no need for you to feel afraid!" *Somewhere in this journey*, I realised with pen poised, *I will have to take a giant leap of faith.*

Wamala was an old lion. He was half-blind, battered and quiet. He walked slowly with me along the concrete patio and into his residence, carrying himself with the grace of someone who has weathered not just a battle or two but war. I had to calm myself to slow down to his pace and wondered if we would ever make the 30 metres into the house. He ushered me into his small lounge room, a "retro" delight and mirror for the all-male (Catholic) residential college of the 1970s that I knew well: *velveteen, and worn lounge set with wooden arm rests, a glass-topped coffee table above a red fraying carpet.* Propped up on bricks in the corner and tilted slightly was a cupboard with glass-fronted doors. It was just big enough to hold two cups with saucers and some bread plates; a couple of forks. A crucifix was nailed to the wall alongside a photo of the cardinal and Pope John Paul II, and a certificate of appreciation from a local school. (The certificate was crooked and stuck onto the walls with glue). He motioned for me to sit down in an arm-chair that was too deep for me and, taken by surprise, I was suddenly relieved of the formality that had dogged me in Rome. He retired briefly, to prepare himself, and returned to sit down beside me.

Like Arinze, Wamala was mentored by an African predecessor. The nation's first African bishop, Kiwanuka, made a lasting impression on men like Wamala, who drew on their example in leadership choices of their own. "As a seminarian I was always in his hands," he said. Like Kiwanuka, Wamala valued the pragmatism of the country's British past,[79] but he also drew on Kiwanuka's application of Catholicism to

---

79 Wamala indicated that British colonialism created an administrative structure with a direct and beneficial effect on the populous. "The British ... did their best," he said. Sanitation measures, promotion of commerce, support for basic education standards, and the centralisation of authority can contain and restrict the fermentation of existing rivalries amongst ethnically diverse peoples. In both Uganda and Nigeria (and other British colonial states as well), the Catholic Church (and other Christian Churches) were very much a part of that secure structure, being commissioned by the British to provide for the society's health and education needs.

emancipation through education, economics, and health to navigate the obstacles of the repressive regimes that followed.

> [Kiwanuka] was conscious that it was not good enough to evangelise the people. Rather, it was important to take them and mould them so that they could eventually become political leaders.

Wamala became one of those leaders Kiwanuka aimed to shape. Having studied at university in Uganda after the granting of independence, he taught in public schools in the turmoil of first the Amin and then the Obote regimes. He guided his students in the arts of peaceful protest, while around him colleagues were murdered for expressing outrage at atrocity. He survived two civil wars and two vicious regimes, which together murdered one-tenth of the country's population, was appointed bishop of the diocese of Kyinda Mityana in 1981 before being made Archbishop of Kampala in 1990 and being created cardinal by Pope John Paul II after the current leader Museveni had come to power. With Museveni, Wamala launched one of the most successful campaigns to combat AIDS, a campaign that pursued the Church's focus (love, support and personal responsibility) in conjunction with the government's focus on practical prevention.[80] The program removed the stigma from those with the disease and provides the medical support that sufferers need through hospitals.

---

80 Uganda is often held up as a model in the war on HIV and AIDS. It reduced the numbers of adults with HIV from fifteen per cent in the early 1990s to five per cent in 2004 (though much of that reduction has been attributed to sufferers dying). From the late 1980s, and in cooperation with the Church, the government launched an attack on the epidemic. Together they created the ABC campaign, (Abstinence, be Faithful, use Condoms). It encouraged government ministries to get involved alongside NGOs and faith-based organisations, and it relaxed control of the media so that a diversity of prevention messages could reach the public. Prevention work also occurred in large part at the grass roots level, through churches, schools and villages. Groups worked to break down the stigma associated with AIDS, and they encouraged an open discussion of sexual subjects that had previously been taboo. (http://www.avert.org/aids-uganda.htm), accessed January 2013.

While armed and violent conflict dogged his earlier years as priest, it continues to challenge Wamala in later life as well. Joseph Koney and his band of thugs are notorious for a murderous and vicious campaign in the north of the country, through which Wamala has suffered personal loss (his niece was raped and murdered as I was on my way to visit him in Kampala)[81] and for which he continues to seek international assistance. Meanwhile, he strives to inject balance into a government that he describes as having become addicted to power, by maintaining a relationship with its leader and advising on political appointments. Where other leading figures will choose a Mercedes Benz, Wamala swaps the personal trappings of his status as Catholic cardinal and political adviser for education scholarships.

At the end of our meeting, I asked him to suggest a worthy cause for a donation and he sent me to the Sanyo Babies clinic, an orphanage for babies under the age of three where beautifully presented women in immaculate clothing served fifty small and sick children with great love and care. I went to the "national museum", a small building under tin, where an exhibition about women's achievement (placed amongst traditional instruments and a diorama of early Ugandan history) showed bright faces who had broken through boundaries despite all: women who had large families of children at home but had seen no private conflict in the pursuit of careers that would secure those children a future. I went to Christ the King Cathedral in the centre of town, to attend an afternoon mass. The cathedral was lined with paintings of an African Jesus and his African disciples; the Christian story within African paradigms. All of the pews were full for the fifth time that day and it sat at least 500. At Rubaga Cathedral on Kampala hill, where the first Catholics had constructed their chapel out of grasses, young men and women welcomed me at the door, took my hand and told me the story of the cathedral, the story of the white fathers, the story of Uganda

---

81 "Ugandan girl murdered in Nairobi", *In 2 East Africa*, 7 August 2011 (http://in-2eastafrica.net/ugandan-girl-murdered-in-nairobi/), accessed 22 May 2013.

and wished me well. They were pleased that I had shown an interest in their church, in their cardinal, in their country ... *and I felt safe.*

How does a place like this produce a man like Wamala, a place that appears to be chaotic and disintegrating, to be fractured by violence and disease? This is a man who advises his own president, but he was also happy personally to serve me fruit and Ugandan tea. The communication frustrations, the concerns about safety and the fearful judgements about individual intentions had threatened to blind me to a *single truth:* Africans in Uganda need love to survive. And Wamala, the prince of the country's Catholics, has a lot of it to give. He thanked Joseph for driving me to his residence to meet him and told the story of his name. "Joseph was a king!" he told me. He took Joseph's hand and Joseph smiled at me for the first time. As I got into the car he asked me where I would like to go next and, waving at the cardinal who stood and watched us out of sight, we drove away together with the windows open and the doors unlocked. Later Wamala would write me a personal letter to thank *me* for *my* interest in him and send it to Australia where I found it under the advertising material that makes up most of the mail ... and for the first time in a long time, *I, like Joseph, would begin to feel alive too.* The wind was blowing. The boat had begun to set sail.

Like Wamala, many cardinals are working together with governments to combat AIDS with positive awareness programs

iii. Cardinal Emmanuel Wamala, Archbishop Emeritus, Kampala, Uganda

(October, 2010)

"... It must be hard, forgiving is always hard, but at the same time, God forgives ... In the north of Uganda the people have been suffering for twenty years under a nefarious group ... you cannot [only] talk of civil war. It is a group that has disturbed the whole world ... their leader has been torturing, killing, mutilating, kidnapping ... A group of twelve female students ... were taken by those rebels and abused, raped, murdered, mutilated ... and some of them never came back ... Afterwards they asked the mother of one whether she could forgive those rebels and she said ... I forgive them ..."

I want to begin by asking you about your journey to becoming a cardinal.

My journey?

Yes, from the beginning.

I think it started the day I was born. The Lord foresaw my path already before I was born. I grew up in a family of great achievers: loving parents, caring parents. And I did my primary education in the school that was some three or four kilometres away from my home. I went to the minor seminary, which is called Bukalasa, the first minor seminary in Uganda. And after that I went to a major seminary where I spent five years. Then between 1955 and 1957, I went to Rome and completed my theological studies, before continuing there for two more years to complete a master's degree in theology. In 1960 I returned home. I was ordained a priest in 1957.

I started my ministry in a parish as an assistant priest. In 1962 I was sent to our university here (our national university) to do a diploma in education that qualified me to teach in the public schools. So after qualifying to teach, in '64, I went and I taught at the minor seminary in Bukalasa where I had studied myself and I was there for four years. In 1968 I became chaplain at the university to the students and to the faculty. I was there for six years and then returned home in '74. I became a vicar-general of the diocese (I come from the south, I was not born in this diocese) ... I served there until 1981, when I was made bishop to start a new diocese some 73 kilometres west of Kampala. And I started that diocese which is called Kiyinda Mityana. I served there seven years, and [then] was transferred to Kampala as a coadjutor. My predecessor was cardinal there. I served with him for a year until he handed over to me and I became the archbishop of Kampala. That was in 1990 and I have been there since. It was in my service here as archbishop of Kampala that the pope elected me one of the cardinals. I think that's the journey you wanted to know.

Was it very surprising when he asked you to be cardinal?
Yes I was surprised because I had no reason to expect it. I never applied for it!

Then you travelled to Rome again, I gather, to be created a cardinal?
Yes I went back Rome in October 1994. We were given the red hat and the ring; this very ring is from the pope. And I was given a church in Rome (St Hugo), in some suburb of Rome (as Rome was at that time. I think they will have been engulfed now within Rome, greater Rome), and then I came back and continued my ministry as archbishop of Kampala.

How did your family feel?
Good! My family was very happy. By the time I was created cardinal both my father and mother had passed away. My brother was a priest

in Masaka and my sister, who was our senior, was a widower. They were both very happy. Yes they were very excited about it.

Did they go with you to Rome?
No. They didn't. A few people went with me from here but they did not.

I'd like to talk a little bit about Uganda. There are a few areas I would like to ask you about: about Ugandan history; the 1960s and up to the presidency of Museveni. The human rights violations, ethnic persecutions and corrupt practices of successive governments (Idi Amin, Obote and Museveni). And perhaps some of the organisations you are involved with. I know that you are patron of the African Prisons Project for example ...
Yes. I am a patron of an organisation called the Ministry After Custody. They try to help ex-prisoners; to rehabilitate them, to bring them back into society, to make them acceptable, accepted by their own people and even to have them restart life. Some have stayed in prison many years and when they come back they are not welcome – maybe they committed a crime in their own village – and so that organisation tries to help them to fit in to society once again.

And you have also taken a particularly compassionate stand towards women with HIV/AIDS ...
Yes, I think you can regard all of us in the church here in Uganda (more than any other organisation) as concerned about victims of HIV. We try to educate people. We believe more in behavioural change than in administering prophylactics. We try to encourage values in our people that will affect their behaviour and limit the spread of the disease (especially in the young people) and we have many hospitals run by the church that administer the programs of prevention of HIV and the care for its victims.

Here in Uganda you have had one of the most effective responses to HIV/AIDS in Africa ...

That's what they say ...

... and I know that you [were] cardinal during the application of that response ...

Yes.

Can you could talk a little bit more about the nation's response to the epidemic and the church's role within that national approach?

See, the Church works through our hospitals. We make sure that at every one of our hospitals there is a program connected with HIV prevention, and care for victims and the people who are affected or infected. So we try, through our hospitals, to get a response and even in the small clinics. We as pastors can only preach to them and encourage them with God. The real implementers of the policies we like to see followed are the hospital staff. It is they who help: with the counselling, the treatment, and distributing and giving whatever the victims need.

We agreed ... to work with the government. Right from the beginning we agreed that we have our own values and we see to them in the fight against HIV/AIDS. But we also work together with the government. The government uses its own means ... that are effective. But we, the Church, are selective. Our gospel is abstinence and fidelity. If you are not married you must abstain from sex. If you are married be faithful to her. But if you are already on drugs and diseased, be open to those who can support you. There is no discrimination. There is no stigmatisation of the victims. They can come openly and say, "I have this problem. Can I get help?" Open communication is very important and we make sure it happens in many places. People in Uganda no longer have to be concerned with any stigma.

How does a man, like you, who occupies a position of real leadership and commands respect amongst his people within his community and indeed his country, negotiate the necessities of leadership [under] the oppression of dictatorships like those of Idi Amin or Obote?

We have had problems in this country over the last well I think, almost 50 years. We became an independent nation in 1962, so it would be 50 years next year. But only four years after independence, in '66, the trouble started both with Amin and with Obote. Amin ruled for eight years but he was attacked and defeated. Obote came back, he stayed here for five years, but then he too was fought against and defeated. So we had two civil wars, one of which was supported by Tanzania.

I think we were fortunate in a way because Uganda never fought for its independence. It was just given to us. The British administered this country for more than 60 years and I think they did their best. They followed the policy that they could in the [face] of new or very different cultures. We had our leaders, whom we respected and whom the British respected. At the time, the British issued the laws but they always implemented their rule with a view to our own cultural structures. That system worked very well. When we became independent, our native leaders wanted to have all the powers and ignore all the kind of traditions we had. I think that was the real beginning of the trouble.

The British approach strengthened the traditions and structures of leadership founding the country. They tried to modernise them, but they always respected them. By comparison, our native leaders decided that they would have none of that. They had to dictate their policies and dictate the law and implement them by force, if necessary, overthrowing one government after the other until Museveni came. He has been with us for 25 years. Now, apparently, he is beginning to be addicted to power as well, I think. So we have problems and now corruption is rampant in every government structure. We have this nepotism ... We don't know how we are going to go with all of this but Ugandans never lose hope. They always hope that tomorrow will be better than today.

Is that what you preached to your people through all of that trouble?
Yeah, we tell them not to despair and lose hope. Because you can't excite them to be false. You can't even justify the way they are being treated. With each day they should try to use their ballots, their vote, but that has not worked, and it can't work when you have rulers who are dictators ... so what can we say? I think we have got to accept it and try to believe that one day, good will come.

So how does someone like yourself ask his flock to forgive the unforgiveable?
(Laughs) well I don't think that there is anyone who is unforgiveable. I think we have to follow the example of Christ: "Forgive them they do not know what they are doing". I don't think that they know!! They do not know that they are abusing their authority! They do not know that they are demoting the rights of others..

But when they are witnesses to gross human rights violations, to ghastly atrocities, to extreme personal loss, it must be very hard for the families of those victims to forgive ...
It must be hard, forgiving is always hard, but at the same time, God forgives ...

Especially in the north of Uganda here ... the people have been suffering for twenty years under a nefarious group ... you cannot talk of civil war. It is a group that has disturbed the whole world, I would say, because now America has come to help us arrest the leader of this group. He has been torturing people, killing people, mutilating people, kidnapping people. In the north, one lady drove a whole group of female students ... I think there were about twelve of them ... the girls were taken by these rebels and abused, raped, murdered, mutilated

They asked the mother of [one of the girls] whether she could forgive those rebels and she said, "I forgive them."

Forgiving is not easy; it has never been easy. But we have to preach it or else we can't move forward. Here we have an ecumenical council that's for Catholics, Anglicans and Orthodox. Then we have an interreligious council and that includes any kind of believers – Muslims, Pentecostals – and we are working together, trying to educate people into justice, forgiveness, and love. People ask, "Why have these things happened to me?" and they question their faith ... forgiveness requires great strength.

I have a quote here: "The Christian advance in Africa was a black advance or it was nothing. The work of teaching, preaching and conversion was almost always born by black leaders." Can we talk about that quote?

Well, at one time I thought I could talk about anything in Africa. Often I realised that I was very wrong. Africa is vast. Africa is diverse. Even in the history and in the practice of Christianity it is very, very, different. For example, I lived in South Africa for one month not very long ago – maybe four, five, six years ago. And I realised that the proclamation of God's word in that part of the world was very, very different from what it has been here. Now even here in Uganda, we have 33 societies, missionary societies, one of which is French, the first one – the White Fathers. Then came the Mill Hill Fathers (who are predominantly British). Then came the Comboni Fathers (predominately Italian). The Comboni were in the north, the Mill Hill were in the east, and the White Fathers were in the centre, the south and the west. But even there you will find differences in the way the gospel is proclaimed.

But what I can say is that in the case of Uganda, the missionaries were very dedicated. The missionaries had foresight. They came determined to educate the people here, the local people, to carry on the work of God. Maybe in other places they didn't think so much about training local clergy, but here they did. Actually, next year we're going to celebrate 100 years of the first priest in Uganda. Christianity in Uganda is only 134 years old next year ... and already 30 years after Christianity arrived, we had our first Ugandan priest ... So, they educated catechists, they educated the teachers in the schools and they educated the local people. In that sense, what we are saying is that from the very beginning, the work of the organisation included the local people. They were introduced to the work of the organisation and they worked together with the missionaries.

Even today, in our liturgy we celebrate the martyrs of North America. Now none of them was American; they were all missionaries from Europe. In Uganda we now have 24 martyrs. None of them was a missionary; they were all local people. So the witness has been very clearly given by the local people, because the missionaries started very early to entrust them with responsibilities within the church and spread the word of the gospel.

There's another element at work here isn't there? That quite mysterious concept of the Africanisation of Christianity? The White Fathers were particularly committed to a deep Africanisation of Christianity in the way that they practiced, weren't they?
Yes they were.

Can you talk a little bit about Africanisation and what that means? And how that applies here?
It applied here because the missionaries believed it was the right approach. They knew they came here to bring the message of salvation, but it is not the only way. And it is surely not for everyone to spread and continue the work and that is why I say that very early on, they began training people, even taking young men to Europe ... They were trained in Malta and they came back and adopted their own people as

ecumenical assistants. So they started entrusting the message and their responsibility was spreading it to their local people. That is why they trained catechists. The catechists here have played and still play a very vital role in the work of evangelisation. That structure, that society, those groups, started to form from the very beginning, to work with the missionaries from the very, very beginning. For example, initially there was one priest to serve an area of over ten square miles: They would train catechists and place them in different centres and trust them with responsibilities of the training of young people and adults – the catechumens – and the priest would go there later as a kind of finishing touch. Yes, catechists did all the work...

In some places, particularly in the West, it is becoming increasingly difficult to find young men willing to enter the seminary. I know, for example, of young African priests who have been relocated to parishes in the United States and to Australia to [fill] the gaps. Is it true that more men are moving into the priesthood here? So many more that they can fill a void in other places around the world?

There are places like that here in Uganda as well where the local people are not easily attracted to other forms of life. Not all areas are the same. You will find an area here in Uganda where they can hardly find a local priest to minister. There are areas like that here as well.

Why do you think that is?
The mentality of the people is not exactly the same. The north is different, the north-east is different, north-west also, the south and so on. In South Africa, where I was for one month for example, it is very difficult to get a local priest. One of the reasons being of course that apartheid played a very big role in stifling any kind of relationship between missionaries and the local people. Here we had "multi-religious" missionary societies. In most parts of Africa they had the "religious". In South Africa most "religious" were Dominicans, Franciscans and so on. So all the young people who wanted to become

priests became Dominicans, Franciscans and so on. Diocesan priests were hardly known in some of these places.

Mozambique, for example, had a longer history of Christianity than many [other] parts of Africa ... They had religious people who had evangelised that area and all priests were becoming Franciscans, and so on. Now when the revolution came in Mozambique and everybody suddenly decided to leave, they didn't have any African priests. The cardinal came here, took some young people to be trained to become diocesan priests in Mozambique and in Limpopo.

So it is not everywhere in Africa that the response is so generous. In some areas, in Tanzania for example, some areas are very, very dangerous and in some others they got no response. As I say, here in Uganda – in the west, in the south – people are more responsive to religious vocations than, say, in the north-east.

The first African bishop, Bishop Kiwanouka, was a Ugandan. Can you tell me what his appointment meant to the future of Catholicism in Uganda and how his practice as a bishop here influenced you as a young man at the seminary?

He became bishop in 1939 and I entered the seminary in 1942. As a seminarian I was in his hands. I was in his diocese and in his seminary, and it was he who [admitted] me to the major seminary, to go and study and to further my education. So I owe quite a lot to him in my priestly ministry. He was a very good man.

What did you take from the way that he practised into the way that you have practised through your life?

Well I think there were different times, different people, even now, you [could] say, a different church, because the Second Vatican Council brought a lot of changes. But he was concerned about the education of the people. Education was a very high priority in his apostolic strategies.

Do you mean the teaching of Catholicism or do you mean education in general or both together?
Education in general! He promoted education in his diocese very much. He was one of the first to open a girl's secondary school (Managongo was first) but his achievement was significant. Of course, the Protestants had theirs already, but he also opened a girls' secondary school. He opened a hospital. He mobilised the Catholics to start co-operating with the nuns. He mobilised them to cultivate and grow coffee.

He had an economic and an environmental impact here. He was conscious that it was not good enough to evangelise the people. Rather, it was important to take them and mould them so that they could eventually become political leaders. He was concerned about harassment and as a result his diocese led all dioceses of Uganda in methods of education, health care and economic empowerment. His legacy continued after him, because he was transferred here. He left his original diocese and came here, and he continued here until independence was achieved [after which time those who followed him or worked with him have tried their best to follow his example].

And were others like you able then to continue his legacy after independence? Or was it just too hard under Amin and Obote?
It was difficult. But we have not given up [laughs] ... because they are still here who lived during his time and who knew the leaders he promoted and who worked with them; they are still with us and they are trying their best [as each new political challenge presents itself] to see that that his spirit doesn't die.

What was the significance of Vatican II for Catholicism here in Uganda?
In my view, Vatican II was significant for a number of reasons: First of all was the openness to encourage [local] values. There were many

cultural values that were quite innocent and not pagan as they are described sometimes. So that is the openness to the cultures of the people: To allow the people, to encourage their culture – the kind of close fraternisation of the Bible and to encourage [the integration of that] culture into the biblical teaching. And that has changed our type of celebrations and made them more vibrant, because people seem to be participating more with the local language and using local musical instruments and movements, and so on. That has enlightened that aspect of worship.

Another strong aspect of Vatican II was the involvement and encouragement of the laity to take up responsibilities in the life of the Church. To know their place, their responsibility in the life of the Church, not to stay at the periphery, always waiting for the priest, but to see that they have a very active part to play in the running of the Church. So we have councils in all our churches, and we have all the groups participating, in many roles ... In my opinion, the outstanding effects on the Church came from Vatican II. We can worship with openness towards the cultures of the people, and [encourage] the participation of the laity in the life of the Church.

Do you think the pope's impact on Africa has been lasting?
I believe so. We sometimes call him "our pope". We had the visit of Paul VI, in 1969, the first pope to come to Uganda and [the first to visit] Africa. And he stayed with us I think for three days and remained in Kampala. He didn't venture outside of Kampala. Pope John Paul II came to Uganda in 1993 and he stayed with us five days. He went to the north, he went to the east, he went to the south and he stayed in the centre. So we call him our pope. His messages are still with us. I remember him because he really [took the] time to see our people and our church. He visited the hospitals ... and as I say he went to every corner of the country. So he is still remembered very lovingly and his messages resound in the minds and the hearts of many.

Did he have specific messages for you?
Yes he did. You see the theme of his visit was "walk in the light". So we had hymns composed for that occasion, an occasion that made particular effort to include the young people. It was nice.

He also ran a number of liturgies that were held in Africa when he was visiting here and then in Rome for Africans too, that incorporated a lot of African cultural traditions …

Yes. He even coordinated the first African synod in Rome and now we have had a second one. But he more or less instituted [the] practice of having the whole of Africa in the synod, and following the same kind of system of evangelising Africa. And over a period of about 20 years he appointed about ten cardinals in Africa.

Can you explain what is described in some of the literature on the growth of Catholicism in Africa as, "the mysterious ripeness for conversion" that seemed to grip different areas of different peoples in Africa between the late 1890s and the 1920s, and the very large increase in the number of Catholics in Africa since Vatican II? Do you believe that Vatican II led to an increase in conversions to Catholicism?
Well, fortunately, we never know how God's power works. A few times I have visited Europe and the people there, and I have wanted to share with them the life of the church in Africa. I will use an example: Europe has seasons like winter, autumn, spring and summer. To use this as an analogy, I think the Church in Africa today is enjoying its spring time … I cannot generalise. I can only talk from our experiences in Uganda. Here, it is more about birth than about conversion. Uganda is almost 80 per cent Christian … at least 40 per cent Catholic, 40 per cent Anglican, and now we have these other groups and so on. So the country is highly Christian. It's not so much about conversion but birth.

What about at the turn of the century when a lot of people were converting from African religions to Christianity?
The conversion from traditional religions to Christianity was steady from the beginning. It was steady in some parts of Rwanda as well. I think Rwanda is 90 per cent Catholic. So there was a rapid growth in the number of Christians.

In the case of Uganda, the invitation came from here to Europe. As I said, Uganda has many different socio-cultural groupings of people here. In the centre we have had a king for centuries. When the British travellers came here in 1862, they went to visit the king, and he said to them, "Go back home and ask the queen to send the teachers to come and teach my people." So the invitation came from the king. That is how the first missionary state of union came to be here. It was by invitation, in 1877. And three years later the French government came. There was a kind of openness on the part of the king to some kind of enlightenment. And that came through religion a desire on the part of the people, especially when they are led by their king, who was called Moutessa.

Would you be prepared to describe who Jesus is for you?
Personally, can we describe Jesus? God is God, Jesus is God, Jesus is a man. He's not easy to describe. What we know is that he loved us and died for us and he rose and is still with us. He's our companion, He's our friend, He's our teacher, and He's everything to us. I find it difficult to give an adequate description ... Yes, He's everything for us believers. He's still our Lord but it's amazing that the same Lord can also be a brother and a companion ...

Were your parents born Catholic?
Not born, no they were not, but they became Catholic for their marriage. Their parents, our grandparents were not Catholic, although they were baptised before they died.

Did they have a Catholic wedding to start with or an African wedding?
Well, they had to follow the traditions of the people but they also had a Catholic marriage…

Well, I guess that's the Africanisation of Christianity in a nutshell isn't it?

Optimistic about the future

4 i. MOZAMBIQUE

Mozambique is in Southeast Africa. It is bordered by the Indian Ocean, Tanzania, Malawi, Zambia, Zimbabwe, Swaziland, and South Africa. It has a population of 24 million who are predominantly Bantu people. The only official language is Portuguese. The largest religion is Christianity with significant minorities following Islam and traditional religions. On average, people live about 52 years. A little over 50 per cent of the population over the age of 15 are literate, and today most children complete nine years of school. Women have at least five children (18 per cent of children under the age of five are underweight). In 2010, 1.4 million people over the age of 15 (11.5 per cent of the population) and 13,000 children were infected with HIV.[82] The country's GDP sits at 12.7 billion USD (2011), and population density is 30 people per square kilometre (2010).[83]

The area that is now Mozambique was originally occupied by migrating Bantu speaking peoples, Swahilis and then later Arab traders, before being colonised by the Portuguese, in 1505, who sought access to the area's gold. The slave trade, historically present prior to the Portuguese, continued under their rule, and human beings were bought and sold by African traders, Arabs, Portuguese and French traders well

---

82 See footnote 40.
83 (http://www.indexmundi.com) accessed 25 May 2013;(http://www.tradingeconomics.com), accessed 25 May, 2013.

into the 1800s if not the 20th century.[84] The Catholic Church has been active throughout that period, though evangelisation only really began in the 1940s – following the signing of the Missionary agreement between the Holy See and the Portuguese government.[85] From that time, the Church received extensive support from the colonial regime, and it became a major modernising and liberalising force during the colonial era. Once 'Africanisation' of the Church and of the Church's social networks began to take place following the Second Vatican Council, Church missions also became an important platform for Mozambican nationalism.[86]

---

84 "By 1790, 9000 people were being exported as slaves from the colony every year. After the British abolished the slave trade efforts by the Royal Navy to suppress it in western Africa stimulated the trade in eastern Africa and the numbers exported rose dramatically, with approximately 1 million slaves exported from Mozambique during the 1800s ...The Portuguese came under increasing pressure to abolish slavery, and in 1869 it was finally abolished in Portugal and India and in 1879 in the African territories; however it was not effectively suppressed until the early 20th century in the central and northern parts of the Portuguese colony of Mozambique." See; Electoral Institute for Sustainable Democracy in Africa, "Mozambique: The slave trade and early colonialism (1700-1926)", (http://www.eisa.org.za/WEP/mozoverview11.htm), accessed 15 May, 2013. See also; Crawfurd, J., (2002) "Mozambique Timeline" (http://crawfurd.dk/africa/mozambique_timeline.htm), accessed 15 May 2013. Macamo, E., (2002) "The Denial of Modernity – The Regulation of Native Labour in Colonial Mozambique and its Postcolonial Aftermath", CODESRIA 10th General Assembly, Kampala 8th-12th December, (http://www.codesria.org/Archives/ga10/Abstracts%20 GA%201-5/colonialism_Macamo.htm), accessed 15 May 2013. Seatizen, (2001), "Slave Trade" In *Ilha de Moçambique*, (http://webspace.webring.com/people/xb/b_veronik/slavetrade.html), accessed 15 May 2013

85 The Missionary Agreement had its roots in Vatican frustration with the 1930 Colonial Act that defined Portuguese Catholic missions overseas as 'instruments of civilisation and national influence'. Local Catholic Churches and the Vatican were not comfortable with the level of control this gave the Portuguese over missionary activities." See page 1 of Dinis S. Sengulane and Jamie Pedro Gonçalves, (1998) "A calling for peace: Christian leaders and the quest for reconciliation in Mozambique" (http://www.c-r.org/our-work/accord/mozambique/calling-for-peace.php), accessed 13 March 2012.

86 Ibid.

Once the Portuguese were recognised by the other European powers as owners of the area now recognised as Mozambique, and until independence in 1975, Mozambique was considered in Portugal to be part of Portugal's world empire. An active policy of racial integration, intermarriage, and cultural adaptation was pursued by the Portuguese who sought a multi-racial society and an expression of Portuguese culture in Africa. But there were clear limits to the country's ability to succeed. Barriers existed between the urban and rural sectors of society. There was limited communication between the two as most rural Mozambicans did not speak Portuguese, and those in the city had access to obvious economic, social, political, and educational advantages. With time, some Africans made a break from the restrictions of rural life and sought education and access to the advantages enjoyed by resident Portuguese. With the help of forward thinking Europeans, they established the independence movement.

In 1975 and after a long struggle for independence Mozambique became an independent nation state based on Marxist principles. Resident Portuguese were expelled overnight, and the country lost much of its educated population. The closeness of relations between the colonists and Portuguese Catholic clergy prior to independence ensured that Catholic clergy were persecuted under the new government; churches were closed, missionaries expelled, and many religious freedoms revoked; Church-owned schools, hospitals, and seminaries were nationalised in a bid for national development, and by the end of 1976, and even though seven of the nine Bishops were now indigenous, any sort of dialogue between the two had ground to a halt. As a bitter war began in Mozambique for the second time, Church criticism of war related atrocities and living conditions were essentially ignored by the government.

The death of the country's first president Samora Moisés Machel[87] in 1986, and his replacement by Joachim Chissano[88] paved the way for a role for the church in negotiations for peace. In late 1987, Chissano agreed to consider dialogue that might end the war and let Church leaders search for the rebels to talk peace. Cardinal Alexandre Dos Santos and Archbishop Jaime Gonçalves took the matter into their own hands. One headed to the USA and then the other to the bush. Finding the rebels they convinced them to meet but the negotiations were not easy. Entrenched mistrust between the opposing parties, alongside foreign interests, had made peaceful dialogue and potential compromise almost unfathomable for men who had spent their entire adult lives at war. Two years later, with assistance from the Vatican, the USA and the Community of Sant'Egidio (an international Catholic

---

87 Samora Moisés Machel was a Mozambican military commander, revolutionary socialist leader and eventual President of Mozambique. He was a member of the Mozambique Liberation Front (FRELIMO), and became the group's leader in 1970 after the 1969 assassination of Eduardo Mondlane. He claimed his radical political stance came from the experiences of parents who were forced to labour for the Portuguese. His charisma and personal style kept his government in power despite the droughts and floods of the early 1980s and the ongoing civil war with the Mozambique National Resistance (RENAMO). In 1986 Machel was returning to Mozambique from Zambia when his plane crashed in South Africa, killing him and most of the passengers on board. *Encyclopedia Britannica,* (http://www.britannica.com/EBchecked/topic/354560/Samora-Machel), accessed 21 May 2013.

88 Joaquim Alberto Chissano was the second President of Mozambique from 1986 to 2005. He is credited with transforming the war-torn country of Mozambique into one of the most successful African democracies. Chissano founded FRELIMO, and was elected president after the death of Machel. He instituted socio-economic reforms that resulted in the 1990 constitution, a multi-party system, and an open market. In 1994, he won the first multi-party elections in his country's history and was re-elected in 1999…since that time he has taken leading roles in a number of international peace keeping and humanitarian concerns. (http://www.icpdtaskforce.org/about/Joaquim-Alberto-Chissano.html), accessed 21 May 2013. See also, "Joaquim Chissano: Democrat among the despots", *The Independent,* 23 October 2007, (http://www.independent.co.uk/news/world/africa/joaquim-chissano-democrat-among-the-despots-397608.html), accessed 21 May 2013.

lay movement that played the role of mediator), they brokered a peace settlement that has lasted for more than 15 years.[89] At the same time, and lead by Chissano, the government enacted sweeping changes, including writing a constitution that provided for a multi-party political system, market-based economy, and free elections.

Between 1977 and 1992, one million Mozambicans died from fighting or starvation, a further five million were displaced, and the country was devastated. By 1993 more than 1.5 million Mozambican refugees who had sought asylum in neighboring Malawi, Zimbabwe, Swaziland, Zambia, Tanzania, and South Africa as a result of war and drought were being returned, as part of the largest repatriation witnessed in sub-Saharan Africa.[90] At the war's end Mozambique was declared the poorest nation in the world.[91]

Alexandre José Maria Cardinal Dos Santos, O.F.M., was born on 18 March 1924 in Zavala, diocese of Inhambane, Mozambique. He attended the minor seminary of the Franciscans in Amatongas, in the central zone of Mozambique, before being sent to Nyasaland (today Malawi), to study philosophy. In 1947, he was admitted to the novitiate of the Portuguese province of the Franciscans in Varatojo, near Lisbon. In 1948 he studied theology at Lisbon, before being ordained priest in 1953 and returning to Mozambique in 1954. He was councillor of the Franciscan province of Mozambique and rector of the new minor seminary of the country in Vila Pery, today Chimoio, in 1972. He was elected archbishop of Maputo in 1974, and was ordained bishop in

---

89 For a recorded version of these events go to the lecture delivered by Archbishop Gonçalves to the Harvard Divinity School, 6 February 2008 (http://www.hds.harvard.edu/cswr/resources/lectures/goncalves.html), accessed January 2013.

90 "Canada's Periodical on Refugees: special issue on Mozambican Refugees", volume 13, no. 6, October 1993. (http://pi.library.yorku.ca/ojs/index.php/refuge/article/view/21751/20421), accessed 15 May 2013.

91 "UNITED NATIONS OPERATIONS IN MOZAMBIQUE". (http://web.archive.org/web/20110516080313/http://popp.gmu.edu/resource-bk/mission/onumoz.html), accessed 15 May 2013.

1975, after which time he founded the "Franciscanas de Nossa Senhora de Mae de Africa", an African religious institute for Mozambican girls. He became dedicated to the victims of civil war and natural calamities and subsequently founded the Caritas of Mozambique and was its first president. He promoted programs to help the poor, refugees and victims of drought. He was also dedicated to promoting new relations among the ecclesial communities of countries which were Portuguese colonies: Angola, Cape Verde, Guinea Bissau, Sao Tomé and Principe. In 1988 he welcomed John Paul II in his pastoral visit to Mozambique, and he was created and proclaimed cardinal. In 2003, he was named Archbishop Emeritus of Maputo.

I met Cardinal Dos Santos early in the evening in Maputo after a dreadful forty-eight hour flight from Rome, in April 2011. I also spoke with Archbishop Gonçalves, at around ten o'clock the same evening, via a speaker phone in my hotel, before leaving the country the following morning.

The beautiful Cathedral of Our Lady of Immaculate Conception, Maputo, Mozambique

ii. Courage

... Therefore, since we are surrounded by such a great cloud of witnesses, let us throw off everything that hinders and the sin that so easily entangles, and let us run with perseverance the race marked out for us ... [92]

I had walked from the Grande Dame of Maputo (the Polana Serena Hotel) a majestic reminder of Mozambique's Portuguese past, and along President Chissano's street. We were heading for the cardinal's residence, an unremarkable townhouse set amongst equally unexceptional family homes. It was late afternoon and the sun was still pounding. The long journey and the blisters on my heels had already worn much of my energy away. I had spent 48 hours travelling from London, with little sleep. I knew that my children were unravelling at home. The usual preoccupations of adolescence were on a collision course with family harmony. With their mother in Rome, London and now East Africa, too much independence had cut them loose from the bonds of social expectations that keep young people walking a straight and narrow line. I was another four days away (it was almost too much to bear) and my concern for their welfare, alongside the complications of travel to date, would drive me to cut my trip to Maputo short. The following morning I hired a tuk-tuk to show me the city's sites before rushing me to Maputo's international airport so that I could fly away home in the night.

Maputo has been called the *pearl of the Indian Ocean*, but the extravagance of the past has given way to a measure of tiredness. The railway station, the municipal offices and the Holy Cathedral have all lost their shine (though not their majesty), and the landscape is still battle-scarred. I was shocked by shell-shattered buildings (their

---

92 Hebrews 12:1

facings torn away to reveal dangling and scattered innards) and the great slabs of broken concrete littering paths, though life appeared to be carrying on regardless of the rubble, and at a pace. Foreigners are throwing money at Mozambican redevelopment and the Mozambicans have reclaimed joy. Graffiti works on the pavements and walls that run beside the sea (all completed by hand and in intricate mosaics) speak of positive futures and self-empowerment. Guns have been turned into inspirational sculptures and artistic expression is thriving.

The man they call "the Cardinal" in Maputo is a profoundly gentle being. Perhaps it is age that has softened his edges. He was asleep when I arrived to meet him and woke up giggling about the fact that no-one knows his true age. Two shy sisters attended to the cardinal's needs. They met me and my translator at the door of his house and ushered us quietly up to the room where we waited for him to get up; he finally emerged, wearing tortoiseshell glasses, a soft cream cassock with pearl buttons and a delicate red trim. There was some confusion about my purpose and it took time to strike upon his passions. Translating each word slowed everything down. Each time I spoke, in English, my words had to be translated into Portuguese. Often the cardinal asked the translator to repeat what I had said. There were children outside, interrupting our conversation. I needed to close the window, turn the air-conditioning on. The microphone kept slipping, until I pinned it onto him, awkwardly. The idea of touching someone so senior and so important in this country just seemed to me to be wrong. I was a muddle of nerves and irritation – the result of an exhausting journey across the world and through a chaotic city – that I found difficult to suppress. I had needed time to centre myself, but had had none. The exhaustion and the worry about my children had made me almost manic.

The cardinal was undisturbed by my inner commotion and after the first hour, as the room cooled in the dying light, the two of us began to reach an understanding; a point at which his pace became cathartic for me and energising for him. The Portuguese and the pattern of his accent lulled me into his story-telling style, a gentle tuneful rhythm that I could feel if not decipher, and I was surprised to find myself at first relaxed again and then, sitting forward on my chair, sailing into the wind with the passion he revealed for triumphs past.

It would have been easy to miss the power behind this man. The weight of his achievements in a country torn apart by war was almost lost in his self-deprecation and his gentle lilt. I had dug deep to have him focus on the public highlights of his calling. The unity of the bishops he had mentored kept the Church alive post-independence and had supported his intention to bring a bloody war to rest. But in the beginning he spoke only of national history and wondered what he could do for me! He was the first African Franciscan in Mozambique, I told him, the first Mozambican priest, bishop, archbishop *and* the first African cardinal. He had been watching his country for almost 100 years. Together with Gonçalves he had engineered peace, saved the Church from dissolution, kept the faith alive. But he still did not quite spark until I asked about the parishes and the communities that lay at the heart of Christian life. Underlying the foundations of Christian society in Mozambique, communities within parishes keep people afloat.[93] The ideas behind those social networks grew out of his earliest priestly formation, a time when he was marooned in a sea of white faces that viewed him as a pariah, called him "the black". Communities were an idea that European missionaries quashed at first sight, but that he was able to revisit following Vatican II. Communities within parishes had given orphaned souls a family and united individuals across devastating pasts.

---

93 Isichei notes that since 1979, "… small Christian communities of perhaps forty families have become common in … Mozambique. Members are generally encouraged to study the Bible, and to apply it to their local situation, which presumes a certain level of literacy. She draws on Clements, "The Catholic Church in Kenya", pp. 6-8, 11-12. See Isichei, Op. Cit., p, 330.

From independence (1975) onwards, a series of appointments, his own as archbishop of Maputo included, saw a new and coherent unification between bishops and priests in the country. Led by himself and his colleague Gonçalves, the new bishops followed the lead of their two mentors with their country's benefit in mind. Despite the banishment of the Church from social infrastructure and public platforms, they worked tirelessly to communicate with people. They publically criticised the civil war (and the foreign interests that supported it) once it began to rage across the country, and they gathered public and eventually political support for peace. They used their seniority to throw punches in high places that would land on the conflict's protagonists, and ultimately they engineered the peace talks in Italy that brought the war to an end.

In 1987, Dos Santos, recorded an interview with the BBC. He told the journalist that the people wanted peace but that they could not find the rebels to talk. A neutral person called the radio station and offered to establish contact with a RENAMO[94] representative who lived in the United States. Already travelling to the USA on the invitation of the National Council of Churches, Dos Santos flew to New York, where he met Artur Lambo Vilanculo at an evening function.[95] Vilanculo put Gonçalves and Dos Santos in touch with a man named Bethuel Kiplagat in Nairobi, an active member of the Anglican Church and the Kenyan Permanent Secretary for Foreign Affairs who organised for the government to speak with RENAMO leaders about a meeting.

It wasn't until Gonçalves was in Maseru (the capital city of Lesotho), that he received a call from a Mozambican man living in Germany

---

94 Mozambique Resistance Movement.

95 In his interview Dos Santos only mentions going to New York to meet Vilanculos. As with his discussion of the motorbike incident, Gonçalves suggested in a subsequent conversation with Ezequiel Gwembe that, due to his age, the Cardinal may not have remembered the subsequent step, which also took him to Canada in search of Vilanculos.

(Artur Da Fonseca). Fonseca told Gonçalves that a meeting had been arranged with RENAMO's leader, Afonso Dhlakama. Gonçalves was told he was flying to Lumbubashi (Democratic Republic of the Congo), but arrived in Gorongosa (central Mozambique) instead. Travelling by night to avoid being seen Gonçalves landed on a runway in a secret location that was marked by hand-held flames before being driven by motorbike, through the dark, to meet Dhlakama in the bush. Gonçalves and Dhlakama talked for two hours before Gonçalves returned, by motorbike and then by plane, to Maseru so that his absence would not be noticed.[96]

Dos Santos and Gonçalves told Chissano that they had met with RENAMO and that negotiations were a possibility. But mutual mistrust continued to dog their plans. Alternate locations for talks were routinely proposed but always rejected by either party on the basis of bias. RENAMO, for example, proposed Kenya but the Kenyan government was allied with RENAMO. FRELIMO[97] proposed Malawi, but RENAMO knew that Mozambican secret police operated freely there. Both parties remained locked in a stand-off that at times seemed almost impossible to resolve.

Somewhere in all this, Dos Santos and Gonçalves thought of Rome. In September 1988, when all seemed to be lost, Pope John Paul II visited Mozambique and gave stern warnings in an official speech. He told the Mozambicans that the bishops were preaching

---

96 In his interview, the archbishop seemed to indicate that a different man rode into the bush to find RENAMO. Subsequent discussions with Ezequiel Gwembe (previous secretary to the Bishop's Conference of Mozambique and good friend and supporter of both Dos Santos and Gonçalves) suggested that the archbishop may have been hesitant to claim that role during the interview without any prior knowledge of who I was, and that it was, in fact, he who had made the trek on the motor bike to meet with Dklakama and RENAMO in Gorongoza. Also supported in Dinis S. Sengulane and Jamie Pedro Gonçalves (1998), "A calling for peace: Christian leaders and the quest for reconciliation in Mozambique", (http://www.c-r.org/our-work/accord/mozambique/calling-for-peace.php), accessed 13 March 2012.
97 Mozambique Liberation Front.

the way towards peace through "dialogue" and "reconciliation"; it was time for both parties to sit down and talk. Both Gonçalves and Dos Santos realised that the Italian government had an interest in Mozambique and as Catholic bishops they could influence the Vatican to facilitate the discourse. The Vatican could talk to President Bush, who could press the Mozambican government into entering into direct negotiations with RENAMO. The Vatican called Bush, and Bush called Chissano, and Chissano agreed to sit down with the rebels in Rome at last. Dos Santos and Gonçalves spoke to Guilio Andreotti[98] (then Italian minister for foreign affairs) who asked San Egidio[99] to provide the facilities. Since then *dialogue* and *reconciliation* have become national words ...

I pushed Dos Santos to explain the logistics of getting leaders of both FRELIMO and RENAMO together, of getting RENAMO out from hiding to talk, and he gave me a detailed run-down of the steps he could remember – from the time he received the phone call, to the point when dialogue finally began in Rome. But his story stopped there. He had fallen and broken his back, he told me, and Gonçalves had gone the last mile alone.

It was a mile that Archbishop Gonçalves filled in over the telephone later that evening, while I was wretchedly tired. I sat in a business centre at the end of a corridor of the hotel, doors closed securely behind me, a

---

98 More Roman Catholic than Italian, Guilio Andreotti served as prime minister of Italy (1972-73, 1976-79, 1989-92). He was said to have met his first pope, Pius XI, as a boy when he smuggled himself into a papal audience. He provided advice to all Pius's successors, at least until John Paul II. John XXIII informed him of the calling of the Second Vatican Council three days before the official announcement. "Guilio Andreotti", *The Economist,* (http://www.economist.com/news/obituary/21577350-giulio-andreotti-many-times-prime-minister-italy-died-may-6th-aged-94-giulio-andreotti), accessed 23 May 2013.
99 Founded in 1968 by Andrea Riccardi and his friends, the San Egidio community is an international group of lay people dedicated to prayer and social action. Their headquarters is found in Rome at the church of San Egidio.

man at the door, privacy guaranteed. Gonçalves filled the conversation with logic and a conviction that frightened me. The depth and volume of his voice beat out the pattern of the war's history over the speakerphone in a clear cadence. It revealed the depth of his intelligence, his compassion, the potential power of his post in a steady, controlled and educated Portuguese. I could see him on the back of a motorbike, either alone gripping the handles or sitting up behind a smaller man – the burden of his mission, no small thing, carried securely on broad shoulders that would front the "rebels", the "bandits", without judgement but with (always with) possibilities. *"These men had spent ... sixteen years making war. For them to stop functioning that way and to ... work very differently was extremely hard for them ..."* He explained the politics of their mistrust to me, the layers of interest that made achieving peace so complicated. Foreigners had done their best to dog efforts at peace. The war was just as much a playing field for on-going tensions between African nations, for the Cold War, and for apartheid as it unravelled across Mozambique's southern border, as it was a war for Mozambique. As he explained the aspects of the battle that rational humanity too often wages with the relentlessly irrational, his voice had a timbre I will never forget.

The evening had arrived by the time the conversation with Cardinal Dos Santos ended and people had come back to life in the cooler air. The cardinal insisted on walking us to the roadside, slowly, still in his cassock and with red socks sticking out beyond the front of his sandals. He apologised for being slow, "on account of my accident", he said, "though those South Africans ... make very good surgeons". The children who had earlier interrupted our time together, now recognised him and waved, while eating and chatting quietly with their parents in the park opposite, under electric lights. Couples were beginning to meander towards the beachfront, holding hands, canoodling. Red-necks revved their engines and flashed their lights to modern tunes without the cardinal even flinching. Perhaps it was the exhaustion but I found myself wanting to hold his hand. I was loath to leave him and perhaps even a little envious of the women who in the night called out to him from the distance and ran forward in their polyester dresses to wrap him up in bejewelled arms with joy. With the footpath bustling with women like these, the Grande Dame of Maputo was a poor alternative to the Cardinal's unremarkable house and his equally commonplace walkway. His was a streetscape that rippled with connections that made me long for home. Notwithstanding the gravity of the battles he had waged in life – the ones I had pushed him to explain to me, the ones that had made the big headlines – it was clear that this cardinal was as much a prince of the Church as he was a king right there on the street.

Cardinal Dos Santos of Maputo, a prouflundly gentle being.

iii. Alexandré José Marion Cardinal Dos Santos, Archbishop Emeritus Maputo, Mozambique

(April 2011)

... there was only a problem; some said that I was born in 1920, and some said that it was after 1920 ... But my mother said that in 1922 I was with my brothers, they were minding me with the sheep. But when I was baptised, the missionary used to guess more or less the age ... and he decided that I was born in 1920 ...

Well ... our history as a Church, here in Mozambique, is different from the other African countries because the Portuguese came to Africa to stay. They never called us a colony; they called us an overseas territory, an overseas province of Portugal. When Portugal achieved independence, Portugal itself was very near to Spain, to the sea, and they didn't know how to expand the land ... so, they decided to begin by exploring the world in search of new lands and when they found them, they connected them directly to Portugal. These countries, Mozambique, Angola and Guinea were called overseas provinces of Portugal. The other European countries, Great Britain, France, Germany, Italy, Spain, they had a different vision. Their territories in Africa were to become colonies.

So, there is a major difference between us and the other African countries ... it meant that winning independence was very hard. It meant that there were wars. Mozambique had to fight, Angola had to fight, Guinea had to fight to become independent, and we wanted independence like the other African countries. But, Portugal said to us, "You are not a colony, you are a province, and you belong to us." So we also had to fight to become independent.

The Portuguese system complicated our lives by defining us as a continuation of Portugal in the ultramar (overseas). The most important consequence was that the standard of education here was very low. Other countries had invested in universities and high schools for their citizens, but we had nothing. The centre of education for Portuguese was in Portugal, and those who sought education went to Portugal to be educated. Other countries could move forward easily after independence because their colonisers had established a system of education for the local people, but we had nothing. So we had to have independence in order to start getting universities, high-schools, and all that. This was not very easy for us, because we had no means. We had no means to build everything from nothing.

The situation was the same in the church. We had few local priests before independence because we had few seminarians, only nineteen ... the first cardinal of Mozambique was Portuguese. With time, the Holy See (the pope) insisted on seminaries so that we could ordain local priests and from that time we began to have seminarians. But in the meantime the Church was run by Portuguese priests. The first seminary was established by the Franciscans – the first, where I was (I am Franciscan also). I was ordained a priest in 1953 when I was 29 years old and I was ordained in Portugal.

After I had been ordained in Portugal, I returned to Mozambique and was nominated for a mission. After that, the Mozambican people started to fight for independence. Once [they] gained it ... things began to change. While we were able to achieve something through war, there were still difficulties ... We had very little financial or material infrastructure to be able to develop on our own. Only now are things starting to improve ... With the help of other countries, the Mozambicans are creating a better life for the people here. But it wasn't until independence that the Church started to become a really local Church as well, because from that time the priests were, by and large, Mozambicans. For a long time though, not many Mozambican priests became bishops. For a long time, the missionaries went on substituting those who left during the war with their own people, and with time they were nominated as new bishops, not Mozambicans. The dioceses however, were occupied by Mozambican clergy.

Can you tell me about the role of the catechists in the absence of native Mozambican priests?
The few missionaries who came here were initially Jesuits and then Franciscans. They entered existing missions and they trained catechists. And then, when the pope insisted that seminaries be created to shape the local clergy, the number of local priests began to grow.

What did your family think when you told them you wanted to become a priest?
It was something new! It was the greatest news! I was not ordained here in Mozambique but in Portugal, because that was where I ended my studies.

Was your family already Catholic?
When I was ordained priest, there were already many Catholics. When the missionaries came they baptised, baptised, baptised and gave catechism … When I went to the seminary, many brothers and sisters had already been baptised in the Church. Certainly we went to school to learn how to read and write, but really the missionaries taught the catechism in school. When I was ordained the first African priest in the country, my family and many other Mozambicans were very happy.

Did that give you a sense of great responsibility?
Sure, yes, because I was the only African priest for a few years, with only the missionaries to work with. The missionaries, like the bishops, had set up "workshops" [or training centres] across the country and especially across the three dioceses; Maputo, Beira and Nampula. The Church was already training priests. Religious continued to come here

as well. If I remember correctly, the first congregation that entered in Mozambique was that of St Joseph of Cluny.

So the Church grew in this way with the missionaries here. There was a bit of trouble here and there. In 1940, the Portuguese government had entered into a contract, an agreement with the Holy See and the Church in Mozambique, whereby teaching was to be done via the Church; school for Africans became available through the Church.

Can I ask about your studies overseas? You were the first to go to become a priest. Going to Lisbon to study must have been very unusual at the time you went?

In Portugal, there was no discrimination, I mean racial discrimination. As I said, we were also Portuguese and we were received as Portuguese citizens from overseas.

Did you learn things about life or about yourself in Portugal that you would not have learned if you had stayed in Mozambique?

Catholic doctrine ensures that it doesn't matter where you study. Catholic doctrine is the same everywhere. You can study in any "workshop" because the church has a plan; it creates its own education for priests. To become a priest you had to complete more or less the same tasks. There was a difference in terms of the regions where you might study, but the training of a priest is universal.

I understand that the training itself is standard across the seminaries. But did the difference in environment have a particular impact on you personally?

It was not easy, it was not very easy. First, because many Portuguese had never seen a "black" and they were amazed to see my blackness. They came to see my hair, for example; the hair after all was well cooked! At first when the young and the kids saw me they said "Look at the black", and they ran to see me. "Look at the black!" they would say. At that time I was at the convent, where they were all religious ... Being alone among whites took its toll on me, so I asked them to send me another Mozambican seminarian, who at the time was in Malawi. Mozambique had no higher seminaries. When the Franciscans first arrived at the Seminário Amatongas, they could stay only until the fifth year. After that they had to send their students out of the country because they couldn't be trained further here. So the other fellow came from Malawi and we in Lisbon together studying theology for a time, but it didn't last. He became ill and returned to Mozambique and I remained, alone.

Apart from the challenge of being the only Mozambican priest, what other challenges did you face when you came back from Portugal as the only African Franciscan? Did you, for example, have big plans for your diocese or for Mozambique when you returned as a priest? Did you have ideas or aspirations or things you want to be achieve?

When I was studying in Portugal, I was beginning to develop projects, even when I was there I saw that in fact the missionaries were evangelising in ways that I did not agree with. So when I returned, I tried to make changes but initially I was unable to have much influence.

How did you want things to change?

First, I could not follow a different path from the missionaries, because I was alone and I had to follow the same programs, the same system of evangelisation. Also the missionaries themselves were not all from the same order. There were several institutes here, [including] Franciscans and Jesuits. These institutes had their own methods, their own systems of evangelisation. Some of these said that we, as Mozambicans, were not in agreement with their directives. They called us "foreigners" and accused us of acting improperly. But in reality we just didn't agree with their decision to educate Africans by force.

Did the Second Vatican Council alter your ability to make changes?
Honestly, it was a revolution, a revolution in the Church. Vatican II made it possible for the missionaries to follow a common path with us and to work in a way that treated people differently. Vatican II opened doors, especially for the laity and that spurred more growth in the Church.

Did that give you a feeling of hope about what could happen here in Mozambique?
Of course, of course! We opened ourselves to a new vision of the Church, a new way of working; a new way of working together that had been unthinkable in the past. There was always conflict between the churches and congregations, which was sometimes difficult to understand. There are many different Christian churches here in Africa, but now there are not so many conflicts between them.

Did it change the way that you celebrate the mass here?
Vatican II was a blessing for us because it decreed many new things. My passion was always to unite the people – to make small communities into a basic union to work together. I worked hard in Maputo for the formation of Christian communities, called cores, cores of the wider Christian communities ... These Christian communities are very strong in Mozambique; everyone has to belong to a community. These communities exist within the parish and the parish has many communities.

I wasn't very happy with the fact that, previously, a person went to church and that was it. Now, people not only go to church but they also meet in small communities or groupings within the church and within those groups they have meetings and discussions. That makes me very happy.

And do they communicate their needs to you and do they have later events to work together, to communicate their community needs to you?

Small communities are "families" who meet on a weekly basis ... they meet and converse, learn and help each other a lot. When a person arrives in a new province, for example, and they have no one to support them, they will become part of a community and that community will make sure they are supported. That community will become their family and they will all help each other. That, to me, is very important because even here in town people tend to be individualistic. Each person thinks only of himself, but brought together under the banner of the parish and of the individual community within that parish, they are expected to think about others as well. If there are big problems, they can bring them to the priest to be dealt with, and further on to the bishop. Often these people have suffered for a long time before they reach us, but once they are here they will be helped. They will have a new family.

Even the president of the Bank of Mozambique is a part of this small world, of such a community. When programs need to be put in place, someone needs a child to be baptised, or someone wants money, they have to go to this community to discuss the matter. I was glad to see the president of the Bank of Mozambique, dancing with the others. He's very happy to be a part of this community. These changes in the Church were made possible in part as a result of Vatican II. The Vatican opened its doors and made it possible for Africa to have a creative approach.

What did independence in '75 mean for the Church?

For the Church, it was the moment for us to grow. Independence meant the growth of everything. We could grow only through self-definition. For the Church, independence meant autonomy and unification. The core of the Church became different; if I asked a person to come, he would already know who I was, the kind of person that I am and as a result would be willing to help. There was a new solidarity and union with independence. It was no longer a matter of just going to church on a Sunday.

Independence also allowed us to be more open to new ideas. We not only had schools, but were also able to create universities. Other countries, for example the English-speaking countries, always had higher education when we didn't. Independence gave us a chance to have higher education. Now we have the Catholic University here in Mozambique, just like in other countries where African languages are spoken.

Considering that you had such a limited national education experience prior to independence, from where did these new universities draw their curriculum?

The first thing I did was this: I ordered priests from Mozambique to go to Rome for university training. The head of the University of St. Thomas had to study in Canada. The religious orders had an easier time. Most of them were not from Portugal, they were from other countries; so it was easy to send their members from here to Europe for further education. Thus, for example, the Jesuits began to work with me, at my university. Although they also have their own responsibilities, they were very helpful in starting my university. For us it was liberating; we can now create ourselves, we can search out what we need because we know just what is needed and we have created it.

We had to have ... priests who had studied in Rome, [like] some of the earlier Portuguese priests who, having graduated with higher degrees, were sent to other countries as missionaries. We had a number here, some of whom had completed their PhDs in Germany, Belgium, France ... Missionaries often followed those who had come here before them, learned about the needs of our country then went back to train their own members to follow them in turn.

Can you tell me about the civil war?

It was a tragedy; what we experienced was a tragedy indeed ... The civil war destroyed much more than the liberation war of independence had destroyed. We suffered a lot during the war of independence, but the civil war made us suffer more. Nevertheless, it seems we have learned that we don't need weapons to build the country, we need a hoe (laughs).

How did you sustain your people during that time?

When the people were very hungry and suffering we kept them going with the help of international organisations, that offered charity, love, etc. I created Caritas Mozambique out of the need to help those who suffered greatly because of the war.

How did you ask them to forgive the atrocities they were experiencing?

The Episcopal Conference found a way to get the men who were fighting in the bush to get in touch with the government, and to sit down and resolve the problem of peace.

How did you do that?

We in the Church were talking against the war. We had made it clear that we wanted peace. We wrote pastoral letters continually (in fact there were about seventeen letters) and the government read those letters. As a result, Chissano, one of our former presidents, summoned all the bishops and said, "Look, you guys are always saying that we must end the war, you are always talking about peace, and union and asking us to talk with those who are fighting. So we are opening the doors for you to speak with the warriors from RENAMO." He gave us permission to find the RENAMO people and to bring them in for negotiations with the government and the bishops. The Bishops' Conference said, "Well, we do not know where to find RENAMO, so we will charge two bishops, who have the habit of walking out there, to find out where RENAMO is hiding and talk to them. Then they chose me, and Don Jaime [Gonçalves]."

At the same time, the BBC did an interview with and asked how our search was going. I said, "Look, I do not know where RENAMO are hiding, I do not know where to find RENAMO to talk about peace." The problem was that no-one knew where the resistance movement was hiding. And a Mozambican who was in the United States heard the interview and called me, saying, "Look, come here to the United States and we will show you where to find RENAMO."

At the time that the phone call came, I had been invited to go to New York with the Protestant Consuelo Cristão de Moçambique, or Christian Council of Mozambique. I used to go with them but this time I hadn't wanted to go, until I heard that someone in New York ... knew where RENAMO were ... So, there in New York, we were talking to the Americans ... about how they could help us achieve peace, when up came this business man who had a company in Nairobi, who said he knew where RENAMO were hiding ...

So I went to Nairobi with this man and the Christian Council of Mozambique, and the president of Nairobi said, "I can make RENAMO come to Nairobi." And he called them. Meanwhile, I went back to Mozambique to call Dom Jaime [Gonçalves] because he and the other bishop [Sengulane – Anglican Bishop from Maputo] had to come with me. So we Catholics, two Protestants, the president of the Christian Council and Sengulane found ourselves in Nairobi. Thus began the dialogue for peace with RENAMO ...

That was just the first step in the dialogue for peace, but we came back and continued to hope. When Pope John Paul II came here [in 1988], he talked a lot about peace ... That message travelled with me when I went again to Nairobi with Dom Jaime Gonçalves, Dom Dinis Sengulane and the president of the Christian Council to see if it was possible to meet with RENAMO again. That time we met with Dlakhama [president of RENAMO]. We said to them, "Look, you're not fighting the Church, you are fighting FRELIMO. I need you – FRELIMO and RENAMO – to come together to establish peace because the people have suffered for a long time!" That was what we talked about.

After that we told Chissano that we really wanted peace and he said, "Okay, let's talk to them." But then I became sick; I had surgery on my back and it was very bad. I never ... got to the talks; instead, Dom Jaime went. But the result was that FRELIMO didn't want the meeting in Nairobi with RENAMO, because representatives of RENAMO had been seen operating there in Nairobi. FRELIMO instead wanted to meet in Harare [Zimbabwe] because that is where Mugabe was. But RENAMO said, "We don't want the meeting in Harare because you are friends with the people there and they will encourage you and not us."

But remember that when the pope came here he had spoken very strongly in favour of dialogue. So at this impasse, I went to Rome where Andreotti was Ministro dos Negócios Estrangeiros and I asked him whether the Italians could bring these two together, whether they could receive RENAMO and FRELIMO for talks.

I communicated the request, Rome accepted, then RENAMO and FRELIMO also accepted Rome as the site for negotiations. But then, as I said, I had a fall. I broke my back in two places and had to go to Johannesburg Hospital for a very difficult operation. Those Jews of South Africa are really the best surgeons! But even in bed, I kept wondering and worrying about what was going on; I phoned Chissano to find out how things were going. The day that I left the hospital they signed the peace deal. But I signed as well, when many people came together to sign.

So that's how it was: peace came to Mozambique through the Church which had always called for an end to the war and a dialogue between the two warring factions. After that, a major part of the process was the return of RENAMO to the country and to politics, and the cementing of those relationships in law ...

iv. Archbishop Jamie Pedro Gonçalves, Beira, Mozambique

(April, 2011)

"... we had to convince them that they should abandon arms and trust in the dialogue process ... These men had spent ten years, no sixteen years, making war ... to stop functioning that way and work very differently was extremely hard for them ..."

How were you able to bring RENAMO and FRELIMO together to negotiate an end to the civil war?
The Episcopal Conference of Mozambique, at the centre of the church, decided to help the government of Mozambique (also known as FRELIMO) and the RENAMO leaders to sit down and to talk together. Both of those parties agreed to a reconciliation. The bishops contacted both the FRELIMO government and RENAMO leaders with the idea of peace. Once the idea was accepted by both parties, it was possible for representatives of both groups to sit down together and discuss how that peace would take shape.

His eminence Cardinal Dos Santos mentioned last night that prior to those negotiations beginning, there was a phone call from a man in the United States who said that he knew where the Cardinal could find RENAMO ... the discussions couldn't begin until RENAMO had demonstrated an interest in the idea of peace ... is that right?
Yes, to contact the RENAMO leaders we needed to find them somewhere. And, yes, the cardinal went to the United States, because we knew there were some people who represented RENAMO in New York. But the RENAMO leaders were not based in America; RENAMO was based in Mozambique ... so in America the cardinal was told that the best way to make contact with RENAMO leaders was

to go to Nairobi, in Kenya, and to contact the government of Nairobi. The government could help us find the leader of RENAMO, he was told. And so he went to America and then on to Kenya to find out if the government [there] would help us to find and meet the RENAMO leaders. But there was another bishop, Bishop Pereira, who had already decided to find where RENAMO were hiding in the bush (and really, they were there!). He met with them there in the bush and through him we passed on our idea for reconciliation between the people at war in Mozambique, in the form of a dialogue. That's what happened: a number of journeys were taken – one to America, one to the bush, one to Nairobi and one to Mozambique – all to find the RENAMO leaders. They were not living in the city [laughs], they were all living in the bush, in the forest, in the place where they prepared for war ... Later, on the day I agreed to take part in the dialogue, we had to go to Nairobi, to the city, to meet with them there. Afterwards, we continued our meeting with the RENAMO leaders in Nairobi.

And how did the dialogue move from Nairobi to Rome?
We went to Rome because, after we advised the government of Mozambique to meet directly with the RENAMO leaders, the problem was to find a neutral place or country where both parties felt equally represented. For example, RENAMO wanted Nairobi but FRELIMO didn't agree. FRELIMO wanted to go to Malawi, but the RENAMO leader disagreed. RENAMO wanted to go to Portugal and once again FRELIMO disagreed [laughs] ... We couldn't continue that way, so we advised them to go to Rome, and the two parties accepted that idea.

And why did you propose Rome as the meeting place?
In part, RENAMO accepted Rome because they wanted to be sure that the dialogue was not organised by the government of FRELIMO. The presence of the Vatican and the Italian government assured them that the dialogue would be sincere. The Italian government,

for example, had a lot of capital invested in Mozambique; it needed peace in Mozambique and [so] it had a vested interest in ensuring that the dialogue was sincere ... FRELIMO accepted Rome because Dos Santos had confidence in the Vatican. He knew [as a result of the Pope's visit in 1988] that the Vatican favoured dialogue.

Can you describe the negotiations?
We had the usual difficulties of dialogue between two powerful leaders. Getting RENAMO to agree to talk with FRELIMO and [vice versa] was the first difficulty. Convincing everyone that there were two parties ... that needed equal representation was difficult. Secondly, we had to convince them that they should abandon arms and trust in the dialogue process, which was also extremely challenging. These men had spent ten years, no, sixteen years, making war ... to stop functioning that way and work very differently was extremely hard for them. Thirdly, FRELIMO wanted to beat RENAMO [militarily]. They were not initially interested in dialogue and they wrestled with the challenge of allowing dialogue to supersede their arms. Fourth, the government did not want a multi-party political system while RENAMO did; getting them to agree to that was another enormous hurdle. Fifth, there was the on-going problem of establishing mutual trust. Was what each one said precisely what they were intending, or was it another thing? The government did not trust RENAMO and RENAMO also did not trust the government. Finally, each of them also had their own [internal] difficulties to contend with along the way, right up until we reached the point of writing the agreement.

Were you ever afraid that the conversations would not result in the peace you were hoping for?
Yes, we were always afraid that the conversations might not come to an end! Each party wanted to believe that it was right, RENAMO wanted to be right regarding the war it promoted and the government wanted

to be right in having rejected and fought against RENAMO. We didn't know at which point the ... government [would] accept RENAMO as a dialogue partner. And also we did not know if RENAMO would be able to renounce their arms. They could have returned to their arms at any stage, right up until the end of the dialogue.

So how did they manage to get past that impasse?
It is important to understand that we took more than a year to talk ... that is why it is very difficult to list exactly what caused the final outcome. Meetings were taking too long, there were further meetings outside of the mainstream dialogue ... there were meetings with chiefs and so on, so it was a big job convincing both parties that they were being equally represented and each one must accept what we were proposing. The main [challenge], from beginning to end, was to convince both parties to accept the purpose of the dialogue. That was the reconciliation.

Did you ever feel that if you left the room the whole thing would fall apart?
No. After having contacted the parties, talked with the leadership of RENAMO and talked with President Chissano, we started to convince each other that it was possible to achieve the reconciliation despite the difficulties ... After we had made contact, because both parties agreed to talk, only the modalities of the dialogue were difficult, the place where we were to meet, when to meet, what time the conversation would take place. The dialogue itself was also not clear. But there was a perception that we had come to the end because both parties had indicated that they wanted to achieve reconciliation.

Can you describe the role played by San Egidio?
San Egidio offered to help the dialogue between the government and RENAMO. They offered help in terms of personnel – people to

mediate, to observe the dialogue, to translate and write up decisions, the place where the dialogue should take place was provided by San Egidio, and they provided ... mediators: one for the Church, one for the government, and one for each FRELIMO and RENAMO.

Obviously, the Church was trusted by all of the parties involved.
Yes. Before going to search for RENAMO, the Episcopal Conference of Mozambique had talked with the government. We had a conversation commission with the government and a search commission with RENAMO. The search commission with RENAMO was built up by the Archbishop of Maputo [Dos Santos], who first went to America and then ended up in Nairobi. And there was the other "talking commission" with the government, which resulted in the government trusting the church.

How was it possible for the bishops to be so united in those first years of independence?
The union of the bishops was favoured by the fact that many bishops had no experience of the life of a bishop. They were young; seven young and two "ancient", with experience. The new ones were anxious to learn how to be bishops ... They were open to all forms offered to them to exercise their responsibilities as bishops. The more experienced were a great support to the new ones. That was why it was easy for the bishops to be united. Out of a group of nine, seven were young, and it was easy to convince them of the ideals that we shared for our new country.

Can you describe how that unity was important?
Yes, yes, that unity laid the foundations of the Episcopal Conference in Mozambique from 1975. For example, as a group, the bishops decided to write letters explaining doctrines; they were unanimous in the production of those doctrines. Further, the faithful followed the

letters we wrote at that time, and those about the great thesis of the revolution and then afterwards, about the problems inherent in the peace. All these were analysed by the united conference of the bishops and [they] helped the Episcopal Conference to gain trust for much of what it did. And it did a lot!

Were there points about which unity amongst the bishops was necessary but not necessarily achieved?
Well, there were some difficulties associated with the united approach that we took. You know that where there are nine heads that think, [those] nine heads will think in different ways, and each diocese was dealing with its own issues on a daily basis, many of which required individual approaches ... That contributed to the diversity of opinions but, in the end, we always managed to guide ourselves using one single idea and ... we programmed all of our actions.

But in the end ... while you say that in the end you always achieved unity, does that mean everyone, or were some pressured into taking the same course of action as everyone else?
We lined up ... from the beginning of [national] independence ... In fact, we were all happy with independence. We were very happy with the government that was formed. But before the creation of the government and the start of the revolution, there were some differences of opinion, sure. There were [some] in favour of the revolution, [some] less supportive of the revolution, and there were those more interested in justice and in the law that would be written for the new government of the country. But as each issue arose (for example; our relationship with the government, our attitude to the revolution, our place in society after the war, our approach to RENAMO), we were identifying ideas among ourselves that would solve problems, before writing about them in the pastoral letters to the people and the country. We wrote as a unit and we signed.

Did the unity of the bishops in those early years provide the foundations for the future Church in this country?

In the early years, we had assemblies; we had to settle the pastorate of the communities. That was done, we had to do it. Before the social problems, those issues were the subjects of pastoral letters ... and the assemblies were granted as a way for us to define the future path of the Church in the new society. We had our first assembly in '77. The conclusions of that assembly guided the pastorate of the dioceses – the communities and ministries – until the second assembly, which was established so that we could evaluate what had been achieved and what was needed. At that second assembly, it was seen that we needed to consolidate and so the assembly was dedicated to the consolidation of the Church in Mozambique. The final result was the unity effort. It arose from the fact that bishops had agreed to accept the guidance provided by the assembly. [So the Church as it is today is the fruit of that original unity, of the commitment of the bishops to work as a team].

5 i. Guinea

Guinea is a country in West Africa. It shares its northern border with Guinea-Bissau, Senegal, and Mali, and its southern border with Sierra Leone, Liberia, and Côte d'Ivoire. The sources of the Niger River, Gambia River, and Senegal River are all found in the Guinea Highlands. It has a population of 11,176,026. The national language is French. Unlike the other countries cited in this book Guinea is majority Muslim. Muslims make up 85 per cent of the population, with Christian eight per cent, and indigenous beliefs seven per cent. On average people in Guinea live 59 years. Women have five children, (20.8 per cent of children under the age of five are underweight) Only 41 per cent of people over the age of 15 can read and write. On average children spend nine years at school, though boys remain considerably longer than girls (ten years versus seven). The economy is largely dependent on agriculture and mineral production. It is the world's second largest producer of bauxite (used to make aluminum), and has rich deposits of diamonds and gold.[100] There are ongoing and significant human rights issues in Guinea, the most pressing of which are the use of torture by security forces, and the abuse of women and children through female genital mutilation.[101] GDP sits at 5.8 billion USD

---

100 Peter Walker, "Mineral-rich but impoverished west African nation is under military rule after death of long-serving president Lansana" ,"Q&A: Guinea". *The Guardian* (London), 24 December 2008.
101 Bureau of Democracy, Human Rights and Labor (2012). "Country Reports on Human Rights Practices for 2011: Guinea". United States Department of State (http://www.state.gov/j/drl/rls/irf/2012/af/208156.htm), accessed 5 June 2013.

(2011) and population density at 40 people per square kilometre (2010).[102]

The land that is now Guinea belonged to a series of African empires (largely Islamic) until France colonised it in the 1890s and made it part of French West Africa by defeating the warlord and then ruler of the Wassoulou Empire (Samory Touré) an Islamic State linked to the Malinke Empire and established in 1878.[103] France and Britain negotiated over the present boundaries of Guinea and Sierra Leone in the late 19th century, and with the Portuguese over their Guinea colony (now Guinea-Bissau) and Liberia.[104] With the collapse of the French Fourth Republic in 1958, and the establishment of the Fifth, France's colonies were given the choice between more autonomy in a new French community or independence. Guinea chose the latter.

In 1958 and with Guinea newly independent, De Gaulle withdrew all administrative support, and French nationals left, taking chunks of the economy with them. The new country aligned itself philosophically at first with the Soviet Union and then China, while still accepting financial aid from the West. Within a couple of years a new and polarising leader, Ahmed Sékou Touré (great grandson of Samory Touré and Guinean president until 1984) established one-party dictatorship, a closed, socialised economy (the state took over farms and other forms of production) and an aversion to human rights, free expression, or political opposition which was ruthlessly suppressed.[105] The imposition of price controls started an era of pervasive black

---

102 (https://www.cia.gov/library/publications/the-world-factbook/geos/gv.html), accessed 25 May, 2013. (http://www.indexmundi.com), accessed 25 May, 2013; (http://www.tradingeconomics.com), accessed 25 May, 2013.
103 "History of Guinea". (Historyofnations.net), accessed 29 May, 2013.
104 Ibid.
105 Peter Walker, Op. Cit.

markets and smuggling even though it was punishable by death.[106] Touré relied on his own Malinke ethnic group to fill positions in the party and government, and his party officials took the monopoly on social and economic life. A police and intelligence apparatus spied on everyone.[107] More than one million people fled the repression into neighboring countries.[108] It has been estimated that almost 5,000 people were executed or died from torture or starvation at the Camp Boiro, a Soviet-style concentration camp.[109] From independence until the presidential election of 2010, Guinea continued to be governed by a number of autocratic rulers, which has contributed to making Guinea one of the poorest countries in the world.[110]

Robert Cardinal Sarah was born on 15 June 1945 in French Guinea. He studied in the seminary of Bingerville in Ivory Coast, and in Dixinn in Senegal before being awarded a baccalaureate in 1964 at the seminary of Jean XIII outside of Conakry. Studying in France and then Guinea, he finished his theological formation in Senegal before travelling to the Pontifical Urban University in Rome, where he obtained a licentiate in theology, and then to the Studium Biblicum Franciscanum of Jerusalem where he obtained a licentiate in Sacred Scripture. Appointed metropolitan archbishop of Conakry in 1979, he was ordained bishop in the same year, before serving as the ordinary

---

106 Robert H. Jackson, Carl G. Rosberg (1982). *Personal rule in Black Africa: Prince, Autocrat, Prophet, Tyrant*, University of California Press, Berkeley/Los Angeles London, p. 211; Ayittey, Op. Cit., p. 106;
107 Ibid., p. 213-217.
108 "History of Guinea" (Historyofnations.net), accessed 6 June 2013
109 (http://www.historyofnations.net/africa/guinea.html), accessed 5 June, 2013; *GUINEA Dying for Change Brutality and Repression by Guinean Security Forces in Response to a Nationwide Strike*, Human Rights Watch, April 2007; U.S.Congress, *Prospects for Peace in Guinea: hearing*, DIANE Publishing, ISBN 1422323315, cited in "Guinea: Free Reign to Security Forces Fuels Violence" (http://www.hrw.org/news/2007/04/19/guinea-free-rein-security-forces-fuels-violence), accessed 5 June 2013.
110 (http://www.economist.com/node/4198911), accessed 5 June 2013.

of the archdiocese of Conakry until 2001. In the same year he was appointed secretary of the Congregation for the Evangelisation of Peoples (*Cor Unum*). In 2010 he was created and proclaimed Cardinal-Deacon of San Giovanni Bosco in via Tuscolana. And in the same year he was made a member of the Congregation for the Evangelisation of Peoples, the Pontifical Council for the Laity and the Pontifical Council for Justice and Peace. Archbishop Sarah was appointed as the president of the Pontifical Council *Cor Unum* in 2009. He was charged with organising Catholic relief around the world. I spoke with Cardinal Sarah by telephone while I was in Rome in April 2011.

Nzulezu school house

ii. Faith

... If your faith were only the size of a mustard seed, it would be large enough to uproot that mulberry tree over there and send it hurtling into the sea! ...[111]

I did not ever meet Cardinal Sarah face to face though he intrigued me nevertheless. His is the only country among those represented here which has a minority population of Christians. And only three per cent of the population are Catholic. Sarah studied to be a priest in the midst of the period of the movement for independence and has practised since then despite the regime that would supress his work. He is an outspoken critic of authoritarian regimes, and is progressive on issues like social justice and economic equality.

In his reflections Cardinal Sarah was very clear about the difficulties he has faced as a priest working under an authoritarian and hostile regime. He saw many of his fellow priests and missionaries killed or suffering. He has had to represent the interests of his people to a government that did not listen and he has faced persecution himself. He worked hard physically and spiritually for 22 years, travelling long distances to offer spiritual support to Guinea's Catholics with a heavily diminished body of priests to share the load. "I had to go on different trips to reach out and meet with the different parishes, catechists and the few priests that I had, in order to encourage them to work with what they had." Many comment that it is extraordinary that the Church has remained alive in Guinea. Recently work was finished on the country's first seminary.

Sarah hints at the need to move forward without fear. He has had to be brave, continuing to proclaim the gospel and fight for a common

---

111 Luke 17:6

view of humanity in Guinea, especially as others have died around him and there has been little, if any, support. Many of his student retreats relied on donations of food and medicines from locals to function, and on the support of adults who were willing to be involved. Despite all he has remained positive in a mostly Muslim country stating that there is scope for sharing between Muslims and Christians. He draws strength from some aspects of Muslim religious practices in his own work as a priest and especially as one who has struggled so fundamentally with the world and the politics surrounding him. He is the only cardinal discussed in this book who contributed to the debate about Muslim and Christian differences that is so prevalent in the West and he does so in charitable terms..

At heart Cardinal Sarah is a conservative. He is troubled by the financial and materialistic cultures that he sees permeating, indeed dominating, Western cultures. Living in Europe has brought those issues into sharp focus for him and they rankle. He writes about the lack of reverence in religious spaces, about modern technology and the fact that it challenges the respect that the Church deserves, and about the personal agendas that drive an individual to take part in the Catholic charity work he sees as president of *Cor Unum*. The culture of individualism in Western society, he seems to suggest, has undermined the selflessness of charity work that relies on volunteers. "It is important to remember that this charity has its origin in God and not [in] personal initiative or generosity."

iii. Robert Cardinal Sarah, Guinea, President of the Pontifical Council *Cor Unum*
(April 2011)

"... I also have learned so much from the Muslims ... The positive influence between Christians and Muslims in Guinea can be mutual; we can help them with our faith and they can help us with the positive aspects that we see from their religious practice ..."

Which of the projects with which you have been involved over the years has excited you the most, both in Guinea and now as president of Cor Unum? Can you describe and expand on that or those projects? What was involved both logistically for you and for the people assisting you? Why was it so important to you?

First, let us take a look at Guinea in the context of the 26 years from 1958, the date of independence until 1984. Guinea [was ruled by] a communist regime with an anti-Catholic tendency. It expressed its anti-Catholic agenda by taking away Church properties and banning ... social action such as running schools and hospitals. Any type of social activity was prohibited. In addition, they expelled missionaries and imprisoned, for nine years, His Excellency, Archbishop Raymond Marie Tchidimbo.[112] As you can see, in this context of a lack of social interaction, the Church insisted on the importance of catechism and focused on forming good Christians through the catechism, Bible, Sacraments and the different human aspects. So, for 22 years, I organised every year a two-week session dedicated to the Biblical and

---

112 Tchidimbo was a Guinean priest and bishop from Conkary through the 1950s, 60s and 70s. He was imprisoned in Camp Boiro in Guinea in 1970 and remained there for eight years and eight months. Tchimbo, Raymond-Marie (1987). *Noviciat d'un évêque: huit ans et huit mois de captivité sous Sékou Touré*, Fayard.

human education of young people. Around 500 to 600 young people participated in these sessions each year. I wanted to help [them] acquire a good human formation, and to deeply and profoundly know the Christian values that would nourish and enlighten their lives and activities. In these sessions, we touched upon problems dealing with marriage, work, money and friendship, all aspects of their lives that could be a problem for [them]. In the formation of the Bible, we went through the Old Testament [but] we couldn't finish the New Testament because I was called to work in Rome. For me, this was a very important task, not only for the present but also for the future of Guinea so that the young people are prepared to live well their Christian faith. A group of young adults assisted me in this work and even the surrounding parishes made contributions of food and medicine since I did not have help from the outside. In addition, important to me were the pastoral visits that I made as bishop to the different parishes of my diocese. Since the communist regime wanted to destroy the family, for six years my pastoral letters were focused on the family. In these letters, I explained what the will of God is for the family and how to live together as a family. This is important because the Church begins within the family. This was my principal concern: to rebuild the Christian families destroyed by the communist regime.

In Rome, I had an enriching experience working as the secretary of *Propaganda Fidei*. I was able to see how the Church works throughout the world – in Africa, Asia, Oceania, a good part of Latin America and northern Canada. I have seen how the Church has grown. If we look only in the West, it seems as though the Church is dying. But, this is not true. The Church continues to expand. For example, in the 1900s Africa had only about two million Catholics, but now it has 174 million Catholics. That shows an incredible growth; even with vocations. Blessed John Paul II said that the Church is now living in a "springtime", a beautiful moment even though there may be difficulties. This "springtime" is also noticeable in the number of saints who bore witness to the Gospel. I have also seen so many missionaries who were killed and who have suffered in the mission. What has also enriched my experience is the contact that I had with the bishops from Asia, Africa and Oceania. I have learned so much speaking with these bishops ... Their efforts to evangelise their people despite the difficulties, since the Church is not always well accepted everywhere, are admirable. Although there is a lack of priests and means, and despite difficult political situations and poverty, the faith is growing in the mission territories.

As the president of *Cor Unum*, my work is different. Nevertheless, I would say that proclaiming the Gospel through charity is a continuation of my prior work. It's about helping others to live the Gospel through charity. It is important to remember that this charity has its origin in God and not from personal initiative or generosity. God is the source of this charity. God is love and from this love we are made capable of loving others and helping them.

Can you tell me about the differences between your life as a pastor in Guinea and your life now at the Vatican? What kind of challenges did you face in Guinea, for example, and what kind of challenges do you face now? Did you have more agency in decision-making processes when you were in Guinea? And did the Vatican help you with the major challenges you dealt with in Guinea?

My life in Guinea was the life of a bishop responsible for a diocese. It was the life of a pastor who lived with his flock. I had to go on different trips to reach out and meet with the different parishes, catechists and the few priests that I had, in order to encourage them to work with what they had. It was more of a pastoral work; a work of encouraging, protecting and teaching those people whom God has placed under my care. On these pastoral trips, there were opportunities for me to share my faith and knowledge with them, to teach them the Gospel and to encourage them not only to have an intellectual knowledge but also to have a personal experience with Jesus Christ. The deep and humble faith of my people that I experienced during these pastoral visits also encouraged and deepened my own faith.

There was also an involvement with the government. As bishop, I had to point out to [government agents] the miseries of the people, and I tried to change their politics so that they would give more freedom and well-being to the people. It was not easy because the government would not always listen to what I had to say and would not accept any different opinion ... I mostly prayed and fasted for myself and my people. Prayer and penance have been very powerful for the conversion of humanity and they are a great sustenance and help in my ministry. Of course, my work here in Rome is quite different. But, here I am also a bishop and I try to live a life of bearing witness to the Gospel as a bishop. Also, it is not so different because it involves evangelisation through charity. Here, I see the universality of the Church and the collaboration between different departments to spread the missionary word. This collaboration is a great help in our work because we cannot face the problems in our society alone. The problems here are different. We live in a Western culture that is secularised and materialistic. It is necessary to proclaim the Gospel without fear, remembering that man cannot just live by materialism but [must live] by the word of God. Here too, I try to pray. Prayer is essential for every priest and bishop. It is my first task. Without prayer our work is useless, for Jesus said: "Without me you can do nothing."

So, the mission is the same with different characteristics. The challenge is to help man not to separate himself from God, to help him see that his well-being is not found only in money and technology but really in God. This is truly a challenge that exists everywhere.

I believe that Guinea is slightly different from the other African nations in the group I am studying in that its Christian population is a minority. Can you tell me how that ratio has shaped your work?

What are the major issues that you have had to deal with in that environment, or that a leading figure of the Catholic Church has to deal with on an on-going basis?

We have to take into account the context that [in Guinea] the Church is in a country where the majority is Muslim. As Christians, we have to bear witness to our faith, stressing especially that God is Father, that He loves each one of us and is close to us and lives with us through the presence of Jesus in the Eucharist. God is not far away but lives with us. The Muslims also believe in God, but they believe in a God who is distant and cannot be reached. Yet, I also have learned so much from the Muslims. One of the things that I learned from them is their fidelity to prayer time. They give a great importance to prayer. This encouraged me not to abandon prayer, which is so important for our life.

As a parish priest, I learned of a Muslim legend which helps to illustrate this point. There was a man named Abdalwanid Ibn Said, who wanted to know who would be his neighbour in Heaven. If we have a bad neighbour on Earth, it is difficult to live with him; [but] we have the neighbour for a maximum of fifty years. What happens if we have him for all eternity? It is better to know who will be our neighbour. He received the answer that his neighbour in Heaven would be Maimuna. The man asked: "Who is Maimuna?" Maimuna was a girl who lived in Kufa. Abdalwanid Ibn Said went to Kufa to find out who was Maimuna. They told him in the village that Maimuna was a crazy girl who was taking care of sheep near the cemetery. Abdalwanid went to the cemetery where Maimuna was with the sheep. He found her in prayer. He noticed with wonder that her sheep live in harmony with wolves. But the wolves didn't eat the sheep and the sheep were not afraid of the wolves. When Maimuna finished praying, Abdalwanid asked her how was it possible that her sheep live in harmony with the wolves. Maimuna answered that because she had improved her relationship with God, God had blessed her and had also given harmony to the sheep and wolves. If we have a prayerful life, God will help us to live in harmony among ourselves even though we may be wolves in our dealings with others. This legend highlights the importance of prayer for a Muslim. This is what I have learned from them. I have also learned about reverence in prayer. Many times we come into Church without respect. There are so many things such as cameras and phones that can be a distraction for us at Mass. We never see this in a Muslim mosque.

The positive influence between Christians and Muslims in Guinea can be mutual; we can help them with our faith and they can help us with the positive aspects that we see from their religious practice.

Finally, can you tell me about the degree to which Catholicism offers women from Guinea opportunities that may not be available to them either in their traditional religious origins or within other religions practiced in your country? What have you done in your position to forward the inclusion of women in decision making processes, both inside and outside the country?

We need to remember that are two types of African societies: the patriarchal society and the matriarchal society. I lived in a matriarchal society where the role of the woman is important. She is the one who decides everything. Also, in African tradition, it is not true that the woman is marginalised or less appreciated, but she has the first place. In African philosophy, there is this saying: Man is nothing without the woman; woman is nothing without the man and the two are nothing without this third element, which is the child. Therefore, this complementary collaboration is a philosophical and social position of so many Africans. The Gospel helps us to understand that God has created man and woman in His image and likeness, with equality in dignity. Because they are physically and psychologically different, they depend on one another. That is why the Church promotes the dignity of women. There are so many catechists and nuns from Africa.

Also, when there is a meeting among men, before the meeting, the men will consult their wives. For this reason, I think that African society's view of women can be a great help for the Church because it is faithful to the Gospel concerning the role of women. I know that in some societies, a woman suffers more because she has to work, give birth and educate her kids. She has the primary responsibility for raising and educating her children. She has a greater weight in the family. But, she does it joyfully because like the Blessed Virgin, the woman is a servant of God and others. Servants should not be understood as a slave but as a ministry, a humble and joyful service of love to the family.

There are many refugee camps on the border between Ghana and Ivory Coast.

CAFDIL, Cardinal Turkson's Foundation for Distance Learning, Ghana (see page 186)

6 i. GHANA

Ghana is an English-speaking nation in West Africa that was formed by a merger between the British colony of the Gold Coast and Togoland trust territory. It is bordered by Togo in the east, Burkina Fasso in the north, Ivory Coast in the west, and the Atlantic Ocean. It has a population of 24 million people, which includes 52 ethnic groups, and is considered "one of the most religious nations in the world", being 69 per cent Christian, 16 per cent Muslim, with the rest practising traditional religions or none at all. On average an Ivorian will live until the age of 62 years. Seventy per cent of the population over the age of 15 can read and write, with children spending on average ten years at school. Most women have approximately four children. (Fourteen per cent of children will be underweight before the age of five). In 2009, 260,000 people over the age of 15 years (1.8 per cent of the population) and 27,000 children were living with HIV.[113] GDP sits at 39.2 billion USD, and population density at 107 people per square kilometre. Ghana is today described as one of the top ten fastest growing economies in the world, and the fastest growing economy in Africa. Gold, timber, cocoa, bauxite, manganese and a number of other exports are major sources of foreign exchange.[114] An oil field containing three billion barrels of light oil was discovered in 2007 and began production in 2010.[115]

---

113 See footnote 40.
114 (https://cia.gov/cia/publications/factbook/geos/gh.html), accessed 15 May 2013
115 "Kosmos Makes Second Oil Discovery Offshore Ghana", *Kosmos Energy*, Monday, 25 February 2008, (http://www.rigzone.com/news/article.asp?a_id=57319), accessed 15 May 2013.

In pre-colonial times the area was inhabited predominantly by a number of Akan kingdoms. From the 15th to the 19th century the Akan people were among the most powerful groups in western Africa. Akan trade flourished due to gold, which along with slaves was later traded with the Portuguese, and then Dutch, English, Danes and Swedes from the 15th century.[116] In 1874, some parts of the area were made a British protectorate after the Dutch ceded their forts, free, to the British in 1872 and after a number of wars between the local Africans (particularly the Asante) and the British over governance.

In 1957 Ghana became the first Sub-Saharan African nation to achieve independence, spearheading the political liberation of colonised Africa. Its first and best known president, Kwame Nkrumah, had been educated in his politics while studying at Lincoln University

---

116 "History of the Ashanti People", *Modern Ghana* (http://www.modernghana.com), accessed 15 May 2013. The Akan people played a considerable role in supplying Europeans with slaves for the trans-Atlantic slave trade. Prior to that role as supplier they bought slaves from Europeans and from further north via the trans-Atlantic route in order to clear the dense forests north of Akanland. Europeans were supplied with slaves by groups from the Benin Empire and states in central Africa (which waged wars on neighbouring states in order to catch people for later sale to the Portuguese) whom they sold to the Akan in exchange for gold. About a third of the population of many Akan states was enslaved people. See Henry Louis Gates Jr, "Ending the Slavery Blame Game", *The New York Times*, 22 April 2010 (http://www.nytimes.com/2010/04/23/opinion/23gates.html?_r=2&pagewanted=1&hp&), accessed 15 May 2013. Gates also notes: "Europeans in Africa kept close to their military and trading posts on the coast. Exploration of the interior, home to the bulk of Africans sold into bondage at the height of the slave trade, came only during the colonial conquests, which is why Henry Morton Stanley's pursuit of Dr David Livingstone in 1871 made for such compelling press: he was going where no (white) man had gone before ... The sad truth is that without complex business partnerships between African elites and European traders and commercial agents, the slave trade to the New World would have been impossible, at least on the scale it occurred." Heyward and Thornton (Op. Cit.) point out that there existed an extensive slave trade from at least 1520, and certainly at least some trading before that as well. By the 1590s slave traders obtained more slaves on the market than from wars. p. 78.

in the United States.[117] There he was influenced both by Marcus Garvey,[118] who became famous for his "Back to Africa" movement, and by W.E.B. Du Bois, an African-American scholar at the time who sought full civil rights, increased political representation, and access to higher education opportunities for African Americans.[119] In addition to an independent Ghana, Nkrumah championed the cause of African unity upon his return to Africa, which led to the formation of the Organisation of African Unity (OAU), now the African Union (AU). The country has not seen the same kind of ethnic conflict that has prompted civil wars in other African countries and since independence has trod a chequered, but evolutionary, path towards political stability. It endured a series of coups before Jerry Rawlings took power in 1981 and banned political parties, after which time he approved a new constitution, restored multiparty politics (1992) and won the 1992 and 1996 presidential elections. As President, Rawlings was succeeded by John Kufuor (2000, 2004), John Atta Mills (2008), and then John Dramani Mahama (2012) via peaceful and democratic

---

117 See "Martin Luther King on Our March to Freedom". *Lokoleyacongo*, 6 May 2012, where Nkrumah is compared with Martin Luther King: "'We are no longer a British colony. We are a free sovereign people,' all over that vast throng of people we could see tears ... And we could hear little children six years old and old people eighty and ninety years old walking the streets of Accra crying, 'Freedom! Freedom!'"
118 Marcus Garvey was a Jamaican political leader and proponent of the black consciousness movement, who advanced a pan-African philosophy that became known as a "Garveyism".
119 William Edward Burghardt "W.E.B." Du Bois (23 February 1868-27 August 1963) was American sociologist, historian, civil rights activist, pan-Africanist, author and editor. He was the first African American to earn a PhD from Harvard. One of the founding members of the Niagra movement that pushed for full civil rights for all Americans, his teachings were an important influence on the civil rights movement of the '50s and '60s. (http://www.math.buffalo.edu/~sww/0history/hwny-dubois.html), accessed 22 May 2013.

process[120]. The country's current and relatively successful policies of freedom, justice, equity, and free education for all are seen to derive from Nkrumah's earlier pan-Africanism and his experiences in the United States.[121]

Peter Cardinal Turkson was born in Wassa Nsuta in western Ghana. He studied at St. Teresa's Seminary in the village of Amisano and Pedu before attending St. Anthony-on-Hudson Seminary in Rensselaer, New York, where he graduated as a Master of Theology. Ordained priest in 1975, he was a professor at St Teresa's Minor Seminary between 1975 and 1992, completed a licentiate in Sacred Scripture at the Pontifical Biblical Institute in Rome, and did doctoral studies in Sacred Scripture at the Pontifical Biblical Institute. Turkson was appointed Archbishop of Cape Coast by Pope John Paul II in 1992, served as president of the Ghana Catholic Bishops' Conference from 1997-2005, as chancellor of the Catholic University College of Ghana in 2003, and was appointed Cardinal-Priest of S. Liborio by Pope John Paul II in 2003 before becoming one of the cardinal electors in the papal conclave of 2005. In 2009 he was appointed president of the Pontifical Council for Justice and Peace, made a member of the Congregation for the Evangelisation of Peoples, the Congregation for Divine Worship and the Discipline of the Sacraments, the Pontifical Council for Promoting Christian Unity, the Pontifical Commission for the Cultural Heritage of the Church, and the Pontifical Committee for International Eucharistic Congresses. In 2012 he was appointed a member of the Congregation for Catholic Education.

I met Cardinal Turkson in Rome, at the offices of the Pontifical Council for Justice and Peace in April 2012 before travelling to his home diocese in Cape Coast a few months later with my son.

---

120 (https://www.cia.gov/library/publications/the-world-factbook/geos/gh.html), accessed 15 May 2013. See also: "Rawlings: The Legacy", 1 December, 2000, *BBC News*, (http://news.bbc.co.uk/2/hi/africa/1050310.stm), accessed 20 May 2013.

121 "Ghana", (http://en.wikipedia.org/wiki/Ghana), accessed 22 May 2013.

ii. Temperance

... These children speak a language that burbles and rains from their mouths like water through a pipe. And from day one I have coveted it bitterly. I wanted to get up from my hammock and shout something that would flush them out like a flock of ducks ... I tried to invent or imagine such a stout, happy phrase. I wanted them to play with me. I suppose everyone wanted the same; to play, to bargain reasonably ... to stretch a hand across the dead space that pillowed around us ...[122]

A shortish African man came into the room in a hurry, dressed in a smart, grey Italian suit with a priest's collar. He did not introduce himself when I offered my hand and told him who I was, but spoke very quickly instead:

"Will this thing take longer than, say, thirty minutes or something?" He was a little skittish, distracted.

"I'm sorry", I said to him, "are you the cardinal?"

"No," He replied. "I'm his younger brother."

"I realise that I sent a lot of questions through to the cardinal, but it needn't take as long as predicted in my emails." I had begun to panic. I had already been gone from home four days and had spent much of them just filling in time. The children were missing me. My husband was over-stretched. What if, after all of this, the cardinal had changed his mind?

"Ok, then we can start," he said. Panic created confusion, which then became impatience. I did not want this low-brow answering on the big man's behalf.

"Well is the cardinal actually coming?", I demanded. Initially he looked embarrassed but then he laughed. It was a "Candid Camera" laugh, a "Gotcha!" moment.

---

122 Kingsolver, Op. Cit., p. 120.

"Actually," he said, in between giggles, "I *am* the cardinal."

With hindsight I would remember that Cardinal Turkson's hair was completely grey and chastise myself for not knowing him better. But really it was the cut of his jib that had deceived me. Turkson's face was youthful, his eyes vibrant and quick, and he carried himself like my fourteen-year-old son might when he had something else he would rather be doing: he wriggled a bit, did not make eye contact and mumbled while looking for the door.

There were other layers that had added to his "trick". Turkson had arrived out of context. He was dressed like an administrator and, like an administrator, had kept me waiting for some time, in a room decked in satin (green and cream stripe), wood panelling and Italian marble that stretched for miles up and down stairwells and across vast, highly polished floors. Perched uncomfortably on the fine furniture, I was dwarfed by the height of the ceilings and an oversized portrait of Pope John Paul II, indeed by the size of the reception room itself where every step I took – spending the anxious moments considering the view or reading the few plaques over and over – seemed to echo my presence to anyone passing beyond the door. The offices of the Pontifical Council for Justice and Peace were themselves intimidating. The enormous courtyard outside was flanked on all sides by four-storey buildings (all rendered in terracotta and covered in balconies) and I had climbed two stories of marble stairs to enter through high French doors. Inside the room where I waited for him, two small, glass-fronted cabinets displayed small and unremarkable tribal carvings – possible tokens of the cardinal's African roots.

But his joke had blown those formal red herrings away. His honesty and openness were liberating, refreshing the otherwise stale formality of the space and more in keeping with the style of an employee who can joke about his boss, than the partner of the firm who upholds its stated mission.[123] Indeed, there was a mismatch between the seriousness of his post and the colour of his character that was hard for me to define until I later travelled across his country. At first glance, he seemed positively youthful, even verging on frivolous. The idealism he expressed in our discussion was both inspirational and endearing. He was what I (and others too) had longed for in the Vatican men I had met. Thumbing his nose at mainstream Vatican pretensions and formalities that had until then made the Church inaccessible to me, he appeared to have embraced modern paradigms in the very way that he chose to function. His personality alone seemed to give the Church a contemporary relevance and practical applicability to the new millennium, and it was no wonder that he had been a popular choice as "next pope" amongst the public.

We talked about his commitment to the plight of underprivileged teenagers and about the links he described as fundamental between education and democratic governance. Perhaps these links were made in the early 1970s, when he was a seminarian at St Anthony on the Hudson, a Franciscan college outside New York. The experience certainly broadened his sense of possibilities; he later established education retreats for students from rural areas in order to fill holes in their formal education and give them respite from abuse;[124] and he maintained wider aspirations for the education of rural West Africa at large via satellite. Once created cardinal, Turkson seized the

---

123 Robert Mickens, senior correspondent and journalist with *The Tablet,* shares my view of Turkson. He describes Turkson as possibly having a "refreshing lack of ecclesiastical ambition ... comfortable in his own skin ... no pretensions, no airs, no sense that he feels his ecclesial rank makes him more special or entitled than others". "He will be a great breath of fresh air in the musty corridors of the loggias of the Vatican," said one long-time Curia official." See Robert Mickens, "The Rising Star of Justice and Peace" (http://jaazsw.org), accessed 24 July, 2012.

124 Teenage pregnancies, and abuse in the home are just some examples of abusive situations he was referring to in relation to Ghanaian minors. See for example: "75,000 teenage girls in Ghana get pregnant every year", *New Strait Times,* 15 May 2013.

opportunity to establish national distance education programs that took early and fundamental learning to children previously beyond the reach of local schools as well. He established recording studios through an organisation he launched, CAFDIL (the Cardinal's Foundation for Distance Learning) and relied on volunteer teachers to record and broadcast classes, many of which drew ideas from the American television program *Sesame Street*.

We talked about women and the Church, about equality of access to spiritual leadership within the fetish religions from which he was descended, and the centrality of women to tribal life. The arrival of Catholic dogma (which forbade women from entering the priesthood) could not eliminate the deep and powerful role of women from tribal life, he noted, nor their access to leadership positions that are recognised by the Church, including in its official catechism. We discussed the differences in the roles he has played as "minister" in Ghana and now "administrator" in Rome. One came with a measure of autonomy that the other sacrificed to international accountability. There are disappointments inherent in that loss, he suggested, something he manages with frequent trips home. Finally, we discussed the future appointment of an African pope, a possibility considering the popularity of people like former secretary of the United Nations, Kofi Annan and Barack Obama, he said. As with the affable Cardinal Napier, the meeting extended well beyond the 30 minutes he had originally allowed, and he lamented the pressures on his time, hinting that he would have been prepared to talk longer if it had been possible.

Later that year, in Ghana with my son Billy, context supported my attraction to Cardinal Turkson. The minimalist, uncomplicated and severely formal spaces of the Vatican offices had shed little light on his colourful origins. Driving from Accra to the Ivorian border, I was warmed by the colours of the boats that lined the seashore, colours that decorated the flags on the masts of fishing vessels moored in their thousands in the lagoons off Cape Coast – flags that flapped wildly in the warm, moist air of the western Atlantic and drew my eyes and my ears to the sound of the busy market and the people that those fish fed on the shore. Colours flowed from women's shoulders, from the cloth that held babies to their backs, from reliefs on the walls of churches and cathedrals, and from the tiled floors upon which they gathered to pray. Colours were painted vibrant and dancing onto coffins carved as fish, or crabs, or books, or birds, or anything that gave away the lifelong passions of the many corpses who now gave cause for grief and family gatherings each and every Saturday. Colour provided the backdrop, the life, the contrast for the stark and ghostly structure that was once Elmina castle (one of the most important stops on the Atlantic slave trade route), for the walls that marked the slums and the villages outside of the city Accra, and for the endless sea of rubbish that loomed as great mountains or flowed as rivers out to sea.

In that context, the Turkson of Rome, that man of colour, certainly represented something both absent from the Vatican's sombre palette and something with which I wanted to align my own sense of self in opposition to Vatican rigidity. The lean-to teaching spaces we passed in the dirt, the children playing soccer on clay grounds, the mud-brick schoolhouses surrounded by mangrove forest, and the tiny, one-room classrooms that floated on sticks above the great lake beyond Axim, site of Nzulezu, the village on stilts, all exuded a sense of optimism and possibility that were in keeping with my experience of Turkson as idealist in Rome. Outside Cape Coast I visited CAFDIL and was struck by the sophistication of the equipment, and the dedication of his team. On our last day we saw children put on uniforms, teenage girls climb into canoes and young adults board buses; all were heading to school along streets lined with posters encouraging electoral participation, responsible citizenship and interfaith collaboration.

From the top of the hill and at St Joseph's Cathedral, where Turkson ministered as archbishop of Cape Coast, he could have looked out and across the salt pans, the dazzling Cape coastline, the town and the crowded streets of people. Standing there in the warm air I indulged in a moment of illumination and imagined everyone leaping into an endless and colour-filled river of possibility. *Perhaps Turkson has thought practically about the way he can influence the old currents to merge with the new,* I thought to myself. *Perhaps Turkson himself represents a return to the river's source?*[125]

Turkson was undoubtedly a visionary, having realised his passion for education (amongst a great many other things) through his seniority within the Church, despite the chaos that seemed to fill Ghanaian weekends with mess and the smell of fish. Furthermore, he appeared at ease in a modern, Western world. Stories were circulating of him charismatically entertaining journalists at dinner parties, and about his bold publication of a document on world finance (from which the Vatican quickly sought distance) that proposed the creation of a global bank after the global economic crisis began in 2008. He was considered funny and entertaining, a well-intended trouble maker, and for me he was a breath of fresh air at the end of a stifling hour's wait within Vatican walls.

But subsequent events a year later left that image confused. Using YouTube video footage about the growth of the Muslim population across Europe to press a point about the anti-life stance of the West, Turkson underestimated Western sensitivity to the Muslim/Christian divide both within the Curia and beyond it, and caused outrage amongst the bishops who were attending the 2012 Bishops Synod in Rome on the new evangelisation. While he claimed that rather than being anti-Muslim he was making a comment about the nihilism in Western society, he was criticised for fear-mongering by using false statistics

---

[125] Turkson brought to mind Ezekiel's vision of the sacred river that flowed from the throne of God: "on the banks of both sides of the river, there will grow all kinds of trees for food. Their lives will not wither nor their fruit fail, but they will bear fresh fruit every month, because the water for them flows from the sanctuary. Their fruit will be for food, and the leaves for healing." Ezekiel 47:12

about a Muslim takeover in Europe.¹²⁶ Later, and just as the Australian Royal Commission into Institutional Responses to Child Sexual Abuse Cases rose into view, Turkson would lay the blame for clerical sex abuse at the feet of gay priests, claiming that African culture was inimical to homosexuality, which protected African society from clerical sexual abuse tendencies.¹²⁷ In both instances Turkson was presented in the press as at best naive, at worst dangerously unqualified to manage the complexities of a highly mediatised Church; I felt a growing distance from him. Highly regarded journalists I spent time with in Rome felt that he had clearly failed to understand the paradigms and sensitivities to which the modern, Western world aspires. And I felt bitterly disappointed as his idealism, rebelliousness, and optimism sank out of view.

Did that make him a charlatan, a swindler, a fake? Had he negated his right, not only to validate the Church for me, but to provide a bridge for his people between his world and mine? I believed in the commitment "my" cardinals had made to the Gospels and to its ethical framework. Indeed I had begun to believe in the same ethical framework myself. But did his blunder have to polarise all of us, to leave us stranded, on the basis of an unexpected, cultural particularity? I was used to social and political commentary in the West that uses a binary equation (good or bad). Entire characters, particularly leaders, are tainted with their individual failings, and public depictions tempt us to call our readers to arms ("You're either with us or against us!") in an empowered declaration of war on everything that we want to believe we are not. As the Western press ran amok with his blunders, I

---

126 Tom Kington, "Vatican tries to create distance from row over Muslim demographics video" *The Guardian*, 16 October 2012, (http://www.guardian.co.uk/world/2012/oct/16/vatican-distance-muslim-demographics-video).
127 Simon Caldwell, "Cardinal tipped to become first black pope in modern times blames gay priests for abuse scandals facing Catholic church", *Mail Online*, 19 February 2013, (http://www.dailymail.co.uk/news/article-2281411/Cardinal-Peter-Turkson-blames-gay-priests-abuse-scandals-facing-Catholic-church.html).

was also tempted to stand on my side of the chasm and point arrogantly to the gulf between us, but I could not. The man's experiences in the United States, his respect for women, his passion for education, even the vibrancy of his country and the evident joy in his people were genuine reflections, and all had struck a very real chord with me if only because they were unexpected. The boldness for which he was admired had also drawn me in. When I began this project you will remember that I wrote: *I wanted to believe that beneath the somewhat harsh and public face of the Roman Curia that he wore, there was a human being with a kindly soul that ached and loved and cringed and laughed, just as I did. I wanted to believe in the power of forgiveness and above all in the power of love* ... and I could not give that up. Turkson *had* to be a bridge for his people between two worlds, if only to satisfy my original thesis that these senior men were driven by the good intent imbibed in the Gospels to take on impossible nation-building tasks. But a bridge linking people across cultural chasms has to run both ways, and ultimately people on both sides have to be willing to cross. Working out if either one of us was choosing not to would be a challenge for the last few interviews.[128]

---

128 Does Turkson's insensitivity or naivety suggest a measure of Afro-centricity in the Ghanaian church or even in other West African nations as well (see subsequent chapter on Ivory Coast)? The Church is usually labelled Euro or Italo-centric. Interestingly, in his 16 years as Archbishop of Cape Coast Turkson never sent a single seminarian to Rome to study. "The Church needs to develop its own philosophy and anthropology", he told Robert Mickens. But at what cost to global unity and to Ghanaian Church connectedness with the rest of the world? See interview recorded with Robert Mickens, "The rising star of justice and peace." Op. Cit.

iii. Peter Kodwo Appiah Cardinal Turkson, Cape Coast, Ghana, President of the Pontifical Council for Justice and Peace

(April 2011)

"... All I am saying is that our world is so very colour sensitive; colour sensitive in the sense that his face is one colour, before he is someone. We don't just look at the endowments or values of a person. If we chose not to go beyond that, we would never really get to experience that endowment ..."

I would like to start with your studies in the States ... I am interested in how an experience of the United States may have impacted on your personal or professional development as a priest. Can you tell me when you went to the States?

To the States! [Laughs.] So you know that I went to the States? We did have a seminary, a bigger seminary, in Ghana for theological and philosophical studies. We had a system of doing a minor seminary and then continuing on to a bigger seminary. I had done my minor seminary, which is basically high school or secondary school studies. And then after my first year at the bigger seminary, the archbishop of Cape Coast [John Kodwo Amissah] decided to send me and another guy to a Franciscan seminary just outside of Albany, New York, called St Anthony on the Hudson. Why he sent us there, I don't know now and I didn't know then. He was a bishop and he was in charge of my formation at the seminary and so he had a right to make that kind of a decision. So I went to New York for four years, from 1971 to 1975.

In the summer of 1974, the two of us were made deacons with the Franciscans, and then in '75 we decided to come home to be ordained priests in Ghana. We decided to complete a little bit of a pilgrimage to prepare ourselves for ordination and so in June '75 we came through Rome [on our way back] to Ghana, and on the 20 July 1975 we were ordained priests in Ghana. That's what took us to the States and brought us back again.

As for the impact that it may have had or did have on my life, it can be seen in so very many different ways: First, I hadn't had a chance to study with the Franciscans before. Until then I had theology with limited interest in Franciscan theology. So for the first time I had to deal with big figures like St Bonaventure and Duns Scotus.

Second, and most importantly, would have been that we were the only two Africans. Everybody else was a Franciscan except for the two of us who were diocesan seminarians.

And third, it also meant that we had a chance to be exposed to Franciscan spirituality. They lived that spirituality. For example, they read the rule of St Francis every Friday evening after Vespers, you know? And at a certain point they allowed us, although we were not Franciscans, to also read the rule. That exposed us, if you want, to a basic spirituality of the Franciscans and that certainly did have an impact on us as well.

Subsequently, after we came back to Ghana, we could talk about exposure to American life, exposure to Franciscan spirituality, exposure to the American university and seminary system, and we could talk also about exposure to the American Church. All of these were and in various ways can be described as influences or impacts that were made on us.

So we came back with a certain appreciation of all of that. Although the African Church in Ghana was not at the same level of growth as the US American Church, some church features were common between them. It was helpful to have been there and to have been exposed to certain pastoral problems in the United States, which were just beginning to bubble up in Ghana.

Did exposure to the US broaden your outlook in terms of possibilities for yourself or for the Church?
Possibilities, yes. Basically they followed an academic program that allowed seminarians to follow two types of programs. The seminarians could, at the moment of ordination, present a Masters in the divinity program or ... in the theology program. The Masters in Divinity required the writing of a thesis of some sort and at the end of it the seminarian was granted the degree by the State University at Albany. Those going for the Masters of Theology needed to do something which could also be approved by the head of the theology department at the State University of New York. I decided to go for both ... which meant that at the time of ordination, I had both a Masters of Divinity and a Masters of Theology.

But that did not immediately prepare me for what I ultimately ended up doing, which was scripture.[129] That was a different story. You know, that is a story that goes way back. It was in the minor seminary or secondary school that I thought I was cut out for science. I thought science was going to be my thing. But gradually, as [I] progressed along the path of seminary formation, it became clear that the gap between science and theology kept becoming bigger, and so it meant that I just had to forget about doing science. When we had finished with our theological studies in New York, and were on the point of coming home for ordination, the bishop came and asked what we wanted to do after ordination; what further areas of study, or areas of specialisations, we wanted to go into. I was thinking that there was an opportunity to go back to my old interest, that's science, and basically I thought I would do physics or something similar. The bishop said

---

129 Differences exist between the study of scripture and of theology. The first refers to the critical and historical examination of the books of the Bible, while the latter refers to the study of Christian faith itself. What is meant by God being Father, Son and Holy Spirit? for example, or What does baptism mean? Theology draws on the Scriptures for support, but also on official church teaching, and the writings of great authorities like St Augustine and others.

that he didn't think he that could answer right away. He went to confer with our professors and they must have advised him to encourage me to go into the ecclesiastical areas of study instead. So when he came and made that known, I said, "If that's the case, then I want to do scripture and I want to do it in Rome."

I thought that I was creating an impossible situation for the bishop and that the bishop would think, "Oh Rome is too far away! You better go and do science." But to my surprise he said, "Fine. Come for ordination and after ordination you can go to Rome." And so that is how I ended up studying scripture.

Studying scripture didn't constitute any really big problem for me, because I didn't have any problem working with languages. Even in the United States, while we were in the seminary, I had started working on Greek, Hebrew and German. So once the bishop agreed that I could go to Rome, I went back to Ghana for ordination, taught there for a year in the minor seminary, then came here to Rome.

Having a background or some rudimentary knowledge of Hebrew, Greek and German meant that I could skip a semester or two. Normally beginners could complete their studies in four years, but I did mine in three and that's what got me going in scripture. With hindsight, I think it was a far better preparation for my ministry than applied physics or whatever I could have done had I stayed to study in Ghana. Scriptures has come in handy. It was a very useful preparation for the teaching and preaching I did in the past, and also for doing what I have to do now – that is for my work on the Council, for taking care of justice and peace. The big contribution of the Church to the discussion of justice and peace used to be all theological. But scripture contributes to any discussion of the issues of peace, justice, economy and politics. So I think that my background in scripture has been very useful. That is the part of my travels that has led to me being where I am now.

You did not ever take out your PhD in scripture, did you?
I was here [in Rome] twice. I came first to do the license. That was '76 to '79-'80. Then I went back to Ghana, taught in our first seminary and helped out in Ivory Coast because at that time they needed professors of the Bible. I came back to Rome in '87 to work on a doctorate. When it came time to defend my thesis, my nomination to be a bishop occurred. Okay, and so my moderator said (and I think I should have heeded his advice), "You are at the end. Just tag on a bibliography."

But in my naivety I thought I could easily go for the ordination as a bishop and then come back here and finish it in an excellent way. But I must tell you, it has not been easy to do that … because after ordination, work began! So the defence has not been done yet, and my doing it subsequently is complicated by the fact that it's not usual to do a defence as a bishop.

Is it not usual or is it not allowed?
I have not come across it. Perhaps there exist bishops who have been ordained and allowed to defend their thesis, but I don't know. I think what I still want to do is going to work out, but then it will be up to the Biblical Institute to decide what to do with the work. It has been a while and I think I just need to create a little real discipline to force myself to do it because it will not come easy. If I were to show you, for example, our calendar for May and June this year! It's horrendous. If I begin after what I have to do here, I will need more than a little bit of discipline just to force myself to take time out to get started! But it's all in the computer here. The other problem is that every year that passes you need to revise your bibliography. The book doesn't stay the same way right? It doesn't stop and wait for you. So I know that is one big area that I need to do work on. But the substance and the argument of the thesis is alright and I've not seen any other work here on my topic.

People ask about the argument and talk about it and the next thing they say is: "When is it available to read?" And I say, "as soon as it comes out." So it is something that I hope to do this year.

Tell me, when did you become a bishop?
In Rome, I was named a bishop October '92, and then I was ordained in Ghana in March 1993. It took from October to March because I was buying time to finish this thesis. I think it was at that time that Cardinal Jozef Tomko asked, "Is the guy already in Ghana? What a waste it is! He needs to be in his diocese for Christmas and all of the Holy Week coming up!"

I was ordained on the Saturday before Palm Sunday. That's how close it was you know, 27 March 1993 in Ghana, and ten years after this in 2003 I was made a cardinal with the last group of John Paul II. It was a large group. There were some big figures among us: Cardinal Okogie was one of us. Cardinal Renato Martino my predecessor here was also part of the group, and Cardinal Justin Rigali, Cardinal Marc Ouellet, Cardinal Ennio Antonelli ... There was a pretty big group.

Do you think it was significant that the Pope appointed African cardinals or was it just that those particular cardinals had reached a certain point in their careers that they were appointed ...
I don't think of an answer to that question. I can say that my ordination was probably motivated [by] external views of Ghana. I occupied the primatial see of the Church in Ghana. Evangelisation in the Catholic Church in Ghana began from the archdiocese of Cape Coast. It came with the Portuguese, in 1482, but they weren't missionaries. The Portuguese arrived as merchants in 1503 but brought chaplains along with them. The chaplains went outside of the castle to do a bit of work: to build churches and baptise people. But missionary work in Ghana, by missionaries who belonged to the Society of African Missions, began in 1880, and so that's where our current Church began.

It all began in the diocese I was in charge of. So I would relate my nomination to an external recognition of the growth of the Church in Ghana. If there were any other considerations, I wouldn't be in a position to know. At one point, the Nuncio called and said a Vatican office was interested in the history of the Catholic Church in Ghana and so I prepared a dossier of how it began, you know, the synopsis of how it started. That was what gave me the impression that something was happening at the time. But exactly what that call was going to lead to? I did not know. I had no way of telling.

Some see the Catholic Church as highly patriarchal, but others have claimed that the Catholic Church offers options to women who lack such options within their traditional tribal religions. What do you think about that?

The tribal religions?

Yes. They described the original tribal religion as being very limiting for women in terms of the degree to which they could actively be involved in their immediate society.

It's all different you know. They get tribal culture mixed up with the core Church in Africa. [We should] recognise that we are dealing with great diversity. You come across so very many different ways of being. If you're talking about traditional religions, for example, in Ghana, there are the fetish priest or priestess. There was no distinction made with regard to gender about who could be serving a fetish. It could be a man and it could be a woman. Right from day one, growing up, we knew that shrines could be taken care of by either of them and sometimes both of them together. So the thing that we were told or taught was that it was up to the deity of the shrine to indicate or to pick whomever it wanted to play that role. In the southern part of Ghana and in the group I belong to, the exercise of a religious function or role in traditional religion was not limited to men. Both men and women could be fetish priestesses or priests.

Both of them could also play the role of "seers" – speaking on behalf of the fetish or coming out with messages. And to that extent they could also play the role of prophets and prophetesses as well. So the traditional religion in that sense doesn't make a distinction between the potential role of men or women in central positions.

The tribal system itself in my part of Ghana was also matrilineal. Parts of Ghana have a patrilineal system. By that, I mean in relation to succession and inheritance. My part of Ghana limited succession and inheritance to the mother's line. And in fact, if it helps at all, you can get some sense of this by understanding the local proverbs. There is a proverb in my part of Ghana that says that a father fries a roast but doesn't eat it; he may roast the corn but he doesn't get to benefit from it. In other words, the father may produce children but the children don't belong to his clan. The children belong to the clan of the mother. If there is a succession to the throne involved, they look for the successor to the chief; and the successor will not be his own child, it will be the child of his sister. So in that sense the role of the woman in the social system was very, very prominent. If you came to a single, individual household, the exercise of power in that house [is] in the hands of the man: the husband, the father, [is] the breadwinner and in charge of everything in the house. So it is a system [with] checks and balances in both ways … the man can play a role but the women at a certain point know that they can determine certain things. You know a man can be anything, but it takes a woman to decide whether he will become a ruler or not.

So do you accept limits for women within Catholicism?

No. You see I will not jump readily from any traditional system to Catholicism or for that matter to any Christian system. They are two completely different systems, although there could be a sense of inequality here and there. But the system I used as an example to describe my part of Ghana is a personal impression, about who and how the culture evolved and developed. If you come to Christianity or the Catholic Church, you also deal with terms which are based on yet another system of thinking. So if you're asking me about the role of women in the Catholic Church as what, as Christians? They are Christians. But what do you mean by limitations?

Are women limited in the degree to which they can take part in decision making?

If it's having a say, then to begin with they have their say as related to the laity having a say in the Church. That's what it all begins with. Then in that sense it's like everybody else in the Church. The Church has laity, clergy and lay teams. So if it is having a say, then the women are treated as members of the laity and they will get to have their say in that regard. That is where determining the role of women in different places and in different cultures is determined as much by different cultures as it is by the Church. In Ghana, our parochial councils and the bodies that assist the priest in their administration of the Church don't make any distinction between men and women. In fact, when I was in charge of the Church in certain places I could only deal with women catechists; so the leadership of a village could be a woman. Until the priest did his rounds and visited a place, it was a woman who led the group community and watched over it, and would preach to them and do everything.

And would the priest take advice from her if she is the leader?

If she was the leader, she was the leader of a local community and therefore we recognised her. Whenever we organised formation programs for the catechists they would come along with a man. OK, so we knew the women who were catechists in certain communities because they showed up for formation programs and they were all treated alike. If I was doing my rounds or pastoral visits and I came to a village or community where their catechist was a woman, well then, that was who I dealt with.

So in that sense, there is really no distinction. Interestingly, if we say that a catechist is a woman and a catechist leads the church, together with a small, organised parish advisory board, men and women might both be present on those advisory boards but the catechists will remain as a liturgical leader. So there will be a scripture leader of the group (who would be a woman) and an advisory board. The advisory board is there even if you don't use it, and the president of that board may also be a woman. There are cases where women who lead those groups, and cases where men lead [them].

Providence is that this happens very easily in our part of the world, probably because the majority of Christians wherever you go are women. There are more women in our churches than there are men. At least in Ghana this is the case. If you were to make some sort of head count of Catholics in Ghana, the women would top the list. So that means that in certain places it isn't difficult to decide on a women's leadership in the community groups.

When you changed from being archbishop in charge of the diocese and came here to your quite bureaucratic position at the Vatican, did you miss pastoral ministering?

It is a completely different type of work. It's a different type of ministry. Being an archbishop in a diocese for this month and that month in Ghana, and being present for the Council here in Rome – they both are positions of leadership, but leadership of different kinds. Here you lead a small outfit. You meet in this small unit or small body, while being constantly aware that you are helping the exercise of leadership by the Holy Father. In Ghana, bishops do that and the ministries support all of that. That's a small difference.

A greater difference is that in Ghana, as an archbishop of a diocese, a lot of far-reaching decisions depend on you alone. For example, here, at the Vatican, we have some situations (as we were discussing before) like the small seminar we are holding here next month on human trafficking, with bishops from England and Wales. We have to coordinate with the police and so on. In such situations I would have to inform the [Vatican's] Secretariat of State. It would not be good if they heard from the local newspapers that the event is taking place. But if it was taking place in Ghana, I wouldn't have to inform anybody. The local church would just take care of everything. And so, once you are in a position like I am in now, you need to have a sharpened sense of responsibility as to what external judgments could be made about Vatican decisions. Last week, we came up with a small document calling for the reform of the financial system, but it was reported in the news as an official Vatican document, even though it was from this office.

So you need to recognise that what you do is easily attributable to the Holy Father. If I did the same thing in Ghana, it would not be attributable to the Holy Father. So yes, in that sense there is a difference.

The second thing of course is that here my work has a more administrative function; at home it is more pastoral.

Do you miss that?

Yes, I mean we still do some pastoral work; but it's not the same type of thing. In Ghana, you're thinking about how to build communities, to build up people, to work with people, to sustain and provide a source of food. It's a more challenging task and it's all day! Here, the challenge is about establishing a credible interface between the Church and the world. But there, we have an on-going need to demonstrate the Church's credibility within society, or to a group of people who may belong to another faith. That was more exciting. That kind of challenge was more exciting.

Do you get homesick?

Homesick? Not really, because for example, this year, since the year began, I've been to Ghana three times. If there is a seminar in Benin, and the seminar begins on Monday, I'll take off on Friday, stop in at home for the weekend or whatever, and continue on to the seminar. I also try to go home for Easter to help out in a parish. This past Easter, one diocese was supposed to be vacant – the bishop retired for health reasons. So I was in the cathedral for all of Easter. The previous Holy Week celebrations I asked a local bishop to find me some parishes or communities where I could serve with him. So I still try to get home for Easter, for Christmas … stuff like that.

Then in August I also carry on a program that I initiated in Ghana before I came here. Every August is a long vacation for secondary schools in Ghana. I developed a growing program that brought 500 to 800 Catholic students from our schools together for about three weeks. Cape Coast has a big educational centre. It's got a lot of secondary schools; so we put together Catholic teachers in these secondary schools as part of a guild of Catholic teachers. And they are the ones who facilitate all the work so that we can offer courses for the students as a way of helping. We started that because we recognised that the quality of education is not the same in all schools. Some are rural and some are urban; this is a way of using teachers from the urban areas to give a little extra help to the students from the rural schools. In the mornings, we hold normal school classes and then in the afternoons we do religion, moral issues, that type of thing. We have been doing this since 1995.

Have you seen the results? Have you seen an improvement in the results of those schools?

When we began, 1995 was the first time, we had 534 students. The highest number we've gotten since then is about 800. It fluctuates in between but we still keep the program going. My successor in Cape Coast maintains the program and that's why I take my vacation from Rome in August. I can visit, look and encourage, and it's good because once they get there, they know they are going to hear about who started the program (me) and so when I show up it's very encouraging for them. It's very good you know from the perspective of continuity. We have students who have come out of that program and have decided to enter the seminary, for example. Some have come out of the program and succeeded in other areas. There is one whom I've followed who became a doctor helping out in one of our church hospitals. Some have become nurses ... it is good.

For me, the other useful experience is that through the program you get to meet people. For example, some who have domestic problems and who otherwise would not have sought help, discover the program is over (let's say it was over yesterday and people are beginning to travel today) and some still hang on. They linger on because the prospect of going home is not attractive to them. And when you do finally enter into a conversation with them, it becomes clear that they are from an abusive home. That signals a more particular problem or issue to deal with: that child is going back to a home where he or she is being abused or is likely to be abused, or has been abused before! It's not healthy, you know? And I can make contact with the parish priest in that child's area and together we can get something done in that home, or we can find a different home for that child. Going through those situations has given me other very satisfying work to do.

There's a very strong educational impetus in Ghana it seems, compared to a number of other African countries.

When I was named a cardinal in 2003, at first, all of Ghana was excited about it. We tried to decide how we could make the nomination beneficial to the whole nation. So we developed a project which we call CAFDIL – Cardinal's Foundation for Distance Learning. It's a project with which we have begun to tackle the lack of access to decent education, to good quality education, in rural communities. We identified and brought some university lecturers together. They took the educational syllabus of the ministry of education of Ghana and produced lesson modules. Then we built the studio and they presented lessons before the camera. The lessons are filmed and then translated into various languages. And then we approve the receivers. So it's like kids in a remote village can still learn what people learn in the big urban centres.

Do you get support from the Vatican for that kind of work?

We've not brought it to the Vatican for help yet. The initial support we got was from the Italian Bishops' Conference. They have their office here in Rome; so you know we sent a project to them and we got initial support from there.

Financial support?

Yes. Since I've been here, everyone has been talking about how important it is to improve government in Africa, in all of the different places, but you can't really and seriously talk about improving governors and politics and rule without serious education. If you talk about the exercise of democratic rights, at least you need people educated to be able to understand what democratic rights are! More ambitious projects can be made possible using technology. We are trying to arrange a satellite link. And when we do that … the project will be not just about Ghana and Cape Coast, but it will be something that all rural communities in West Africa or [all of] Africa can benefit from. If that link works, then we see it as a big way of dealing with the gaps in rural education in Africa. Wherever there is a footprint of that satellite, people of any village will have access wherever they are. We just have to communicate the wavelength and any community will be able to do distance education. And this is also possible because West Africa, for example, has decided to adopt a common educational system.

The whole of West Africa?
The whole of West Africa. It just means that we follow the same levels, the same exams and all of that.

In this particular project I am talking about the basis started from Cape Coast. Some from the archdiocese of Cape Coast, and their studio, are in Cape Coast. The bishops of the conference in Ghana know about the project but the actual implementation is basically in the hands of the archdiocese of Cape Coast, and I follow the progress from here. For example, I've learnt about another project called "one computer per child". Through that I can see how we can project the lessons to each child through their lap-top. The internet makes all of this possible. And if all of that works very well, it will provide one of the big solutions to this problem of education in African communities. I know India already has initiatives of that nature.

Is it something that you can influence from your position here?
No, I actually thought about it before I came here.

But now that you are here, are you able to influence ...
Well I like sometimes to make a distinction between what I do there and what I do here. The focus of my work over here is the world Church, and I like to maintain that focus. I do not want to confuse that with the small parochial communities and the Church in Cape Coast. If I come across someone who visits our secretary and talks about a project like that, I can mention that to him ...

But I don't consider myself being ready to promote that. I hear actually that the new archbishop of Cape Coast wants to promote it and he can; he's got very many ways of doing that from Ghana. I like to maintain the work and vision of this office for everything that we do here.

What kind of problems [do] you think are evoked in imagining an African pope? Do you think there are problems? Do you think it's possible? Do you think it will be important? I'm sure that everyone will ask you this question.

I was going to say that is especially what I faced here when I arrived in 2010. You know, everybody who wanted an interview invariably asked a question about this. And I have always said that, in principle, everybody who accepts to be ordained a priest potentially accepts to become a bishop; it's not about becoming a bishop, I suppose; it's not about becoming a cardinal, I suppose; it's not about becoming a pope.

There must be an Obama factor?

The possibility is implicit. Now I will be frank with you. The possibility is real [that] anybody can become a pope, every cardinal especially can become a pope. From history way back and the northern part of Africa we did have people who were very close to this. Before I came to Rome I also used to follow the race: I used to watch whenever there was any conflict and I used to keep tabs on the identity profiles of all the candidates – which African had a chance. First it was Cardinal Gantin, then there was a drop in his popularity and it became Cardinal Arinze. The possibility is there and a lot of people are looking for it, particularly as they can also now see possibilities. Think about Kofi Annan who became the secretary of the UN, or Obama leading the United States. I do think about this.

Do think that it would make the Church more attractive to non-believers?

It's difficult to tell what the result or the impact of that would be. It would probably be an equivocal or ambivalent type of experience that we can have. While there might be excitement about having a black leader of this universal Church; you still need to work with a whole lot of other [circumstances]. One, the Church in Africa is growing very fast, but its level of maturity is variously judged by people within the Church. And mature just means its theological maturity or sophistication, you know.

Two, when someone becomes the pope, like Benedict, he still makes use of a whole lot of other support systems; organisations, theologian support, whatever. So while the leader himself needs to be a very well-prepared person, he's not supposed to be omniscient. He needs the external support structures as well and structures that are willing to support him.

Three, people in the Church do not also cease to become sons and daughters of various religious cultures. There are, there are still, parts of the world where the prospect of an African or black leadership may seriously constitute a problem. Stuff like that is not normal to some people. There are some communities in the world whose experience and exposure to people in Africa are still very, very limited.

When I went to the U.S., we were the first blacks or Africans who had studied together with people from the United States.

Did you [run] into problems?
No, no problems, but there were a whole lot of funny curiosities. Like, how will your skin look like when it gets burned? ... I had a friend back then, you know, we still correspond, he's in some place near Pittsburgh ... once he came to my room, you know, and he said, "I really wanted to see if you burn" and he lit a match ... (laughs.) But we understood. We understood their curiosities because we were the first blacks for them. They had questions about our hair and, "How do you look when you blush?" Or, "do you ever blush?" (Laughs.) But no, this is ... very, very natural. And it was fun. And for the same reasons we also had our own curiosity to satisfy. So all I am saying is that our world is so very colour sensitive. That's the point I want to make.

Hence I asked the question.

Yes, it's still very colour sensitive; colour sensitive in the sense that a person's face is one colour, before he is someone. We don't just look at the endowments or values of a person. If we choose not to go beyond that, we will never really get to experience that endowment. And we need to recognise that the Church is made up of all different people. But things are changing very fast. Globalisation, the communications systems, all of that can help such people deal with all of these challenges quickly. So in fact, some of these considerations may be taken care of at a far greater pace than we can anticipate. There are a whole lot of missionaries travelling now and meeting people, also through social media, which helps them get in touch with people and breaks down barriers so that these issues may well eventually disappear. So to respond to your question; for me, I reckon the reality of an African or [other third world] leader of the Church is very real. He may come from Africa, he may come from Southeast Asia or Latin America, but all of those, any of those would for me be a clear and manifest demonstration of what people mean by a universal Church, a world Church.

Do you think the global south is adequately represented here at the Vatican?

Definitely not adequately represented. For example, there are two cardinals from Africa in the Roman Curia now. Two secretaries I think; culture and healthcare workers, a couple of them, you know like in some universities in Rome; a couple in some orders of the Church. From India there is currently no cardinal in a Roman career. There is a bishop from Hong Kong; there are some bishops and some secretaries from Latin America. If you take a number from the northern part of the world and compare the south with them, the scale will tip in a particular direction, but again that's something that needs to change. John Paul II signalled a big breakthrough in this regard, opening up pathways.

Benedict didn't appoint any African in the last [round of] appointments?

Not in the immediate past. But in the consistory before that, three cardinals were appointed from Africa: there was Laurent Mosengwo; there was Robert Sarah; and there was Joseph Mazombwe from Zambia. So hopefully things will change.

Hey, thanks.

Anytime! I wish you success with the book.

Oh I brought you some socks. They have kangaroos on ...

Australian kangaroos!

The affable Bishop Ahoua of Grand Bassam who had us over for a long lunch. "The information Westerners have is fabricated"

Top: *After civil war, Abidjan, Ivory Coast*
Below: *President Houphouet-Boigny's massive Cathedral, Abidjan*

7 i. IVORY COAST

Ivory Coast borders the northern Atlantic Ocean, lies between Ghana and Liberia, and shares borders with Burkina Faso, Ghana, Guinea, Liberia, and Mali. Like Nigeria, the country can be broken roughly in half: about 40 per cent each to the Muslims and Christians with the rest claiming a traditional religion or none. The country has an estimated total population of about 22.5 million. Most people live until their late fifties. Only 56 per cent of the population can read and write. On average, children spend only six years at school. Most women will give birth to approximately four children (30 per cent of children under the age of five are underweight). In 2009, 3.4 per cent of adults (450,000 people) were infected with HIV, and 63,000 children.[130] GDP sits at 24 billion USD (in 2011), and population density at 62 people per square kilometre (2010).[131] Cote d'Ivoire is the world's largest producer and exporter of cocoa beans and a significant producer and exporter of coffee and palm oil. The country also produces gold. Seventy per cent of the population work in agriculture. Since the civil war of 2003 there have been on-going assaults on the country's economy with the nation's biggest challenges now being political instability and a downturn in infrastructure.[132]

Ivory Coast first came into existence as a French colony in 1893. Prior to French colonisation the area had been home to five flourishing African empires: The Muslim Kong Empire, which was a focal point

---

130 See footnote 40.
131 (http://www.indexmundi.com), accessed 25 May 2013; (http://www.tradingeconomics.com), accessed 25 May, 2013.
132 (https://www.cia.gov/library/publications/the-world-factbook/geos/iv.html), accessed 16 May 2013.

for agriculture and trade, the Abron kingdom of Jaman which was established in the 17th century by an Akan group, the Abron, and three other kingdoms, the Baoulé, Indénié and Sanwi, the latter two being Agni. All three resisted French subjugation. Descendants of the rulers of both Indénié and Sanwi tried to retain their separate identity long after Ivory Coast's independence (as late as 1969). The Sanwi of Krinjabo also attempted to break away from Ivory Coast and form an independent kingdom.

The new colonial government exploited natural resources and introduced a forced labour program to meet the labour demands on French plantations and forests. Africans in Ivory Coast were officially declared French "subjects" without rights to representation in Africa or France. Local rulers were expected to obey existing antislavery laws, to supply porters and food to the French forces, and to ensure the protection of French trade and personnel. French colonial policy presupposed the inherent superiority of French culture over all others and French language, institutions, laws and customs were extended across French colonies. French remains the official language today. Africans in Ivory Coast were only allowed to preserve their own customs insofar as they were compatible with French interests. Africans were also drafted for work in mines, on plantations, as porters, and on public projects. They were expected to serve in the military and they were subject to a separate system of law.

French citizenship was granted to all African "subjects" after the end of the Second World War.

At that time the government recognised the right to political organisation, and abolished various forms of forced labor. The country achieved full independence in 1960, with Houphouët-Boigny its first head of state. A considerably more conservative leader than most African leaders of the post-colonial period, he maintained close ties to the West and rejected the leftist and anti-Western stance of many

Ivory Coast: Bishop Ahoua 213

leaders at the time.[133] This approach is seen to have contributed to the country's evident economic and political stability during his leadership which lasted until his death in 1993 and which remains apparent, at least in the seat of government, Abidjan, in the vast lagoons that separate different arrondissements, the 1970s architectural expression that lines the city streets, and the modern freeways that circle through parkland and in and out of districts like any modern day city in the USA. Houphouët-Boigny has been followed by four subsequent heads of state, including Bedie, Guei, Gbagbo and Ouattara, and two separate civil wars since the turn of the 20th century (2004, 2011). Both of those saw a drop in the quality of life, a rise in the country's national debt, ongoing civil unrest, and the marginalisation of northern migrants. In 2011, thousands of people were killed in escalating violence between pro-Gbagbo and pro-Ouattara partisans and at least a million people fled.

Bernard Cardinal Agré was born on 2 March 1926 in Monga, Côte d'Ivoire. He is the archbishop emeritus of Abidjan, and a cardinal of the Church. He was ordained priest in 1953, serving as vicar in Dabou and then as teacher and director of the school between 1953

---

133 Unlike Kwame Nkrumah who pursued the idea of an Africa strengthened by the unity of its components (Pan-Africanism), Félix Houphouët-Boigny sought a solid Ivorian economy first (Houphouëtism), which was largely reliant on a labour force bolstered by migration into Ivory Coast and from Ghana, Nigeria, Mali, Niger, Guinea, Togo, and Benin particularly after 1970. Specialisation in export products took the country into the international trade circuit, and supported the country's economic performance, which was unmatched in the sub-region. As a result, Houphouët-Boigny maintained his reputation and popularity, and an ongoing policy of paternalistic regulation of the socio-political space was apparently justified by the creation of wealth which ensured political stability for some time. However, Houphouët-Boigny's reliance on the support of his tribal brethren (both within Ivory Coast and in the form of an immigrant labour force who were given voting rights) sustained an attitude of exclusion, and lead to subsequent clashes between the excluders and the excluded. Furthermore, the opposition's hostility to foreigners voting in national elections contributed to the rise of xenophobia, and bolstered the ill feeling that supported subsequent conflict. See Akindes, (2004), pp, 10-16.

and 1956 and then as rector of the pre-seminary in Bingerville until 1957. Agré studied at the Pontifical Urbaniana University in Rome and earned a doctorate summa cum laude in theology. Between 1960 and 1962, he was pastor of Notre Dame in Treichville, and created a domestic prelate. He also served as vicar-general of Abidjan, and was in charge of private education and of the seminaries between 1963 and 1968. Appointed bishop of Man (1968), he served as president of the Regional Episcopal Conference of Western Africa between 1985 and 1991. He was transferred to the see of Yamoussoukro in 1992 and promoted to the metropolitan see of Abidjan in 1994. Agré was created and proclaimed Cardinal-Priest of San Giovanni Crisostomo a Monte Sacro Alto in 2001, and he participated in the 2005 papal conclave.

Bishop Raymond Ahoua holds a PhD in Biblical Theology from the Catholic University of Eastern Africa (CUEA). His dissertation was published by Peter Lang under the title: "The Transference of the Three Mediating Institutions of Salvation from Caiaphas to Jesus: A Study of Jn 11:45-54 in the Light of the Akan Myth of the Crossing of a River". He is a member of the Pan African Association of Catholic Exegetes (PACE). Among other interests, Bishop Ahoua writes novels to evangelise the young.

I first met Cardinal Agré at his residence in Abidjan, in September 2011. In the same week I also met Bishop Ahoua at his residence outside of a UNESCO world heritage listed town called Grand Bassam which is about an hour's drive from Abidjan.

ii. Prudence

... The vendor ladies squatted, scowling, resting their chins on their crossed arms, behind fortresses of stacked kola nuts, bundles of fragrant sticks, piles of charcoal, salvaged bottles and cans, or displays of dried animal parts. They grumbled continually as they built and rebuilt with leathery, deliberate hands their pyramids of mottled greenish oranges and mangoes and curved embankments of hard green bananas. I took a deep breath and told myself that a woman anywhere on earth can understand another woman on a market day. Yet my eye could not decipher those vendors: they wrapped their heads in bright-coloured cloths as cheerful as a party, but faced the world with permanent vile frowns. They slung back their heads in slit-eyed boredom while they did each other's hair into starbursts of astonished spikes. However I might pretend I was their neighbour they knew better. I was pale and wide-eyed as a fish. A fish in the dust of the marketplace, trying to swim, while all the other women calmly breathed in that atmosphere of overripe fruit, dried meat, sweat, and spices, infusing their lives with powers I feared ...[134]

Outside of Grand Bassam, a UNESCO World Heritage-listed town on the eastern edge of Ivory Coast, a man in a short-sleeved, blue and green surfing shirt knocked the caps off a couple of long necked local beers. Handing one to me he asked me to explain myself; where did I come from? What did I want to know? Did I, or did I not, know the saying "Hakuna Matata" from the blockbuster film *The Lion King*?[135]

---

134 Kingsolver, Op. Cit., p. 100
135 "Hakuna Matata" is a Swahili phrase that can be translated to mean: "There are no worries." The phrase was popularised by the 1994 American animated musical drama film called the Lion King, produced by Walt Disney Feature Animation and released by Walt Disney Pictures. See (https://en.wikipedia.org/wiki/The_Lion_King), accessed 1 May 2013.

I obliged with a rendition of the chorus, and he replied with a laugh so deep it was almost hard to hear. Below us in the garden, a table dressed in cotton cloth and silverware sat elegantly shaded by plantain tree thatching. I had brought the best wine I could find in Abidjan, but he produced better, three bottles which he had attendants uncork and decant for his guests: myself, my son, my friend and two novices who assisted him in his work. He offered a simple buffet – fish, vegetables and fried plantains, with fruit to follow and coffee later.

The formality was short lived. As we sat to eat, the gates of his compound opened and a car arrived to deliver two more people. Vivienne and Robert, both teachers from town and close friends of Bishop Ahoua, emerged from their vehicle screaming with laughter and taunting one another in French before calling out to all of us at the table and gesticulating wildly about the adventures they had had on the way there. We were introduced briefly in English, before the conversation lunged forwards in rapid French again, becoming more raucous as Vivienne occupied the space with her infectious personality and self-deprecating sense of humour. Vivienne's jokes left most of the party in tears, with the bishop eventually rising to dry his eyes away from the table (though still sporadically doubled over in fits of joyful hysterics), before her claim to a potential acting career – talent foregone by the necessity of high school, she told us (eyes twinkling) – lead her to sing hymns for us all. The novices, and then Paul, Robert, and finally the bishop himself rose from their seats to join her in gentle and tuneful song, while she remained singing but seated at the table's head, posing beautifully for my son's camera.

From Abidjan we had been driven by my friend to Grand Bassam, out through the bomb blasted streets of the city towards the ocean and the forest that runs along its edge. The bishop's residence sat on about an acre, a relatively informal but two-story brick home, with surrounding gardens and a vegetable patch that provided for most of our meal. It was a warm day, and humid, and it was nice to be out of the smog. Abidjan itself had been relatively uninviting. Smashed up by the civil war only ten months previously, the streets where we stayed near the presidential palace were dirty and chaotic. The Chinese hotel I had chosen sat adjacent to parkland. We were woken both by the smoke that wafted in through the window from fires lit for morning meals in the small piece of land beyond our window, and by the dense smell of cigarettes smoked by Chinese businessmen that crept under the door. Cement dust had settled on most surfaces, giving the entire place a visage of grey, and the streets ran with hawkers who were at once menacing and dogged in their attempts to shove cheap plastic souvenirs in through the car windows.

In many ways my experience of Ivory Coast was like a scene from a modern James Bond movie[136] or perhaps in a more literary sense a reminder of the writing of Graham Greene.[137] At the border where my son, Billy, and I crossed from Ghana, trucks revved amidst the clouds of hot yellow dust initiated by their wheels, razor wire marked the passage that separated the two nations. Green clad soldiers roamed around; some bored, hunched forward to light cigarettes that they smoked lackadaisically, their guns dangling from their shoulders, brown berets angled, lace-up black leather boots, beneath socks that held tucked military trousers, kicking at the brown earth. Others were straight backed, highly alert, one hand on the butt of their weapon, the other holding the barrel, and watching for people like me seeking entry. We were interrogated by three such men, at gun point, and after our passports had been confiscated momentarily. They sat us under corrugated tin on a wonky wooden bench that rocked us off balance,

---

[136] I was thinking of the film *Casino Royale* (2006) which featured Daniel Craig (as Bond) in pursuit of an international bomb maker to an embassy in Madagascar.

[137] Green wrote four major novels in which the context is based in Catholic theology including: *The Power and the Glory, Brighton Rock, The Heart of the Matter,* and *The End of the Affair.*

and stared at us menacingly before questioning why we were there. As my passport disappeared into the neighbouring building I asked myself the same question. The fluorescent colours on our bags and clothes contrasted too sharply with the broad neutrals that defined the border. They drew attention that we didn't need. Layers of mosquito repellent clothing that we wore self-consciously made us sweaty, and uncomfortable, the colour of our skin another cause for their concern. Billy was fourteen but looked an adult, and the sophisticated camera equipment on his back suggested to them that he was working. "Perhaps for you?" the largest man asked leaning towards me, his English breaking as he invaded my space. "He is your cameraman? You are a journalist?" "No," I told him over and over, my French clearly incomprehensible, "He is my son. Please check the passport. I am here to see the cardinal, *Cardinal Agré*." Mention of the cardinal's name was enough to break the impasse. The previously intense, black, and frightening face in front of me cracked into a broad and insanely easy-going smile of wonderfully strong and healthy teeth. He sat back against the wall and reached out across the table to engulf my hand with a huge hand of his own. "In that case," he said to us in English, "Welcome to Cote d'Ivoire!"

The border crossing was the first of a number of surprises. The second came the following day. When I met with the cardinal I was told that he was unhappy with the questions I had emailed. The political sensitivities in Ivory Coast at that time made it impossible for him to discuss politics in any shape or form, and it was his intention to send me on my way.[138] The cardinal had been caught in a high profile division amongst the bishops of Ivory Coast that was driven by politics, the recent election of Outtara, and the subsequent civil war. The Episcopate was deeply divided by the political crisis that erupted in December 2010 and that led to the war. The elections of 2010 were

---

[138] "Ivorian Cardinal appeals to French to restore calm", 20 November 2004, *The Tablet*, (http://m.thetablet.co.uk/article/1982), accessed 1 August 2012.

meant to end a ten-year socio-political crisis in the country, but the former president (Laurent Gbagbo) presumably lost the elections and the declared winner Alassane Outtara was largely considered a foreigner who heralded from Burkina Faso. Some church leaders made divisive statements on the television and in the press on the political crisis. Various discussions I had with Jesuits had suggested an unspoken allegiance between the cardinal and the deposed president on the basis of ethnic ties that did not sit well with expectations of political neutrality from religious leadership. On behalf of the Ivorian Bishops' Conference, and supposedly without consultation with his colleagues, he publically condemned United Nations enforcement of the democratic elections that installed Outtara to office and led to the ten-month war.[139] Subsequently some bishops had publically disagreed with his pledge of religious allegiance to the nation's corrupt but now deposed president, exposing a rift. Furthermore he was, in that very week, appearing before a military court investigation into the murder of past president Robert Guie.[140] Perhaps the border guard's amiability was brought about by ethnic as opposed to religious affiliations shared with Agré?

Unaware of those issues when emailing my questions from Australia some months earlier, I had assumed he would be willing to discuss topics that ultimately became volatile. I had blundered in naively, only to find myself confronted with an assumption of mal-intent.

A foreign mother and child assuming themselves in charge, suddenly slapped down to nothing by what they all saw us to be ...[141]

Threading the needle of diplomacy was not going to be easy in

---

139 "French undermine Ivory Coast, cardinal charges", *Catholic Culture,* November 24, 2004, (http://www.catholicculture.org), accessed 1 August 2012.
140 Ange Kessi ordonne l'audition du cardinal Agre: Enquete sur l'assassinat du Gal Guei Robert", *La Nouvelle,* 16 September 2012, pp. 1-4.
141 Kingsolver, Op. Cit., p. 100.

such circumstances (the cardinal would say later, "What I don't like I don't do!") and without warning I began to waver on a precipice; the wrong facial expressions threatening to push me over the edge. But just as I began to feel myself toppling, my adolescent son (by this stage bored with the on-going translations between English and French and oblivious to the rising tension) interrupted the intermediary to ask if he could have a small passage he had written translated for the cardinal. In it he described his educational background, as a high school student in Australia, and his hope to create a short documentary from his experiences in Africa entitled "Embracing the Stranger". Would the cardinal consider answering three questions from him instead?

A white woman and her son carrying expensive camera equipment at the Ivorian border is a picture out of focus. Within a setting of armed conflict and social instability ostensibly brought about by the international enforcement of Western concepts of democratic process, it is natural that we were viewed with at least some reservations, and so too by the cardinal when we first met, with or without my email blunder (not that we understood that at the time!) The cardinal appeared annoyed, his impatience with my written approach came across as irritation and evoked in me illogical generalisations about West Africans being "volatile". But Billy's audacity repositioned the lens. A little taken aback by the boldness of his gesture yet touched by the naivety of Billy's appeal, the cardinal made a last attempt to maintain the upper hand with me. He belittled *my* skills by asking me, in perfect English this time (despite the apparent necessity for a translator) to guess his age: "You know nothing about me!" he cried, holding out his autobiography, which was written entirely in French and suggesting that I leave and read it before returning to Abidjan a second time. "Can you even be so foolhardy as to guess my age?" Seeing a potential change in the atmosphere I grabbed at a last chance. "That would be impossible." I said to him, before considering him carefully, "It is clear from your seniority that you must be around the same age as Cardinal

Wamala ... but to look at you I couldn't say you were a day over sixty. Eminence, how do you do it? You look fabulous!" It was enough. Like the border crossing we all became people again in a moment; mother and son travelling through Africa, human, faulty, but driven by good intent; he a man, mortal and imperfect, and ultimately vulnerable to flattery. A common thread stitched the flaws in our humanity together at last, and drew him out from under his red hat.

He smiled and paused before changing the topic entirely, standing to explain his daily exercise regime, and saying that he rides three kilometres per day on the exercise bike in his bedroom before bending upside down to show us how he stood for five minutes each morning to get the blood into his head. His hat fell off, and the large and heavy golden cross around his neck hung down somewhere near his chin and he mumbled through the folds in his white and red cassock as he stretched his head towards the overly thick red socks on his sandaled feet, clearly unconcerned about undermining the formality of his post in his attempt to impress me. "We can meet again", he told us once he was upright, his hands held out in front of his body, his arms perpendicular to the ground. He was balancing perfectly while gently squatting up and down to demonstrate the strength in his legs. "But come on Thursday at ten." When I did arrive and before we started recording he handed me four personally typed pages of answers to a number of my original questions.

In between, on Wednesday, we found ourselves lunching with the bishop, our third surprise. The laughter and the wine had wiped away my nerves. The bishop's generous nature (and possibly the wine) encouraged me to raise certain topics that had been out of bounds with Cardinal Agré. Politics, sources of conflict in West Africa, syncretism, polygamy, and female circumcision had already been conceptualised where I came from in very particular ways that were not at all in keeping with Ahoua's views. The confidence that he displayed in his convictions also caught me off guard and challenged me to accept their validity. The Muslim/Christian divide, for example, so heightened in Western consciousness, does not exist in West Africa. In fact, he said, there is fluidity between religious denominations that flows across families with ease in West Africa, particularly Ivory Coast, a measure of flexibility that was also raised by Cardinal Turkson when pushed by the media to explain his Synod blunder, and which I encountered possibly every time I had an opportunity to engage with local people.[142] Many families have Muslim and Christian devotees within the same community. In some instances religion was presented to me like fashion, and everyone has to wear clothes. The Muslim/Christian divide that we Westerners look for in explanations for conflict in Africa is a convenient construct, a simplification of otherwise highly complex ethnic and tribal paradigms that are unfamiliar in the West.[143] It justifies international intervention into African conflicts when there are actually valuable resources at stake and accounts for Africa's supposed unwillingness to embrace democracy on a national level, he said.[144] In fact, he continued, Africans are not ready for democracy because democracy's requisite sense of national mission has not yet

---

142 Isichei, Op. Cit., p. 198, discusses an early fluidity between Christian denominations in Africa: "Denominational hostility may have been confusing and disconcerting to new Christians, but it made it clear that there were many possible paths to the Christian God. Africans were empowered to find new paths of their own."
143 John Allen, senior correspondent for the *National Catholic Reporter* and prominent author, draws on Matthew Kukah a priest and intellectual who holds a master's in public policy from the Kennedy school at Harvard and a doctorate from University of London and writes on civil society, democracy, and Christian/Muslim relations. Kukah, he says, is required reading across Africa. In his blog, "All things Catholic", Allen notes that Kukah (like Ahoua in Ivory Coast) has claimed that conflict in Nigeria is NOT about tensions between Muslims and Christians.
144 "The United Nations Environment Programme (UNEP) has found that over the last 60 years, at least 40 percent of all internal conflicts have been linked to the exploitation of natural resources, whether high-value resources such as timber, diamonds, gold and oil, or scarce resources such as fertile land and water. Conflicts involving natural resources have also been found to be twice as likely to relapse." (http://www.un.org/en/events/environmentconflictday/), accessed 11 June, 2013.

been achieved in places like Ivory Coast, not because the country is divided between Muslims and Christians, but because there are so many separate ethnic identities and communities.[145]

... the concept of nation has not yet been learnt [here]. A country is a territory and there are many "countries" in Africa. It is not enough to cut up a piece of land and say this is a country called Ivory Coast. You have to put the people, the tribes and the ethnic groups together. When they have come together and they consider that they to belong to a community, only [then] will we have a nation ... If I am like a general, I am going to fight. My strategy is there... My planning is in place ... Everything is clear ... But if the soldiers are not committed to fighting, then I will never have a victory. So, everything does not rely on the one single person; the people surrounding him must also have the same vision.

Until that time comes, he noted, a social contract only exists

---

[145] The forcible process of democratisation began in Ivory Coast as in other countries in 1990 (after 30 years of single party rule) exposed the social divisions of a society whose components (ethnic groups and immigrant populations) were poorly integrated, and brought sensitive issues that had previously been repressed into sharp focus. The underlying essence that pervades a vastly genetically and culturally mixed society (components of which often share links beyond national borders) makes citizenship problematic. "Recognition" within that diversity is dependent on the nation's capacity to produce wealth and ensure (at the very least) the equality of its citizens in the face of poverty. The questions of political representation and of immigration in a new context of economic contraction make them political instruments. As the economy goes downhill, the management of the distribution of national wealth in a region where Ivory Coast continues to attract immigrants because it offers a comparatively better life style to that of its poorer neighbours, becomes the deciding factor. See Akindes, OP. Cit., pp. 17-25, and 40-41. Some argue that the West patronisingly resists the establishment of democracy in places like the Democratic Republic of Congo, and Ahoua inadvertently makes reference to that Western position as well. True independence in resource rich Congo would perhaps draw upon Lumumba's brand of militant nationalism which would exclude whites from the Congo, and put resources out of Western hands. See "Is the world ready for a democratic republic of Congo?" *Lokoleyacongo*, 14 May 2012.

between a community's king and *his* people, for whom he has a very real and tangible duty of care.[146]

I have a king, I have a mayor, I have a prefect, [and] I have the leaders of political parties. I have all these people. But [only] a king ... provides for that which the people need to live normally, socially, to function together.[147]

As the great gulf widened between us Ahoua continued to build a bridge for me, filling in the gaps in my understanding of syncretism and polygamy, for example, and subtly drawing attention to not only a lack of patience in the West, but to the Western tendency to infantilise the average African. Religious sceptics at home had belittled African

---

146 Existing political divisions in Ivory Coast are a good example of the way in which national unity is destroyed by the competing ethnic, as opposed to religious, rivalries that create the ethnic mosaic in Ivory Coast. Conversations I had with various Jesuits in Abidjan gave me an overview of the country's recent socio-political history: The western region of the country initially felt excluded by the first President Houphouët-Boigny, while the north felt excluded by the first president's heirs. Northerners are still seen as foreigners today and they continue to be associated with Burkina Fasso, the country that shares Ivory Coast's northern border (and vaguely, with Islam). The former president, Bedie, belonged to the central region of Ivory Coast. In order to win the elections Outtara and Bedie made an alliance which, generally speaking, joined the north and the centre of the country together. Laurent Gbagbo, who lost the elections, was supported by people from the west and the south. On the surface there appears to be a political divide between Laurent Gbagbo and Alassane Outtara, which is vaguely interpreted as native Ivorian vs. northern (or Burkina Fasso) foreigner. The latter's depiction as "foreign" is all the more entrenched through the support he has from France, the former colony. Add into the mix the ethnic identities of the vast immigrant population and it becomes clear why, deep down, Ivory Coast is a nation struggling to build its unity from broad and fierce ethnic complexities.

147 Ahoua's comment mirrors and perhaps makes possible through the simplicity of the African King/people dichotomy, the social contract discussed in Jean-Jacques Rousseau's 1762 treatise, *Du contrat social ou Principes du droit politique*. The heart of the idea of the social contract may be stated simply: Each of us places his person and authority under the supreme direction of the general will, and the group receives each individual as an indivisible part of the whole ...

Catholicism as syncretistic. *"After Mass they might cut off the head of a chicken to cover all bases..."* one said. But that is a misunderstanding that fails to allow both for the luxury of time enjoyed by the West over the last two thousand years (Catholicism has only really been officially African since Vatican II), or to validate the powerful attraction of the gospels to Africans broadly. It is arrogant to assume that Africans are incapable or unwilling to practise the religion in its strictest form, he said, and ignorant to suggest that Africans at large have been victims of Christian programs of religious indoctrination that they are happy to discard or merge with traditional, African tribal, religious practices in times of need. Cultural practice and religious belief are entwined as much with the practice of Catholicism as they are in traditional beliefs. It is a question of form, not of substance. The accusation of syncretism is simplistic and ignorant, and undervalues the deep commitment that Africans in general have chosen to, and do, make to a spiritual life.[148]

"Ivoirians are miraculous believers", a Jesuit in Abidjan later told me. "Even though some defining cultural practices continue to share links with traditional religions that cannot be revoked overnight, Ivoirians are quite determined to choose and practice their Christian faith with every ounce of their strength, and that means combining cultural traditions with religious (read Christian) life."

So too the claim of indoctrination: Eating at a restaurant before I left, one well educated friend had become angry when I suggested that Africans in Africa were choosing Christianity because it answered an inner calling for something else. *"I don't buy it."* She told me. *"They were forced to go to school in Catholic schools. Of course they think that they want to be Catholic. They are indoctrinated!"* But the bishop's experience stood in stark contrast to that view. Born into a

---

148 An aversion to unorthodox practising of Christianity was made by Cardinal Wamala as well. "I don't know if these so-called priests and the Church should not be scared ... Many such people have emerged in Uganda and gone. I advise Ugandans neither to follow nor listen to them because they intend to divide the church," (http://www.cardinalrating.com/cardinal_121__article.htm), accessed 22 May 2013.

polygamous family of some 30 children, and raised and educated in a traditional culture and religion, he saw the way in which the Catholic brothers lived whilst working as a builder in a seminary. Without understanding what he saw, he said, he considered their humble generosity and kindness as leaders of a community to be enlightened, so he sought out and then chose that way of life for himself, despite the fact that it meant rejection by his family and community for many years on the basis of a cultural clash. It was clear that Ahoua had not been indoctrinated, though I suspected that his choice was the same adolescent-like rebellion I had also considered possible in Arinze's case. He would later describe the great gulf that exists between the older (Agré) and younger (himself) generations, and indicate that it was *impossible* for Agré to interact with the younger generations on their terms. Like the first African Catholics of old, Christianity (and in his case the post-Vatican II version) had been his key to the modern world.

Married clergy became part of the same discussion, as did the supposed tolerance of polygamy. It is common for me to hear at home that African priests regularly take a wife, despite the vow of celibacy. This is not only a misunderstanding of the centrality of the catechist (or often married lay clergy) to Christian life in Africa, but also a deeply offensive assessment of those who take their commitment to the cloth very seriously, and their parishioners who demand it. *"People would say, "That's enough!" ... They would say that his willingness to be a priest is not there."*

The tolerance of polygamy is similarly misunderstood, he suggested. A disjuncture exists between traditional African religion and culture, and Christian life that is not yet resolved. The two have to live side by side but the fact that they do does not mean that Christianity, Catholicism, is not practised by the book. *"They can't say, 'Oh, it isn't in our religion,' our Christian religion and so on. The village has its pride and polygamy is tolerated within the tribe. People who are not prevented by their religion from taking many wives, continue to do so... [but a polygamist cannot be a Christian], absolutely not!"*[149]

The truths I assumed self-evident about Africa were quite fairly, and indeed brazenly, depicted by Ahoua as an expression of arrogance, a mask for personal insecurity, fear and ignorance that derived from my Western, feminist origins. There was a potential for such misrepresentations to affect conflict, and even unhappiness, he suggested. If I have learnt anything it is that intelligent deliberation requires I listen carefully to the experiences of the members of the culture (both Catholic and otherwise) in question.

In discussing polygamy, for example, Bishop Ahoua described his own experience of polygamy (as the child of a polygamist) as relating to the care rather than the abuse of women, and rocked my expectations of his views as a Catholic priest. My Western background has led me to position my understanding of polygamy around male sexual convenience alone. But in cultures where community identity and belonging are valued above individual aspiration, polygamous marriage can be seen to support and validate not only those women who seek higher honours within the community, but also those who would be otherwise outcast by a failure to wed, he said. Furthermore, as the "modern world" encroaches more and more on Western Africa, access to sex (and exposure to disease) outside of marriage becomes readily available via the internet. Single women can be prostituted and neglected by married men, he said, their subsequent isolation made all the more acute because the centrality of marriage to female status continues to be fundamental to female identity and community acceptance in places like Ivory Coast. I assumed that he was talking in support of polygamous marriage but in fact he was merely acknowledging its existence as a better alternative for women when their world was in a process of change.

---

149 Numerous historians describe the out casting of polygamists. Isichei, for example says, "... many of the older men had been disconnected for polygamy." p. 240.

It is what you call "successive polygamy". Today you will be with your official wife, then [later] with [another woman], then after tomorrow you will have a third, and so it continues. So what is needed is not liberation from polygamy, but to train people to have a right to know – this is the type of lifestyle that will empower women with more rights, more respect, and more dignity.

Ahoua's point was that the evolution of a society has to run alongside an evolution in morality. It is not enough to modernise, he said, rather men and women must both be granted equal access to the benefits of that modernisation as it comes. Cardinal Polycarp Pengo of Tanzania (interviewed by Gerard O'Connell, see Appendix) describes the private and psychological challenges of polygamous marriage for wives of the same union in terms of "hatreds and antagonisms", and disempowerment. He says, "[When] you find [a] woman who is faced with the situation where her husband has another wife [she] says, 'OK, because I'm a woman, I have no voice' ... You really have to say, it must come to an end!"[150]

What happens then with female circumcision? Ahoua claimed that there was no need for female emancipation in Ivory Coast. *"The modern fight ... The feminists call it feminism. That does not exist in our society and is it even harmful to bring it here ... What you see is*

---

150 Buchi Emecheta's classic, *The Joys of Motherhood* grapples with the private issues associated with massive social change in Nigeria in the 1940s. Through the life of Nnu Ego, she describes the loss of status traditionally attributed to Ibo motherhood as a traditional Nigerian life merges with the modern world, and the bewildering and devastating impact of those changes on one woman's life in particular. Emecheta depicts not only the social necessity of polygamous marriage for women without familial support, but also the private and destructive psychological challenges (including jealousies, conflict between women, etc) that such marriages entail for wives in the same household. Nnu Ego becomes the traditional "mother sacrificed"; her centrality to family survival, both psychological and physical, is left unacknowledged and ultimately negated as the mismatch between traditional life and the lure of modernisation pull her family apart. Buchi Emecheta (1979), *The Joys of Motherhood*, George Braziller Inc., New York.

misinterpretation." He said. *"It is written in the books, talked about at the school and people [learn] that women here are oppressed."* He described his society as matriarchal; *"I, myself, was sometimes deprived of food by my mother, which was kept for my sister ... This should be a reason for the liberation of men!"* but went on to say that young people (men and women) choose genital cutting the same way that "... *young people want to have a tattoo.*"

Was I supposed to take his word at face value? Having just lunched with Vivienne and watched the interaction between the sexes at our table (having travelled in Africa four times!) I was quite willing to embrace the idea that my assessment of Western Africa, including my generalised assessment of West African women, had been skewed in advance by misinformation. Indeed I wanted to grant every person I met ownership of their own choices, if only because I had denied them that agency in my assessments in the past. Vivienne was a powerful presence during the meal and she openly encouraged the men at the table to wait on her and to defer to her opinion. Furthermore, her husband had been left at home to care for the children while she lunched with these quite senior Catholic men. Vivienne was very much in control, both at our table, and at home. Had she been circumcised (something I did not ask her) it could not have been about repression and control.

Nevertheless circumcision remained a moot point for me. Apart from my concerns for the physical and emotional welfare of circumcised women whose health is under threat and sexual expression curtailed, my fear was that some women in Africa were potentially isolated from a society that emphasises community over individual aspirations when they objected to their own cutting (out of self-preservation) especially where the procedure stood as evidence of a willingness to belong. Was Ahoua saying that circumcision was just as much an expression of a willingness to belong to a community, as a tattoo or piercing might present as a free expression of individuality that is applauded and often exists as a precursor to belonging to a group of "like minded individuals" in the West? But that was too much for me. There were indeed limits to my ability to throw my own values away in the search for insight.

> ... the prevalence of a practice, and the fact that even today many women endorse and perpetuate it, should not be taken as the final word, given that there are also many women in African cultures who struggle against it, and given that those who do perpetuate it may do so in background conditions of intimidation and economic and political inequality.[151]

I do not believe that Ahoua was arguing in favour of female circumcision, nor was he demanding cultural relativism on my part. Rather, like Turkson, he had possibly discounted or even underestimated Western (and therefore my) sensitivity to the issue and stumbled (perhaps it was the wine?) into the topic of circumcision as part of a much broader discussion about the dangers inherent in an assumption of knowledge arrogantly claimed and defined within Western theoretical constructs about female repression in Africa, and the Church's supposed unwillingness to do anything about it. Despite his protestations to the contrary, it was clear that female empowerment was very much at the forefront of his consciousness, and that he not only drew on Christian morality but also did so while maintaining a clear view of the African experience (both male and female) of social upheaval. Our discussions about polygamy and female circumcision could have been evidence of the hypocrisy for which the Church is damned in the West, yet his take on them reduced them to being just two of the many challenges depicted in a very complicated portrait of struggle. By focussing on them alone I could have obscured the whole picture.

---

151 Nussbaum, Martha (1998), C. *Sex and Social Justice*. Oxford University Press, 1998, p. 122.

Marching into Africa with the privilege of a highly sophisticated education experience and the connections and confidence that experience had provided, I had clung to atheist and Western feminist reasoning in analysing social, religious and cultural paradigms that I really knew nothing about, just as I had weighed up my fears of the "African other" in deciding to march at all. My earliest pre-occupations with carjackers in Johannesburg, murderers and rapists in Uganda, rebels in Ivory Coast, night-time burglary, rubbish and disease were small fry next to the sophisticated manipulative potential of the educated intelligence I owned. *I* was a threat. I had the ability to misrepresent what I was seeing to an educated (and therefore powerful) audience in the West, and yet I had been embraced and nurtured nevertheless. My search for friendship had been answered in Africa despite my judgement of the average African as dangerous (and the average African woman as repressed), an indiscretion that was *forgiven* time and again. Ahoua was telling me that having been granted access to an inner sanctum I now had a duty of care, and I needed to *listen*.

... *However I might pretend I was their neighbour they knew better* ...

Expressing my concerns about travel in Khartoum to Wamala the previous year, Wamala had replied, "There is no need for *you* to feel afraid." I thought that he meant there was no danger in Khartoum (despite the civil war), and I had scoffed at his confidence when I returned home. But now I think that he had recognised the things that would make Africans anxious about me. It had taken almost a year but I think I was at last taking that giant leap of faith I wrote about in Kampala; shedding my arrogance, embracing compassion, landing with confidence and with relief.

Michelangelo's *Pietà* in Rome was suddenly so beautiful, so endlessly patient with the failings of others. Her suffering, the suffering that I had wanted her to represent as a mother was just a human condition, and a fairly disquieting echo of our mortality. The mastery of that suffering was the stuff of living, her gift to everyone else.

> A group of twelve female students ... were taken by those rebels and abused, raped, murdered, mutilated ... and some of them never came back ... Afterwards they asked the mother of one whether she could forgive those rebels and she said ... I forgive them ...

Michelangelo had depicted Mary's strength as divine. Enter *enlightenment*.

On the way back to Abidjan we faced our last Ivorian surprise. My friend was eager to get onto the road. We had been with the bishop most of the day and the traffic was building. As we drove along the highway, bumper to bumper, there was suddenly a sense of urgency. "Uh, oh", my friend said. "Something is happening. Something is happening. There is trouble brewing." A police car, sirens blazing and loud speaker protruding from the window, stopped in the lane beside us. Policemen leapt out and wove their way on foot, at pace, in and out of the crawling cars in front of us while blowing piercing whistles as they ran. Up ahead, a Ute, heavily laden and covered with canvas, swerved across our lane and down a side street out of view. The police gave up the chase and made their way past us and back to their car. Supporters of ex-president Gbagbo attacked three police stations while we slept two nights later. They stole an armoury of weapons, and caused the airport to close. They had apparently crossed the border from the refugee camp in Ghana that we had seen before we crossed over four days before, and were driving a white ute with an overloaded tray and canvas cover along the highway from Grand Bassam. As we drove to catch our plane the following morning, hoping that the airport would reopen in time, bodies littered the roadside not far from the airport. But we were Westerners, and we were moving on. There was no need for *us* to feel afraid.

Cardinal Agré, Ivory Coast

iii. Bishop Raymond Ahoua, Bishop of Grand-Bassam, Ivory Coast

(September 2011)

"... My Father is a polygamist. I come from a family of four wives and around thirty children. My mother was the second wife. So we have to consider that these people [the family of this polygamist] are trying to move away from their traditional religion towards ... Christianity."

Why don't you start by telling me why you became a priest?

Why I became a priest? I have been asked several times why I became a priest, but I never got the right answer. Well, I decided to become a priest as a young man. Really, I was trained in building and after my study I worked for almost three years, [before leaving to] become a priest. I decided to change my life because I had seen other priests serving young people. I found that they were not interested in themselves and that they were happy in their work. At that time there was a prophetical message to my society, to the young people of my background, in the form of a big feast they would have in the village when a man and a woman had their tenth child. Giving life is considered the most valuable contribution to society and so people are shocked if someone like me chooses to be a priest instead of getting married, choosing a kind of life that involves caring for many other people. So I was subjected to many questions as to the worth of my life, for example. "What is the use of my life if it is not for me, but for others?"

And at the time, what was the Church like in Ivory Coast? When was that – which year – do you remember it?

I joined in 1979, early 1980. But let me tell you, I am not from a Christian family so I did not know anything about the Church.

Why did you choose the Church then?

I chose the Church because I was starting work as a builder at a school that was run by the priests and it struck me that they had a certain lifestyle. They were Italian priests but they were also our lecturers and I could see them doing God's work. One of them, whom we call "le grand" – it means "the big man", was the one who had to unload the cement from our truck ... white [sacks] of cement. He went close to the truck's customers and put one sack of cement down, then another. So you see, first of all, we are not a normal family group from colonial times. If white people saw our lecturers doing manual work, they would either say "these people are crazy", or they would see that there is another way of living and behaving. That's all. I did not intend to become a priest because at the time I didn't know what that meant. I didn't know anything about the Church. I just wanted to train in the seminary, so I started praying for an adventure, and I discovered mid-term that the cost of that adventure meant being a priest, or a member of a religious order.

And did your family accept your decision?

My family is a very special family ... There was a lot of tension in my family because I wanted to train to be a priest. You need to understand that a child is an investment here. He goes to school and if he manages to do something good, and especially when he starts working, then he was a worthwhile investment because he brings some money into the family, some support back to his family. This is the first point. So in the family, my father was opposed to this profession, due to that fact that he had spent a lot for me and I wouldn't be able to help my younger brothers. I could be a provider for the family. My mother, she was very practical, she said, "As you will have no children, you cannot be accepted in our society." And I was considered as a dead person. By becoming a priest and having no children, I was cutting off the line of children after me.

That must have been devastating.
Well, I remember that we talked through it and one evening after we talked, I said, "Listen, we have many children in the one bed ..." and so forth and so I said goodbye. That was all.

You are very brave.
You know, after one year I had to decide and so I decided.

Did you study overseas? Were you sent off to study?
Well that became a bit of a problem because I met with the bishop and spoke to him about my vocation; he said there was a problem about his submitting me due to my tribal religion. He sent the catechist and the priest to meet my father but that did not work. He literally would not receive them. It is not good for you to be near your family, when there is so much tension between the family and your situation. So he decided to send me to another country.

To Togo?
To Togo. He sent me to Togo and I spent four years there.

And then you came back straight afterwards?
I came back after two years but it was like I was in exile from my family.

Is it still like that?
No, it is not like that anymore. After that, okay, the tension continued for six or eight years but it did eventually die down.

So tell me about Ivory Coast at the time? What was it like here?
Living in Ivory Coast was very difficult in those times ... the north was not very populated then and they said it was not much use trying to develop there…

So going to Togo was a really big move for you?
Yes, at that time, yes. You had to go up in a truck to the north ...

But also psychologically it would have been a huge distance ...
Psychologically, there was a lot of problems surrounding myself and my personality, but I was not in any trauma because I had begun to see how I wanted to live my life.

And the Church?
The Church and the catechists. There were no Christians in my family. The catechist was a man, there were some in my village, in my tribe, and there were priests.

Did you have much contact with priests or was it mostly catechists?
One or two of them. There was one who taught me at school there. But we didn't see the Church as such. We were living with the catechists; what they told us about the Church was what was relevant for us. For us the Church *was* the catechist holding the service, and the catechists were like parish priests or curators. Those people were living God's word, it was just like Christ.

Do syncretism and polygamy cross into Catholic traditions as it is practised here? And if so in what ways?
Firstly, there is the issue of our religion; that is an interaction between the catechist and Catholicism. I'll give you an example from my own background: My father is a polygamist. I come from a family of four wives and around thirty children. My mother was the second wife. So we have to consider that these people [the family of this polygamist] are trying to move away from their traditional religion towards ... Christianity ... Secondly, within their culture there is a particular way of thinking that [makes doing so problematic]. We [Catholic leaders] have to enable them to enter Catholicism through a process that will

take their own struggles [with the changes in expectations] and their growth into account. We say that these people are being converted to Christianity, that they are moving away from the past. But life is a slow process. [We must be patient]. We must find a way to show them that while they are entering into Christianity, they have not lost all of the elements of their religion or other traditions of the past. There must not be a conflict between their past and their present, between their traditional religion and their present, Christian life. It is simply a process that has not always been completed before they join us. But I am sure that one day it will come, as they grow as Christians.

Even theology is an issue: The traditional religions, for example, show us that there is only one God, the creator of heaven and earth, the creator of everything. But this is also the case in the Catholic Church. From the outset, when we say that there is only one God, they ask me, "What about Jesus Christ?" And I have to tell them, "Jesus Christ is a theological matter. [Don't worry about that for the time being.]" So there are only a few elements of Catholicism that we can initially accommodate within our culture. To put Christianity into our hearts and our daily lives takes time. So at that moment, we can't talk even about syncretism. It is a fact that these people are holding two or three religions in their lives at the one time. It is part of a process.

So what we would describe as syncretism of the home is not syncretism as such?

Ever since I was born I have been told that there is only one God, the creator of heaven and earth. I pray to this God. The mystery of Jesus Christ is still a theological mystery which, when we are raised in the Christian tradition we can understand. But how can you explain these elements to someone like my father, who has never stepped into a classroom? When he says, "I pray to God", and you try to tell him that his God is the father of Jesus Christ, it has no context for him." Judging from [the Christian] side, we decry his religious practices as syncretism, but for him there is still one God. Now he is talking about our God, the father of Jesus. Okay, our God is a Trinitarian God, but it is very difficult to explain that to him. Even at the stage in his growth as a Christian, these elements are gathered together, sometimes they are one entity. So if you were to ask him, "Do you have two or three or four religions in your life?" he would say, "No. I pray to the one God."

I found a nice book in Ghana, in a tourist shop in the national park, which was written by a catechist about the representations of Christianity in the symbols of the Achan. It was very interesting for me that Christianity was being interpreted from within an African ethnic past. Can you comment? [152]

Well, there is a process of marriage between them, of one overlapping the other. We have to consider that the African religion is entering into Christianity or is being brought into Christianity, that the two are being married together, or alternatively, that Christianity is entering into the traditional religion. I will put it like this: When a man has for a long time been living in an African context, in an African religion, and he [decides] to change to Christianity, then little by little Christianity will overlap with his traditions and move into his past, and he will perhaps reinterpret what has been before. But in the meantime, he needs to

---

152 While noting that it is not possible to generalise across the African continent, Cardinal Arinze also spoke about the overlap between African traditional religion and Christianity in terms of his childhood in Nigeria (geographical neighbour to Ivory Coast). In his interview with O'Connell, he draws parallels between Igbo and Christian names, and the ever present sense of God being present in everyday life. "It was not a life in which the individual forgot God, in which man was regarded as supreme It was a life in which man obviously recognised beings who were invisible and superior, and to whom he referred, and whom he did not ignore. "O'Connell, Op Cit., pp. 14-16.

ask God for direction. It is not [simply] that the African religion is overlapping with Christianity or the other way around.[153]

So is the view that Christianity had been there all along but was being interpreted with African symbols? That is quite different to what you are saying.

No. You have to move the African symbols from the context of religion, into the context of liturgical celebration. That celebration is an expression of the soul, the body and the cultural elements that are expressed during the Mass, during prayer and so on. For example, to strike like this [Ahoua takes his fist and strikes his chest] on my chest is a sign of pride in my culture. It might say to some men that he cannot defeat me. I can use words, or I can just strike my chest. Either way, it is a sign of boasting. This is liturgical but it has nothing to do with the doctrine. Doctrinally, the faith is expressed through my celebration of the liturgy. For other things, I can use signs from the Achan tradition. This is a language, a language [in which] to express something. The language must be recognised, it must be understood by the people right in front of me.

So this all leads on to the Second Vatican Council obviously?

Yes, but I don't think that this is very important.

It is interesting though. Don't you think that it leads into a discussion of the power of Vatican II and the way in which it gave Catholicism to its people?

---

[153] Again, as Arinze points out with O'Connell, "We can say that the African Traditional Religion was the religious context, the religious background, from which most Africans come, except in those areas that have been heavily Muslim for centuries. Of course, in some parts of Africa, the Traditional Religion would not be as strong – in some parts of eastern Africa, for example. In other parts it is very strong, as in Ghana, Benin Republic, and parts of Nigeria. There must be no generalisation. But one thing is clear, it permeated the atmosphere, and it was a major influence in African culture and still is." O'Connell, Op. Cit., p. 16.

Well, we have to use those symbols. There are some elements that we could describe as "African law" that will contribute to the power of the liturgy. For example, when we read the Gospel, especially in the south, the Achan area, we sit down [whereas] normally [as Catholics] we stand. When we celebrate things in the Achan culture, we sit down. Sitting or standing both *say* something. Here, if we have an important message to deliver to someone, then we need that person to sit down. If we have a testament to deliver to someone, you will want that person to sit. "Please" they will say to you, "I have something very confidential to tell you, so please sit down." Every person will sit down in that situation. They won't look at you, but instead will bend their head and open their ears to listen.

So it's more about form than substance?
Yes. So in this context and since Vatican II, we are allowed to use *meaningful* symbols, *meaningful* expressions of the body and the language, which can contribute to a better understanding, a better celebration of the liturgy. But this is a liturgical matter.

And how did that alter the nature of the Church in Ivory Coast? Did it make it more accessible to people?
Well it is a fact that Vatican II made those provisions, and those provisions promoted the Church to a certain degree. But it is one thing that the Church said they would do it, it is quite another to implement those provisions. The implementation of that new element, which Vatican II delivered to the Church [has been] a bit slow here, a bit slow.

In view of the fact that you are a young man of the Church here and Cardinal Agré is an old man of the pre-Vatican II Church, can you describe the differences between the two of you?
The difference comes from two sources. The first is from the Church; the second is from society. In society, I think we work parallel to one

another. For example, in the past, when I wanted to greet an elder person, someone a bit older then me, I would cross my arms and bow a little. Today, it is different. When I greet you today, I say, "Good morning!", and I shake your hand. Even a boy of five or ten years of age [does that]. So this separation between social classes, between the young and the very senior people in society, does not exist anymore. In the past, however, it was felt and in the Church too, because it was felt in society.

So, the bishop, the priest, and so on, even though they were committed to working with the people, they were not within the people, so to speak, in the actual mass of people. Today it is natural to see no distinction between a chaplain and a youth group leader on the basis of age. They come with the same mentality and so they are close. The people, the priests and the bishops are closer here to the average Christian than they ever were before. Even in a parish with 60 villages, each of which I would visit only once every three months or once a year, there might be a distance between the bishop and those people, because they don't see one anther too often, but culturally, we are still very close.

So is that a problem for someone like Cardinal Agré?
No, it is impossible. It is not difficult. It is "impossible". You can feel the difference. There is a difference between attitudes amongst people from rural areas and urban areas too. They feel a difference between [traditional and] modern attitudes. Agré is the same. It's the problem of a generation.

Does that makes it harder perhaps for him to relate to the young?
Not hard. I say *impossible*. They do not understand each other.

The difference between you is that sharply felt?
Let me explain it differently. The difference is not put there to prevent one class from interacting with another, to separate one group from

another. It's just there because of time and culture. If you take Viviene [the woman who joined us for lunch]: Just listen to her and you will see how what she says reflects her urban background. It is the same for the way that religion is practised by people from a certain area. People agree to behave in a certain kind of way. You might meet someone at school who has grown up in a village and you will see the difference. People will interact, but the closeness that we are talking about is quite impossible.

So is the current Church flexible in that regard? Does it cope with those changes?

The Church – yes, especially with the priest and so on. Yes, even the bishops.

Is polygamy therefore still tolerated as part of that process of moving towards Christianity?

Well, I think it is a special [case] as far as how people ... across this area, feel. Polygamy is tolerated. It is tolerated, accepted within the society. Society does not exist separately from the Church. They can't say, "Oh, it isn't in our religion," our Christian religion and so on. The village has its pride and polygamy is tolerated within the tribe. People who are not prevented by their religion from taking many wives, continue to do so. The day before yesterday I met a young person, he was about 45 years old, who has two wives. He is tolerated. We don't feel that there is something strange about his life, because we know that that is a condition of life for him.

And he is a Christian?

No. He is not.

So if you are a polygamist, you cannot be a Christian?

Absolutely not.

Can you start as a Christian and then have again a second wife and then stop being accepted?
At that moment you have to stop being accepted.

So you can no longer attend a Church?
No. Newcomers sometimes are tolerated. Newcomers attend services but [distantly] and they cannot take communion and so on.

What about priests who have partners and family. Is that common here?
I don't have statistics to say exactly, but I think that the percentage would be very, very low. There would not be many. No. People would say, "That's enough!" He would not have people to support him getting married. They would say that his willingness to be a priest is not there.

In the West when we hear about conflict in Africa, for example last year here in Ivory Coast, we view those conflicts in terms of the Muslim-Christian divide. Can you tell me what is really going on? If it is not a Muslim-Christian conflict, can you explain in your words what the real issues are, for example, in the war last year?
Well, whatever happened here we call it a situation of politics. I mean, first of all that international politics played [and plays] a big part around this area. There is an interest running from Congo-Brassaville, to Nigeria, to Ivory Coast and up to Ghana. [There are] problems because of our oil.

So what about the conflict last year?
Obama came to Ghana and he said that 45 per cent of the oil used in America should come from the Gulf of Guinea. Okay? So the first problem is oil.

The second problem is a problem of resources. The lack of resources in Europe. They have to take them from Africa. We sensed this problem when I was in Kenya. There is also the problem of cocoa and we are getting problems of resources.

The third problem is that of importing democracy. Go around and you will see the difference between the past and the present. The solution is not a matter of being for or against democracy, because one way or another, the people are ruled by their chief. Where I come from, I have a king. He automatically defines my allegiance. That king is more important for me that an international leader who will be there for three, five, or even ten years. That is another key element to reading correctly the Ivorian political situation.

The fourth problem is associated with issues that exist between the north and the south, and between Muslims and Christians. But this, let me tell you, this is a fabrication! It is a fabrication that is being constructed by what I call an international community. I know which country in particular, but let's just call it an international community for now. Let me give you an example. The cardinal of Dakar called me, "Your Excellency, I heard via the media, specifically the foreign radio station operating in this area of West Africa, that in Grand Bassam two mosques had been set on fire." He was calling from Senegal and he was also worried that the famous 'war' between Christians and Muslims was about to start. Well, let me tell you that in my family I have some brothers that are Muslim and we have never had any problem. Many others are also not Christian and we have never had any problems – until politicians transform a non-political situation into a political situation! So I say: "No, excuse me, no mosque has been burnt here." "But please my Lord," he said, "It has been said on the radio, and even people from the good mosque have been interviewed and confirmed that the mosques are burning!" And I said, "No my lord, there is no mosque which has burned". "But they say two mosques!" And I say, "Please, let us cut it short. I am not speaking to you from another planet. I am in Bassam. No mosques have been burned, neither by a Christian nor a Muslim nor anyone!"

So it was manufactured.
Manufactured. In fact something [did happen] on Friday. There was this young girl with a friend who was, let's say, 100 metres from a mosque. ... not far from the actual building ... Wind blew the dust into their eyes and they started crying and saying that [someone had] put a grenade into the mosque. From that misunderstanding, the story was fabricated that one or two mosques were burning, and five minutes before the cardinal from Senegal called me, the parish priest of the town came and said, "The Muslims are marching to the church to burn [it]! So what shall I do?" So I said, please go and remove all of the documents that are in the church and let them burn the church!" ... but ... it was nothing ... you can go and do your investigations but you will find that no mosque was burning, and certainly not two!

If you go to Korogov and after that to the conflict zone in the north part of the country ... one of my classmates is a bishop there ... and he said to me, "Whoever would say that this place is not Christian is not speaking the truth." It is a fabrication. We also have a parish there where every year we have more than 50 baptisms!

So do you think the political conflict you are seeing is not about religion it's more about ethnic groupings?
It's not even that. It is about resources. That's all. It's what I said earlier.

What about the conflict last year with Gbagbo. I heard that his judiciary backed him as did the military, and a lot of the senior officers in both were members of his ethnic background. Would that be accurate?
Well, I read a book written by one political leader, I don't want to say who, and he said, in the very first sentence, "I became a rebel because in Ivory Coast, Gbagbo is planning genocide similar to that of Rwanda." Okay so that's one thing.

The rebels backed Ouattara?
No, at that time there was no Ouattara. Ouattara came [more] recently. Ouattara never declared that he was part of the rebels. He was a candidate, an opponent of Gbagbo that's all.

Last year, at Christmas, a French priest was passing by here. He said, "Thanks be to God that we managed to save the Ivory Coast, because we prevented genocide." I say "My father, congratulations!" Then I said "Father, which genocide are you talking about?" And he said, "the situation here is similar to Rwanda. Listen, I have been here for the last 20 years ..." Now he lived in Uganda, Rwanda, Burundi. And he said, "so I understand the situation there. I came back to Ivory Coast in 2010 and I am very familiar with these kinds of problems."

Rwanda has two ethnic groups. They can speak about genocide. But in the Ivory Coast we have 50 different ethnic groups! Which ethnic group will kill all the other 50? And so far, there is no covenant that allows this between one ethnic group and another. How can we speak about genocide? But they will still use the idea of genocide as a justification for military intervention in the Ivory Coast.

We know this about Europe and especially UN/American policy towards Africa. It is a cliché and one that does not apply everywhere. Nevertheless, they apply the same cliché to different areas. The UN will throw around a fabrication to justify intervention. Let's say everybody can pray, but he cannot apply the idea of genocide to Ivory Coast. We have more than 50 ethnic groups. It's impossible! What's more, all of the leaders in Gbagbo's government, his wife, all of them ... are a mixture of different ethnic groups!

Incidentally, what happens to the children? Which ethnic group do they belong to if the parents are from two different groups? Do they join the father's or the mother's group?
Well [according to] national civil law, that they belong to the father. This [means that] they are called to some ethnic group, they train for

some dance and [suchlike]. But they belong to the mother's group, especially when it comes to the Achan group; anthropologically, Achan children belong to the mother's group, which is matrimonial.

I know they are a bit complacent, because the father gives the name and so on, but we say that the blood is given by the mother.

So if the parents were to separate, the children will go with the mother? Or ... with the father?

Well, they should go with the father, but the court might ... decide differently ... It is not automatic that they go with the father or with the mother.

What happened to the unity of the bishops last year? I know there was a division here. In Mozambique the unity of the bishops was very strong and helped to bring the civil war to an end. So I am interested in the bishops' conference in Ivory Coast, they weren't united?

I have been asked this question several times and my answer is this: It is said that when we take the life of Jesus we have four Gospels. Each one says something about Jesus Christ and at the end of the day all of them know that the Gospels did not exhaust the life of Jesus. It's the same here, everybody knows what happened. There was a moment when the bishops questioned what the international community [the United Nations] was doing here [and insisted] that the constitution be respected. People of this country (white also) must be respected. Nobody from abroad must decide for them.

This is what was said in a pastoral letter written by the bishops. After that, another bishop wrote giving his opinion on the same issue. Personally ... I do not see anything wrong [with that]. If as a scholar, as a bishop and as a leader, I have a contribution to make, to enlighten the path of the Christian, I will do it. Unity does not mean we all have to agree, all of us, in what we say. No. If we agree in what we say, we are united in saying the same thing, but that is all. But if we do not agree in what we say, if I have a personal contribution to make, then I think that I can offer it to people to help them [analyse] the situation and to decide without undermining the unity that exists between the bishops. I can recall when I was in Kenya there was a referendum about a new constitution in Kenya. The bishops there said, "No, let the Christians decide for themselves, but give them all of the facts. Put the facts in front of them, so that they can deepen their knowledge and be aware of what they are voting for in this constitution."

That is the democratic process. But if some people are not united from the outset then they might be hostile towards one another. Even if they are not united [but] they disagree about essential issues, then they will want to fight, but this does not happen within the Church or among the bishops. We have strong characters, we have strong people.

Did any of the bishops become politically aligned?
You cannot prevent political alignment in the context of Ivory Coast.

Why is that? Why can't they stay neutral?
No one can remain neutral in politics because if I give you a card, I seize you and say, "go and vote!", then even as a bishop you vote for the candidate you want. Myself? I have only my passport. I have not been registered [on the electoral roll]. I came when the election process was ending, so I never voted. Okay, but if you ask me to be neutral I say, "No. What are you asking me to do? If I have two candidates I have to vote for one or I don't vote. If I have five I still have to choose someone."

As an individual you could do that, but what about as a group?
As a group, we don't go to vote together. Let me explain the various situations; a broader interpretation is not possible when a foreign element becomes involved. A foreign interpretation will not provide

an appropriate understanding of what is really going on. For example, you may see me with a politician, but we might have been at school together, from secondary school and upwards, so I see him as a friend. Even on the day of the election I don't vote for him, but let's say the day before the election it's his birthday and he asks me to [attend his birthday party]. I will go, because for the last 20 years he has been my friend, my classmate or my "brother". Just because he's a politician and it's the day before the election, I would say that even the devil wouldn't stop me from going to his house ... [My] being with someone does not mean that I support his political interests! This has been another misinterpretation [both] within the country and outside it.

So, ethnic similarities do not imply necessarily that you will vote for the same ethnic group?
Absolutely not.

So does political leadership come before ethnic similarity?
No, no, the thought is one thing, the ideology is another. Recently, people have been trying to set up ideology [on] an ethnic basis but ... there are so many ethnic groups, so many. I think some ethnic groups have grown to 20 million people. What do you do with them all? ... Also, the ethnic groups are intermingling, the people are being mixed together. This is done on purpose, so that some from there could go to do secondary school here and some from here could go there. Now there [is] also inter-marriage. I don't know, I try to understand but it's difficult for me to figure out such a thing, unless I believe what is said on the radio which sometimes, as I say, makes no sense.

Pope Paul VI had quite a democratic vision for the Church. With everything that you've said about ethnicity not being as clear cut as it may appear to be from the outside, do you think that it is possible that the laity could elect who should be appointed bishop, rather than the appointment coming from Rome?

The appointment of a bishop by Rome does not come only from Rome. From the little that I know about the appointment of bishops, people at the grassroots are consulted. There are many investigations at the grass roots by the nuncio. Those at the grassroots *are* consulted and a lot of investigation occurs at that level, because the bishop must provide for the people's needs. His people know what they need more than those who are in Rome. Among many candidates, one must be more popular than another. So I think that they look for the most suitable person, because the most popular candidate must be able to gather ... the people together. For example, the priest might say that the Mass must be in Latin or something like that and African people are sensitive to that [because Latin holds little relevance for them]. So according to the historical context we need more or less the right person.

In view of the fact that the global south isn't really equally represented in terms of cardinals, do you think that the bishops should be involved in the election of the pope?

For me, this is not an issue because the Church is living in a historical context which is itself a process. One fact, for example: people say here [in the Ivory Coast], that the south is more developed than the north, so there is political injustice. And I say, "Oh, I am from the south. I don't feel guilty." The first white people came from a ship that arrived here in Bassam. When the missionaries who arrived here with schools and education first came *here*, everything was a forest. They started ... here and little by little they went to the north. So, education started from here. Before it reach the north, [there was] a gap of maybe thirty years. Why should I feel guilty because Christianity started from here? Okay the Church started to seriously develop in some places before coming to Africa. The process of growth in Africa will come. Maybe one day there will be so many bishops, so many cardinals, that we will participate in the election of a pope ...

So you think the Church has to reach a certain level of sophistication that it hasn't quite reached in Africa?

They said, "let us build a university" – Yes. Then they say, "Maybe we need a university to [show] that we care [about] education." But we have only primary schools, there are not yet secondary schools, why should we [have] a university? Let us wait until the turn comes when you have finished secondary school and then we will think about building a university. Otherwise this process will skip some steps forward.

It requires patience?

Exactly.

Somebody said that Africa wasn't ready for democracy. Do you think that's true?

I've been thinking about democracy as an idea that runs through schools, politics, education and so on. Democracy involves an election and a candidate who wins the elections and becomes the president for five or ten years and so on. But who is living with the people? Who is caring for the people, [regardless of what] happens? As far as I am concerned, I have my king, which ... is more important to me than a president, because I can go and talk to my king. I know what he does for the people. I have a king, I have a mayor, I have a prefect, I have the leaders of political parties. I have all these people. But there is a king who provides for that which the people need to live normally, socially, to function together.

You cannot come to the people to really campaign and say "I am the president of this party!" You will start a conflict ... *You* know your candidate and after the election you will say that he is the president of your whole country and this is true. But here the concept of nation has not yet been learnt. A country is a territory and there are many "countries" in Africa. It is not enough to cut up a piece of land and say this is a country called Ivory Coast. You have to put the people, the tribes and the ethnic groups together. *When* they have come together and they consider that they to belong to a community, only [then] will we have a nation.

Do you think that the Catholic Church can do that?
No, the Catholic Church cannot do that. It cannot be conducted within the Catholic context. Catholicism cannot provide for a whole nation, for one full area.

Do you think that opposing socio-cultural groupings can be brought together across ethnic boundaries?
This is possible.

Is the Church working towards that?
It is possible ... I think the Catholic Church has done more in that regard than other denominations.

So it has been successful?
Well, the results are there and they are very positive but there is one thing with the Catholic Church that is important to recognise: We don't portray what we do too much, because our achievements are a part of our life mission; they are part of our inner mission. We don't need to show people that we mandated to do something and that we were successful. We're not publicising [things]. [They just happen very quietly.]

Can you tell me about women in Ivory Coast and in what way the Church here is liberating for women. Is it or is it not?
[Laughs] You have to understand that our society is made of young people who have a different culture to yours. The traditional fight that you talk about, men against women, and women against men, that does not exist here.

Do you mean a traditional fight or a modern fight?
The modern fight ... The feminists call it feminism. That's does not exist in our society and is it even harmful to bring it here.

Why?
Because the oppressive side of the man against the woman is not there in [this] society. It is a traditional part of regular life. In some societies, let's say, Kenya, where genital cutting occurs, there will be a lot of NGOs going against this. But it is not the parents of the people or the leader of the village telling the young men or the young women that they must go to have what is called this "genital mutilation". They go themselves.

They choose it?
They choose it. The same way young people want to have a tattoo and so on. So the fight, the real fight, is not there. It is a fight that is made up by social workers. And what has been seen, what you see, is misinterpretation. It is written in the books, talked about at the school and people [learn] that women here are oppressed.

Do you think that the church liberates women here, that it takes them out of polygamist marriages and puts them into one-partner marriages, for example? Does the woman have a voice in the laity that she wouldn't have otherwise?
[Laughs] I ask myself if you understand what I am saying. Let me tell you the points of your departure.

We say especially with our tribal groups that we have a matriarchal system. I, myself, was sometimes deprived of food by my mother, which was kept for my sister. And this has never been a source of conflict between my sister and me, woman against man. It's never been a source of conflict. It [is] the same for all [who] live in the matriarchal system. This should be a reason for the liberation of men

... But when that liberation occurs, the system in place will have been destroyed and the new system, which has been put in place, will have nobody to support it.

The Church is liberating as you put it, yes. In the sense that for the Church: one man, one woman. Every person has been created in the image of God. Male and female – he created them. So from this point of view, there is no debate. This is the ideal. Now, officially everything is okay. But go into a society, remove your glasses and look. What do you see? People are married, sure, they are not allowed to have a second wife, but even when they have no second wife they will have a mistress, maybe two, maybe three and so on ... Can this system be approved of as a better one than polygamy? Today we have the mobile phone, today I am in an office, today I have transport and so on, and we also have many hotels. Well ...?

It's still possible, it still exists, it is just not official or honest?

It is what you call "successive polygamy". Today you will be with your official wife, then [later] with your second, then after tomorrow you will have a third, and so it continues. So what is needed is not liberation from polygamy, but to train people to have a right to know – that this type of lifestyle that will empower women with more rights, more respect, and more dignity.

And that is how the Church is liberating because it's teaching morality.

Exactly, I called it formation. There are many meetings and so on.

You mean in society?

In society and even within the Church. What is more interesting for people I think is that in the past ... society was hospitable. Today, people are selfish. We used to have sharing, but now we have greed, individual greed. If I'm going to steal a lot of money, I steal it, and then I put it in a bank in Europe or elsewhere and so on.

The same concerns existed in the past as well. There were even tales told in which a spirit, or a god who could be transformed into a human being, will come as a foreigner and test your hospitality to see how you will help. If a pauper comes to ask you for something; you should try to help. These days, people know that "the more I have the better it is for me!" I try to test people's values about that. Maybe you have a new value, you go, you come, mobility makes it easy for you to come and go as you please. Okay, I understand that. Everybody is on the internet, Facebook, Skype and so on. We see everybody relying on technology (which is good, which is good), but it has no [positive] impact on their spiritual life. We see both sides. Their spirituality has disintegrated and they are not happy but it is difficult to understand exactly why. I can say that it is the same for the priests. Many priests must really define their values and stick at them.

So it was a challenge even in your Church?
Yes it was a challenge. "I've chosen to be a teacher, I am a teacher, and I want to be one and to stick to it ..." It involves commitment.

One finds that in Australia, too, you do one thing for a short time; then you find another thing and move on.
This isn't just because [people] want to change. It is because they are not stable.

Do you see internal stability as the biggest challenge then?
The biggest challenge ... For the young of today everything is a must. To have more is a must.

What do you think of Outtara? Do you think he is a visionary?
Outtara is a great man. The problem is the context. Just let me give you an example. I can be a captain of a navy ship, but if you put me in an airplane I would not be able to fly it ... this is what I call a context.

You think he's a great man but he is in the wrong place?
No, that is not what I am saying. Things might be very different if the context were different. What I can say is that as a bishop I have a vision, I have a plan, I have a strategy. If I am like a general, I am going to fight. My strategy is there – it is clear. My planning is in place – it is clear. Everything is clear. But if the soldiers are not committed to fighting, then I will never have a victory. So, everything does not rely on the one single person; it is all of the people surrounding him, the vision, and so on. The people surrounding him must also have the same vision. We have so many great people here, but it is a context. Because people say "let's save the country", but some will say "I want to but I don't belong to your party". So instead of having 80 per cent support you will only have 60 per cent.

But he is a great man in your eyes ... he is a good guy. He's got good intentions?
From what I know. As far as my knowledge goes.

Tell me what do you think of the West? How do you conceptualise the West?
Negatively.

All negative? For what reason?
For what reason? What happened on the 11th of September, 2001? Bush himself asked, "Why do people hate us so much?" And the answer was, "Because you are very arrogant."

By the West do you mean the United States or you mean the whole West?
I don't mean West as a country I mean West as a culture. It has been like this from Greece, from Rome from Britain. Since Alexander the Great up until now it has been the same system. Their intentions are good.

Outside though they show a mask of solidarity – humanitarianism, education for everybody ... But we know that is a mask.

Do you think that Western arrogance has affected cardinals as well?
It affects them because what they are being fed is a kind of lie. The information they have is fabricated ... They are not even interested if there is other alternate news or alternative facts and so on. Today, what is trusted is the internet. This is what I call co-fabrication. Because when you write on the internet, whatever you write on the screen will be accepted . You can send it to the internet. But even if I am an eye-witness and I want to send [reports of] what I see with my own eyes to the internet, if there is no power or electricity, I can't. Meanwhile you will send whatever you want there and everyone will believe you, just because they have seen what you have written on the internet. These days, technology is seen as more reliable than eye-witness accounts, and this is what I call fabrication. Whatever happens here, or in Western culture, or for bishops around the world, I cannot take the time anymore to sit down and listen if those people are not concerned with facts. If a black man speaks, he is considered biased because he is African [rather than as] reporting something that he has seen.

IV. Bernard Cardinal Agré, Archbishop emeritus Abidjan, Ivory Coast
(September 2011)

"... The bishop Nosho, Papa Nosho of Abidjan, sent me your questions. Those questions don't work very well for me. I don't know you. Because the political situation it is very, very sensitive here, it is difficult for me to answer some [of your] questions. Some of the [answers] would affect my ability to control political issues. I can't comment on politics. I would prefer to keep quiet because of the situation ..."

I am 86 years old. I have been a priest for 59 years. I was ordained in 1953. I was a priest from 1953 to 2012 ... I have been a bishop for forty-four years. I was ordained a bishop in 1968. I am from the diocese of Abidjan and I first worked in Dabou as an assistant parish priest.

I was a headmaster of a school, a primary school, from 1953 to 1956, and from 1956 to 1957 I was the director of the primary seminary school (for those who want to become a priest) in Bingerville. Bingerville is the second capital of this country. It is not far from here. From 1957 to 1960 I went to Rome to study canon Law. I came back in 1960 when the country became independent. At that time I was the parish priest (not the assistant parish priest) of the parish called Notre Dame de Treichville. It is another part of Abidjan. It is [beyond] the lagoon, when you cross the bridge. I was the general secretary of the archdiocese in that year and the vicar in charge of Catholic teaching. And I was a lecturer of law in what you call the high seminary. In 1968, I was appointed bishop of a new diocese, called Man, in the northwest of the country. I was a bishop in Man for twenty-four years from 1968 to 1992. And in 1992, I was appointed as bishop of Yamoussoukro, a new diocese. After two years in Yamoussoukro, I was appointed bishop of Abidjan. I was bishop of Abidjan from 1999 to 2006 and I resigned as bishop in 2006.

My relationship with Cardinal Yago (because you asked a question about my relationship with him): when I read your question I felt that for me the golden age of the Catholic Church in this country was during the time of Cardinal Yago ... because of what he did for the Church. In 1960, I worked for Cardinal Yago ... From 1960 to 1968, I was his secondary ... So you cannot oppose us to one another. I worked in the light of Cardinal Yago. I think that during that time it was a golden age.

You asked about Houphouët-Boigny and his relations with the Church. When Houphouët-Boigny became the first president of this country I was 34 years old. I had a doctorate in theology at that time. I was a mature adult. I had been a priest for seven years. I had a good relationship with [him]. Sure there were some difficulties ... Sometimes I was asked by Houphouët-Boigny to be his spiritual father, to give him some spiritual advice. I went to see [him] when he was in hospital in Geneva during his last days in December 1993, and when he died in Yamoussoukro I was the bishop [there].

Houphouët-Boigny was known as the father of the Ivorian nation. That title is good for him. He had a good, a great, vision for the country and he liked the people of Ivory Coast. Despite his relations with some friends of colonisation, say France, Houphouët-Boigny knew how to get what he needed from that relationship. He understood that some aspects of that relationship could benefit the country. I know that during [his] time, everything was not always ideal. The man had some difficulties. But you can see that he made a good effort and he took care of the welfare of the people in this country during his presidency. He also took care of national infrastructure. He built buildings and bridges, he provided good education and health services, and all of those things.

[Re] my apostolate method: I think that the method of apostolate changes all the time. When the missionaries came to Cote d'Ivoire, there was what you would call in French "Societés des Missions Africaines" (SMA). They were based in France and they did something very good for this country. After the establishment of a native Ivorian clergy they, they tried to form or build a new Ivorian ministry. Today those French priests are still welcome. There is also acculturation, which [is one] of the concerns of the clergy – to move together with the lay people. How do we do that? I see the answer in the liturgy, in the way of doing things during the Mass, and so on. I think everything is not OK when you talk about acculturation and the Ivory Coast. There are some good things, but there are some failures as well.

Human beings need conversion. What is important for me is the key phrase "conversion of heart". Conversion in the way that we live in Africa, in Europe, in Asia and in America. Christians across the world have the same problem. The conversion is to be converted to Christ. To follow what the Christ demanded of us in terms of how we live our lives: That is the future of the Church in Africa. In that case, you can say that the Church in Africa is young compared with the Church in America, in Europe, in Australia.

What are the strength and the weakness? When a person is young, he has a greater sense of possibility. You can do a lot of things when you are young. – for God and for human beings. You will see that youthful strength in the Church if you go to Mass here. You will see the liturgy in the Cote d'Ivoire. There are many people during the celebration of the Mass. There are a lot of young people who would like to be priests, compared with in Europe. We have a lot of vocation, a lot of community and religious congregation. And the Christian lay people are engaged in the society and in the church. That we can see. That is very important for me.

But the fact that you are young means you can also make mistakes that young people make. You don't have enough experience when you are young. The Church in Cote d'Ivoire is still fragile. You cannot say the Church is [very] mature. It does not have a [great] tradition like the churches in Europe or in America. To be more adult, the Church must have more autonomy in some areas: Conception, education, formation, evolution, planning, tradition, formation, funding and [the like]. For me, that is a weakness for our Church. So we think that we have to work. The Church in the Ivory Coast is at least 100 years old, so it's not too bad. But it is better to think that the future is ahead.

Is peace possible?

Yes, for me peace is possible, but under some conditions. First of all, there must be a conversion of mind, of conscience and mind, of young and adult, of men and women, [of] those in positions of power and those not in positions of power. Hate can destroy people but love can build them up. So we must be united. To be in the Church you must strive to be honest. It is better to work for the truth, to work for love, in order to live together, if that is what you want. It is true that the peace will come in the actions we take towards peace. Yes, you can say, "peace is possible" but only if you decide to put love everywhere.

I'd like to talk to you about your experiences or the differences in your experiences, working in the three dioceses: Man, Yamoussoukro and Abidjan, and the challenges that you faced moving between them.

My life was very lively, I was in Man, I was in Yamoussoukro and then Abidjan. Again, if someone asks me what is I most loved ... I would say Man because it was [my] first-born ... First, I was consecrated in my twenties and thirties. And then, I came to Yamoussoukro [which] I liked because there were many professors, many students and the intellectual milieu was very good ... I wanted to do a lot of projects [there]. In two and a half years I founded three parishes. I launched a radio station. I also launched the first radio in Man. [It] pleased me very much to work there, around the basilica.

And then the Pope said to me, "we must send you to Abidjan". That was difficult for me. But when I arrived [there], well, it is my country, my region, [but] politically, so much has changed. There was the coup d'état, then the war, but I was here in a milieu that I liked. There were many intellectual people and many hard-working people ... my diocese was partly urban and partly rural, so I was inside both and I liked that. I was also happy with my ministers, for twenty-four years. When I was first in Abidjan, I moved to Man, then to Yamoussoukro. I was the founder of the diocese of Man. I was also the one who founded the diocese of Yamoussoukro, then I came back to Abidjan. Man was different because it was a rural area, but I liked [it]. I spent twenty-four years there. When I went to Yamoussoukro, I also liked [it there]. In Yamoussoukro, there were more intellectual people. There was a school of engineering; there were lectures, students going to the university. I liked it there because I like to work with that kind of people, to help them.

In Yamoussoukro, I built three parishes. I had some projects for Yamoussoukro but only spent two and a half years there [before being] asked to move to Abidjan. I wasn't happy, but I moved. When I came to Abidjan there was a [tense] political situation ... it is the capital, so there was a lot of change. There was a coup d'état in 1999, then the war of 2002 happened while I was still the bishop ... But I was also happy to be there, because there were both urban areas and rural areas in the diocese. I helped them to work together. Now I am retired ... I work as much or maybe more than before, because I [have established] a foundation for education, health and development. In this foundation, I have many engineers around me. I have people who reflect and who try to change the country. I do a lot of work on health; for example, we [are promoting] a plant that is rich in protein, in iron, in vitamin C, vitamin A ... the moringa plant. Yesterday, I received, ten kilos of seeds, next week there will be another ten kilos of seeds and the week after, again ten kilograms; I am going to make 100 hectares [for harvesting] the leaves [and another] 100 hectares [for] the seeds.

It is to care for the population. I have land to grow corn to give to the people to eat. Corn [mixed] with the moringa is given to the animals.

[Which] of the projects you've been involved in excites you the most? What things do you feel most passionate about?
First of all, giving the word of God. That is a passion of mine. Because, all people need to come closer to God, either in Man, Yamoussoukro or Abidjan. That is my passion. I love God. I love people. When I teach people the word of God, people go to God and [they are] together. So for God, I give the word. People and God are like a triangle. When people go towards God, God sends men towards each other. If other people go together with God, they come together as human beings. If man is ready to go to God, then he is ready to go towards other human beings. You are not isolated; you are not alone. It is a social dimension of a human being.

Today, the entire world is [about] finance, the world of the economy. One of the causes of the crisis is putting God outside of the economical milieu and the financial milieu. They say that [when] God goes outside, it will be man against man. Those who are strong will kill those who are not strong. For me, it is important to put God between man and man. God will help men see the human being in others. That is the reason why I became a priest, if God is not my passion, it is a lie. My second passion is human beings.

So, you have seen the communication that I have had with you. That is because of God. Otherwise, I have other things to do. I could have said, "Go away. I have other things to do. I don't want to speak to you. But because of my passion for God, I told [you], like [I would tell my] my little sister or my daughter, "here you go, we are communicating".

Can I ask, which aspects of your work do you dislike?
What I don't like, I don't do ... But I like everything I do. I learn a lot. It is passion. I like praying, reading, writing and human relationships. Those I like. But what I don't like I don't do.

A short while ago, the man with whom I had a meeting was a Muslim. I had a rapport with him. He is a trader. I need him to get the moringa seeds. He is Senegalese. He ordered in Senegal, yesterday, ten kilos of seeds of this morning; I paid him. I told him, next week, [I will order] another ten kilos, making ten times ten kilos; I am going to help the people of my home, the children who are not well nourished [because] there is no milk. This plant is a solution [to] infant mortality. I put a lot in Cote d'Ivoire. That is my goal.

Can I ask about Vatican II and how it is changed the church in the Ivory Coast?

Vatican II had wanted to simplify certain things. Some priests and bishops, headed by Archbishop Lefebvre, members of the Society of St Pius X, have rejected the way of saying Mass since Vatican II.[154] It was a difficult beginning; such men refused to move from Latin. That kind of resistance was difficult for the faithful and for the church as well. It existed here as well. I spoke French and found it difficult to translate the Mass into another language.

You have written that you studied in Rome. Apart from the religious and theological lessons that came from that, what else did you gain from that international experience?

There were many experiences. When I were there in 1957-60, we lived a residence of 120 students [including] 80 Anglophones, so we were practically forced to speak English in the refectory, because we had to change tables regularly. It forced us to get along with the

---

154 Marcel Lefebvre was Superior General of the Spiritans (Holy Ghost Fathers), and following Vatican II formed the Society of St Pius X, a conservative movement that defended the Tridentine Mass, along with pious practices, beliefs, customs and religious discipline often associated with the period before Vatican II. Pope Benedict XVI lifted the automatic excommunication it had incurred when Archbishop Lefebvre consecrated four bishops in 1988 in defiance of Pope John Paul II while pointing out that the Society had no canonical status in the Catholic Church. Isichei, Op. Cit., p. 326.

Australians. I spoke with the Archbishop of Tokyo Shirayanagi (he is no longer living), for example. Of those who studied with me in Rome at St Pierre, five became cardinals. We knew each other well. We had Shirayanagi, we had Văn Thuân, from Vietnam, who worked in Rome and is there now. There was Arinze from Nigeria and Wamala from Uganda and me, so five cardinals from the same class. That was a lot. [It] opened my eyes to international affairs. The affairs of Cote d'Ivoire interest me, but the affairs of Vietnam also interested me very much, Japan as well, the US and Canada. In fact I made many voyages. Not yet to Australia, but to the Philippines, London. These trips were a result of my having studied in Rome, because Rome gave me English and Italian. The time there served me well. I also learned ... a little German, but German is a very difficult language, difficult and fluid.

My eyes gave me many opportunities to love everyone without distinction: To see that some Ivoirians are actually intelligent when I might have assumed them to be stupid, that some French people are also intelligent when I might previously have assumed that they were stupid. It puts things into perspective. You cannot say your culture is the centre of the world. You try to put in a kind of relativism among you and other people. So you learn to love people. That is very important. I learned more relativism towards culture and to like (to love) more people, to accept a person's good qualities and his weaknesses. Philippe, whom I met, an Australian, he was good like everyone. He told me that the entire world has something in common. That was the learning experience.

How you think the Church liberates women in Africa? Where I come from, the Church is seen as very patriarchal; I believe it is seen quite differently here ...

The Church does not [differentiate] between men and women. Unhappily, it didn't always go well. It is necessary from time to time to be reminded that women are the equal [of men]. That was the lesson that my mother gave me in childhood. She was very intelligent. I believe one of my friends had said something bad to a girl, the girl thought it was me and told my mother. It wasn't me, but my mother taught me a lesson. When I got home, she picked me up like a flower. And then she hit me on the buttocks and I cried a lot. I cried because I thought it was unjust that she hit me. I loved my mother. I cried a lot. After, she sat next to me; she told me "do you understand? You [must] respect me." I said "yes, mother, I respect you. I love you and I respect you."[She said] "you see, the young women, when you see them, it is me. The way you respect me is the way you must respect them. The older woman, when you see them, it is me, too. The way you respect me must be the way you respect them." ... All my life. I have respected young women, ... old women ... I learned that fundamentally, from my mother and she was very Christian. There was promotion [of girls] at school ... [and also] at the Mass ... I think for me, the Church did a lot [and] for girls at school. [They taught us] that women are equal to men. There are women religious, who do work, like the priests. Human [equality] and the training of women were launched at church, in schools, at meetings. In the Catholic movement, it is that. [It is very strong] in the Cote d'Ivoire.

... It is the business of the Church. What my mom said, it is applied to you also when you came. "Why would you want to let [her] go like that? She made the voyage to meet you. You must respect [her]. She is also your mom." ... And I continue to pray for you, what you are doing for your soul, for your work, for everything for you in your life. It is very important. I am available for you; I am available for everyone. I don't know what you want to do with this interview, but even after we finish here, I am available for you. If you don't finish this time, I am still available.

Yesterday evening, I was with an agricultural engineer. He came to see me here and we discussed agriculture, how to do cloning, etc. He said to me, "Eminence, they tell me that you are a theologian.

How is it that you know so much about agronomy? Did you study agronomy?" I told him that I studied at the school of agronomy, in fact [because] it interests me! So, I read many books on the economy, on finance, that interests me [too] because everything cultural is good for me ... the work that [the engineer does] interests me. I wish I could read what you are doing, especially because you came here.

Billy and the novices after soccer at the Jesuit Seminary in Bamfoussam, Cameroon

8 i. CAMEROON

The Republic of Cameroon lies in the central West Africa region. It is bordered by Nigeria in the west, Chad and the Central African Republic in the East, Equatorial Guinea, Gabon, and Congo in the south. Cameroon has a population of 20,549,221. Unlike other African nations mentioned here, the country is divided roughly in half between those with indigenous beliefs (40 per cent) and Christians (also 40 per cent). Twenty per cent are Muslim. The country is officially half French and half English, and most people live to about 55 years of age. Seventy-six per cent of people over the age of 15 can read and write. On average, children complete ten years of formal schooling. Most women have four children (16 per cent of children under the age of five are underweight) and in 2010 5.3 per cent of the population over the age of 15 years (610,000 people) were infected with HIV, and 54,000 children.[155] GDP sits at 25.2 billion USD (2010), and population density at 41 people per square kilometre (2010). Because of its modest oil resources and favourable agricultural conditions, Cameroon has one of the best-endowed primary commodity economies in sub-Saharan Africa, though corruptive practices continue to act as a deterrent to foreign investment.[156]

Prior to independence the area now known as Cameroon had been inhabited by the Sao Civilisation and the Baka hunter gathers in the south. The Portuguese reached the coast in the 15th century. The Fulani created the Adamawa Empire (Muslim) in the north in

---

155 https://www.cia.gov/library/publications/the-world-factbook/geos/cm.html, accessed 16 May 2013. For HIV statistics see footnote 13.
156

the 19th century, and various ethnic groups of the west and north-west founded powerful chiefdoms and fondoms. From 1884 Cameroon was a German colony until after World War I when it was divided between France and Britain as a League of Nations mandate. France integrated the economy of Cameroun with that of France and improved the infrastructure of its territory using capital investments, skilled workers, and continued forced labour. The British administered their territory from neighboring Nigeria which roused complaints from their indigenous citizens that they had been neglected. In 1960, the French-administered part of Cameroon became independent before the southern British part, which merged with it in 1961 after considering a merger with Nigeria. The country was renamed the United Republic of Cameroon in 1972 and the Republic of Cameroon in 1984.[157]

Since 1982 the nation has been governed by a multi-party presidential regime under the leadership of its authoritarian president Paul Biya. It enjoys relatively high political and social stability (which has led to the development of agriculture, roads, railways, and large petroleum and timber industries), though large numbers of people still live as subsistence farmers. Divisions between the English and French speaking territories of Cameroon continue to exist, as dissatisfaction with endemic government corruption grows.

Christian Wiyghan Cardinal Tumi was born on 15 October 1930 in Kikaikelaki, a small village in the Nso klan, situated in the northwest region of Cameroon. Tumi was ordained a priest in 1966 and served as a vicar in Soppo for a year in 1967, before becoming a professor at Bishop Rogan College's seminary. Tumi trained as a teacher in Nigeria and then in London between 1969 and 1973, before earning a licentiate in theology in Lyon, and a doctorate in philosophy at the University of Fribourg, Switzerland in 1979. He returned to his diocese and became rector of the seminary in Bambui in 1979 before being elected the

---

157 DeLancey, Mark W., and Mark Dike DeLancey (2000): *Historical Dictionary of the Republic of Cameroon* (3rd ed.). Lanham, Maryland: The Scarecrow Press.

first bishop of the diocese of Yagoua, and then archbishop in 1984. The following year he was elected president of the National Episcopal Conference of Cameroon before being named Cardinal-Priest of Santi Martiri dell'Uganda a Poggio Ameno in 1988, and then Archbishop of Douala in 1991. Tumi also participated in the 2005 papal conclave.

I met Cardinal Tumi after driving eight hours in two directions to find him in central Cameroon. We met at his diocese in Douala, next to the city's great Cathedral in September 2012.

Sunday school, Bamfoussam, Cameroon

ii. Courage

So is that it then? Does it end with "enlightenment"? Yesterday I was an atheist; will tomorrow I be a believer? How much of my identity do I need to discard before I strike upon some part more worthy? And how much should I appropriate? I could find a convict in my past, better still an Aboriginal, to undermine the disgrace of my white fortune. But there is nothing of use to me here in Africa, bar the crystal clear outline of my own reflection in the black eyes that have spoken to me ...

There were still three conversations to be had, two in Cameroon, and the last back in Rome with the legendary Monsengwo. Billy and I were on the last phase of our journey, comfortably surrounded by the apparently nonsensical chaos of Western Africa, in Cameroon, "little Africa", surrounded by roadsides of Mazda 323 parts and trucks carting sand to the edge of the sea, and entire families loaded onto motorbikes with only plastic bags protecting them from the oncoming rain.

Billy and I drove in a 323 in Cameroon in our search for Cardinal Tumi. He is a big man, probably almost two metres tall, and he speaks with the deepest and most perfect Oxford English, enunciating each syllable as he speaks so that his mouth forms wonderfully slow and carefully considered shapes below his nose. And he, like the others, wore a soutane, black this time with black buttons, almost severe though its severity was softened by the quality of his voice, the gentle way that he met me at the door. I had learned something about him earlier, in Abidjan, from a Cameroonian Jesuit who had challenged government corruption and been moved from the country to save his life. He told me Tumi had taken them on. Yes. Tumi was a big man, he said. And so he was.

Comfortably large and strong and clear eyed he told me about government corruption, and the extermination of the government's opponents, and the actions that he personally took to demonstrate against the government's extremes. He told me about his work in justice and truth, in schools, in society, in politics. He was the man his parishioners would have had as president, had he been willing. He is a man of great integrity, of courage and strength, and also a man with a sense of humour. Billy and I drove one of those Mazda 323s for eight hours from Douala to find him in the forests surrounding Bamfoussam, but he took off before we got there – to see his mother. What man in his eighties still has a mother? Cardinal Tumi's mother is the oldest woman in the country ...

Leaving the city we crossed a huge body of water speckled with sunlight and topless men paddling wide canoes that were loaded with sand on route to ships that would transport palm oil, sand, and wood to Nigeria. A big pink bus, over loaded with passengers, overtook us just outside of the city. Ironically it was called "The Vatican Express". There were suffocating diesel fumes, chaos on roads without markings, no traffic lights and apparently no rules. Indicators were just a hand – waving left or right. At the market, boys and girls sat separately, the girls in beautifully printed clothes and with scarves to match. Half a cow travelled by, on the back of a motorbike, and trucks were lined up on the road side, their trays filled with the same sand brought by canoe. On the right, bags of corn chaff were being sold for pigs to eat. Industrial activity flanked the left. People were busy working. As the rain fell more solidly the road dissembled into pools of mud. People and cars picked their way through. Others jogged.

Toward Bamfoussam the world became instantly lush. Villages filled with small and sturdy dwellings made of bricks, and a huge rubber plantation rose up out of the trees. There was another village, with an "institution de beauty" – a place to have your hair done in a shack by the side of the road. A truck loaded up with family and friends drove off towards farm work and its passengers waved to us with one hand while gripping the truck tray with the other. Huge avenues of electricity towers headed off into the distance, and then a train line that ran through the city and beyond.

We drove on to Mbanga, the next protectorate after Douala. The train there weaves its way south west to Kumbah then back to Douala, before heading towards the Northern provinces. There was a secondary school, and then mountains draped in glorious rainforest that rose in sharp peaks not too far away. It looked impossible to tame the mud. It oozed from the forest floor and out onto the wide road, sucking up around our sandaled feet and ankles when we took a break outside of the car. Suddenly another town appeared, and another market – it was quieter than the last – and fed by the banana plantations, and the acres of orchards (paw-paw, orange, pineapple ...). And the road which kept going up and into the endless forest ahead and as far as our eyes could see.

In every town we passed there was another church, with a tower and ringing bells that drew small groups of people out of the forest to pray. They emerged from tiny weather board homes with corrugated tin roofs and small square windows with plantation shutters. They peeked out from under the lush cover of the forest. Most of the homes were worn and weathered. They leant to one side, and were stained by the same red earth that lined the streets. Outside Mango a small herd of cattle with metre-long horns wandered down the road. We stopped at another small weatherboard shack (about two metres wide and one deep) that sat patiently on the road side; "garage moderne". There were coffee plantations near Nkongsamba, the first developed town of Cameroon, filling the air with the smell of rich beans, and everywhere children who played in the water that pooled beside the street.

A break in the downpour let us stop for coffee, water, biscuits, bananas. Peter (our driver) stocked up on cabbages and sweet yam from the small village stalls, casually tipping great buckets of both into the unlined boot of the car with a rumble. There was another clap of thunder and we jumped back into the car and began our climb into the mountains. Towering blue gums that lined the roadside climbed with us and sucked the water out of would-be swamps. Boys who made pocket money by filling the holes in the road with dirt for passers-by, cheered as we tossed coins onto the road for them to find. They danced and laughed wildly in the rain that was falling again in torrents and gathering in huge creamy puddles beside the road. Great slabs of mud slid down the mountains not too far away. Houses began to ooze their redness, their tin roofs glinting within the leafy drapes of forest when the sun poked its nose out from under the heavy clouds. The thunder kept rumbling alongside the flashes of lightening from which I ducked for cover inside the car.

    Like many African drivers, Peter drove like a maniac. He grabbed at the bitumen and took advantage of it greedily, heedless of both the wet weather and oncoming cars. His enthusiasm was bolstered by the Nigerian gospels that sang out from the car's battered stereo – a mass of wires between speakers balanced precariously front and back. Slowing to avoid pot holes in the dilapidated road beside Thomson's Night Club – "le repere du jazz" – a motorbike slammed into the taxi that had been tailgating us for miles. The motorcyclist fell into a cement drain before climbing shakily back to his feet. A woman with water on her head jumped off the road, screaming but not spilling a drop. The speakers and the gospel singers tumbled in with the vegies into the back, their voices rising in the drama, along with Billy's as he yelled expletives and grabbed for extra seat belts.

    Bamfoussam is a busy town, a bustling African space in the heart of Cameroon. It had once boasted an airport, now abandoned and peopled on its far side by a small village. We sought the Jesuit mission across the runway and found ourselves swallowed up by hungry forest and more mud. As we drove slowly, the sounds of misery rang through the hot, wet air and in our open windows. A corpse was being carried above a distraught group of mourners. Momentarily caught in the deep mud, our 323's wheels revved and spun beside the grievers, kicking dirt up at the group as we passed in fits and spurts before they broke free and allowed us us to escape our shame and head back along the run way and through the old airport gates.

Sometime in the following hour we found the Jesuit Mission hiding behind high walls and extensive gardens on a hill outside of Bamfoussam. The superior offered us beer and coca cola before gently telling us that the cardinal was gone. "He left to visit his mother in the south west." He told us, "You should meet him back in Douala." He said, "But first you will need to stay for the evening. At night the roads are littered with thieves."

There was laughter then, a kind of release of pent-up energy, a celebration of the "madness" and unpredictable character of Africa. We were relieved that the driving was over – for now. We passed the afternoon at the seminary, touring the flower-filled grounds and meeting the pigs, before playing soccer with the young men who had left their families to complete their two noviciate years. That night I would write about talking to Evariste (a novice who had come from the Ivory Coast) while watching my son play soccer with beautiful young men from nations right across the West. Outside, bells rang regularly to signal a change in the timetable. I took a cold shower and readied myself and my son for the evening meal.

The seminary had a refectory with seven ot eight circular tables. We sat with three others. One was 19 and from the Republic of Congo. One was 22 and from Chad. The last was 26 and from Burkina Fasso. They practised their English and shared vegetable soup, before couscous and a salty sardine stew. The end of the meal came suddenly. A rush of wooden chairs on the hard floor, out and then in again, before silence while the superior said the final grace. I took books, written by Cardinal Agré, to the superior for his library, and then sat horrified and embarrassed as the disgrace of Australia's Catholic paedophiles spread across international TV.

The air was filled with the sounds of insects at first night fall. The generators were switched off and it was pitch black in the room. There was no more TV, no internet, no phones. It was peaceful. Outside the soccer pitch gave off a sweet smell of grass. There were roosters coughing up a last crow before settling, and the sows, feeding piglets, were uttering their last sleepy grunt for the superior who scratched their noses lovingly before putting them to bed.

In the morning St Joseph's Cathedral in the town of Bamfoussam filled up with a thousand worshippers, the choir belting out African melodies, backed by the parishioners who clapped from their seats. The congregational response echoed deeply and sonorously between walls lined with the twelve Stations of the Cross with the characters represented by disciples with African features. On either side, a huge and beautiful crucifix towered above an African Mary hand-painted in traditional dress and looking up towards her African son, Jesus Christ. Outside the cathedral children of the congregation played, some were being watched or held by adults, while others were busy on the dusty sports field at the front of the Cathedral, playing as if their lives depended on it. Beyond the soccer field the beauty of Bamfoussam spread out across the valley and hills.

On our return journey there was the infamous African roadside check: police whistled us off the road because the Mazda's papers were out of order, and uniformed guards threatened to end our passage at gun point, before an inevitable contribution to their lunch bill (passed through the half-open window) saw us on our way. Arriving in Limbe we saw rehabilitated gorillas and chimpanzees, and the same massive industrial harbour that had taken possession of the sand brought first by canoe and then trucks. Then we went on to Seme Beach, lunch and more coca-cola, after a high-speed drive through endless palm forests. Water flowed in wide streams and great rivers, arriving from the mountains. In the shallows, and amidst more tall palms, taxi drivers drove straight into the river to wash their cars clean. There was another police block, though this time the officer recognised Peter from his community in Boya and they shook hands before he moved the block away.

A year earlier I would have felt frustrated by the Cardinal's spontaneity. I would have seen it as an enormous inconvenience and an interruption to the achievement of my end goal. But then I saw his decision to leave as a great gift. He had dragged me deep into the heart of his country and forced me to stay overnight in a space that had filled me with peace. The complexities and dramas of African (at least West African) life had played out in front of us as if summing up a year of virgin experiences in one final fanfare; the paddlers, the markets, the cattle, the cars and the pot-holed roads, the miserable and haunting funeral in a dark heart of forest edged by a plundered airport, the beauty of the seminary that carved order, peace, and curiosity out of the apparently troubled chaos beyond its walls and that offered us refuge, the great cathedral crammed full with parishioners, the police blocks, the beaches, the families.

It took three more days to meet the Cardinal but we filled in our time well. The archbishop's drivers took us to their local markets and helped us shop for dresses for my daughters and material to take home. We drank coffee together and walked through the river that flooded the street stalls, me with my only clean sarong pulled up at the waist, they with their finely tailored trousers pulled up to their knee caps and with leather shoes slung across their shoulders, laughing at Billy as water dripped from his nostrils. I bought each of us an umbrella and we ran between leaking, hessian bag-covered walkways. During those days the archbishop's secretary gave me his papers on Vatican II, and organised a meeting with the archbishop in case the Cardinal did not arrive. And in the final evening's twilight, while I waited for Tumi to come back to Douala, I sat in the gentle rain at a hand-built pebble-clad shrine to Mary Magdalene outside that beautiful cathedral, and I said my first prayer.

iii. Christian Wiyghan Cardinal Tumi, Archbishop Emeritus Douala, Cameroon
(October 2011)

Your Eminence, could you tell me a little bit about the Church in Cameroon?
Of course. I was made a bishop of all the Church in Cameroon. The early missionaries came from Germany in 1894 . The first Catholic missionaries came from Germany I think in 1894 and they settled their first missionary activity in Marianburg, which is now in the diocese of Edéa. [It] has been declared a centre for national pilgrimages, because we consider it to be the birth place of the Catholic Church in Cameroon. Of course they didn't know how to speak German at that time, so the mission did not last long, and then because of the First World War they had to leave the country, and again with the Second World War. So, then various missionaries came in and in the English-speaking part of the country the Marianne Fathers came in 1922.

On this side of the country (French-Speaking) it was the Holy Ghost Fathers. After the Germans (who were called the Palatine Fathers), the Marian Fathers came and they went to the hinterland, that is to Yaoundé. Germans were already settled here and German missionaries too. The Protestant missionaries came earlier to Cameroon, more than 40 years before the Catholic missionaries came in. The only difference between them was that the Protestants went in for the elite. We went in for the population and that is why today the number of Catholics is far bigger in Cameroon than the number of Protestants. Yes I think the Catholics are currently at approximately 35 per cent, the Protestants about 25 per cent and Muslims about 15 per cent of the population. So the Church is young in Cameroon. And quite a number of dioceses are now preparing for the celebration of 100 years of existence as the Catholic church on the 25th of January [2013]. The national celebrations have taken place already, in Marianburg. About 25 years ago, we celebrated [the 75th anniversary] too, but now we are a centenary church.

When the missionaries came their first object was to build a local church. The Marian Fathers from England did not recruit young people into their congregation or their society, they preferred to form the local clergy before beginning to encourage other younger people to enter into the society. Now they have Cameroonian Marian Fathers. They have started coming in. So in the English-speaking part of the country there were not many missionaries and not many congregations, whereas in the French speaking part there were many. The Holy Ghost Fathers, the Jesuits, the Xavarians were here. So now they look for the local clergy which is growing by leaps and bounds. All of the seminaries are almost full. We cannot take all of the young people who want to become priests. So we have to discern very carefully. But the majority of the bishops are Cameroonian. There are now three European bishops out of a total of 24.

Yes I have heard that number before, 24 yes.
Out of 24 and quite a lot of them don't feel at ease but we try to tell them that the Church is one. They would like to hang around near to Cameroon, so.

You know the Church's history and [its] political history is a history of evangelisation. And every Catholic Christian should feel at home, everywhere in the world, in any Christian community in the world.

Do you think evangelisation has made an impact here?
Well, we are the fruits of evangelisation. It has made an impact with many Christians, and many Christian families. I am not saying they will have no downfalls. But I am saying that they are living the Christian life as it should be. The matter of faith is an on-going formation; you

know you have to pray every day that the Lord should increase our faith. A Christian cannot reach a point and say, "Now I've had it!" There is always need for more. So there is no doubt that the Church is established in Cameroon, there is no doubt about that. But we still need missionaries. Yes, we still need missionaries. The whole Church is missionary so the missionaries are still welcome. Even though we have enough local priests, diocesan priests, missionaries still have their place.

And do they still come?

Yes they came.

For example, I was in Kumba where a part of a congregation is coming on Saturday, [they will be] in Kumba in a matter of days ... they still are coming. And I will receive, the archbishop receives, quite a number of congregations in this diocese.

Where do the missionaries come from mostly?

Most of them come from Italy now.

Oh Italy, not France?

No not France. There are a very, very few from Lichtenstein. There are very few vocations now. The countryside [hosts] quite a number of missionaries, principally from Italy. Other congregations have recruited from Asia – India. The missionaries come from India through European congregations that have many Asian priests [among them]. For example, we have also Sisters of St Anne here and the majority of them are from India, but their mother house is in Italy.

I think the majority of their sisters are Italians. There is a local congregation. Now I think the majority of them are Cameroonians. But their mother house is in Italy. It was founded there and they came to Europe. There are few vocations [in the West] now, so quite a number of their vocations come from Asia, from India and Africa.

Why do you think that is happening?

I think it is generally due to the situation of the Church in Europe and America. The Pope said once, "Where the faith is, [even] where the faithful are tired, we are still a youthful Church". The majority of our Christians are young people. The Church is still active. It is not as I told you some moments ago that we are barely celebrating our centenaries. Whereas in [Europe] they are celebrating a millennium Christianity, you know? And so one can understand. But I have always been very surprised when I have taken part, happily surprised [to see that there are] youth riding with the Pope.

In Italy or here?

In Europe.

Mmm, they love the Pope?

He is not as dramatic as many tend to portray him. That is my impression. It is true that the practice is different in a formal sense, but you know, I think they want us to practise Christianity in another way. I met a German man of middle age, he was in his 50s, and he told me that his children practise more than him [as a means of protest] against their parents! [laughs] You know I was surprised to hear that the children practise more.

So it is still alive but in a different, perhaps a less measurable way?

Yes, you know I always say the Church is of divine foundation. It is the church of God, you know? And Christ has said, "I will be with you until the end of time." So the Church continues all around the world. Now there are some missionaries from Africa who are going to Europe and to America. Quite a number of African sisters and priests are going to Europe.

Are they successful there?
Quite a number have studied there. You know, quite a number. Of course whether in Europe or in Africa we do the same studies as far as intellectual information is concerned because it is the central church that directs the formation of young priests, so it is all the same [training] that they receive; the same demands. We tend to be stricter here because quite a number are from non-Christian families, you know; quite a number of those who want to become priests were baptised as adults. But more and more now are coming from Christian families that have already had the Christian tradition set in place.

So if they come from a non-Christian family how does that make things different?
It makes it different because the fundamental Christian exercises are spontaneous with a Christian child. Sometimes [the others] don't even make the sign of the cross. They don't know how to do it ... Quite a number have not had this early formation in the family because they were not born into a Christian family ... Some were [born] into paganism, [grew up with] pagan practices, and so on. I met some missionaries and Patrick Fathers from Ireland, I met them in northern Nigeria, and they told me that they now see a difference between priests. The early priests were not from Christian families and the priests today who come from Christian families.

What's the difference?
The difference is that those who come from pagan families tend to fall back to paganism when they reach a crisis. They are more influenced by pagan practices [than by Church ones]. I was born to parents who were already Catholics. I have never participated in a pagan sacrifice. I grew up in the Catholic school, as did my parents and so forth. But those that do not have this spontaneously [to] want to pray to God, to

our Lord Jesus Christ, [but] are spontaneously pagan, ... they want to go back to a traditional interpretation of the rites.

Are they more likely to tolerate syncretism in the Church do you think?

Not syncretism. [It is better to speak of enculturation]. There are some of us who do not really know our culture. For example, those of us who grew up at a time when missionaries were cut off from the pagan environment; there were Christian villages where other Christians lived. If you saw a Christian child with a pagan child, well there would be some sort of punishment ...

But it is not like that anymore.

No.

Now there's a combination of culture and Christianity.

Now they co-habit. People live together.

Quite happily?

Yes. That is why there are quite a number of problems. Pagans tend to have more influence on Christians than Christians [have] on pagans.

Is that because there is an ethnic connection?

I think it is because their faith is not solid. There are many who still live in fear. When one lives in fear one tends to go towards a traditional way of dealing with a problem you know, [like] witchcraft, and they still believe in witchcraft.

The pagan religion is not systematised. Today in Cameroon it is difficult to know who is a pagan.

Yes I have heard it said that it's hard to tell between a Christian and a non-Christian in Cameroon.

Yes. It is still hard to tell now. When we were kids, those who were preparing to be baptised did not bear Christian names. You were only given a Christian name the day of your baptism. So you could recognise those Catholics who came from paganism. But today everybody is John, Mary [or] Peter so you don't know who is baptised and who is not.

That's the situation today.

Are there other things that make it difficult to tell between a Christian and a non-Christian?

No you cannot say, you cannot say. It is difficult to know. In the area from where I came, often non-Christians did not wear clothes, and now everybody does. And when somebody did something stupid [laughs] he was told that he was acting like a pagan.

There's no doubt that the very fact of learning catechism was a kind of intellectual formation; the very fact that they had studied. There was much theology, so to say, even though we did not understand what they were saying. For example, can you imagine that in primary school we had to learn the definition of 'god'. God is a supreme spirit who alone exists of himself and is infinite in all perfections. We did not understand what that means! The students were studying metaphysics. That is the metaphysical definition of God: A *supreme spirit* who alone *exists* of himself and is *infinite* in *all perfections*.

As a child you are already being lifted up to a more sophisticated level of education than someone who has studied nothing. You begin to question. You want to know the answer.

Yes, yes. And also, the first schools in Cameroon were Christian schools and those who were not Christians were hesitant to go to those schools because there were afraid of being converted. They thought they would be converted by force.

... the first college in this country was St Joseph's College, Boya, founded by the Marian Fathers, but everyone went there ... [inc;uding] Muslims ... it was the first catholic university for central Africa. So when it comes to education we do not make any distinction, so everybody goes, you know and so ...

Is the church still highly involved in education and health here?
Yeah, yeah.

And working with the government.
Yes. We cannot open a school here without the authorisation of the government. Yes the government gives the authorisation. Upper level primary, secondary and university ... the government has to give permission. It doesn't help us financially, the parents pay the fees. [Well] the government gives some help but it cannot go very far. But parents pay fees. And that's why in rural areas there's a problem, where quite a number of parents can't pay fees. But there are some scholarship foundations to help so that a child who can't study in the university but should study [will not miss the opportunity just] because he has no means.

Do you have an active program for girls as well?
Oh girls, yes, yes. Especially girls, they are probably the majority at school now. Oh yes, yes. There is a Catholic country school in my village and the majority of the students are girls. There is quite a number. It is difficult now to find a child of school-going age that stays at home. I think the majority of children go to school now. Except in the northern part of the country, this is very much influenced by Islam. Yes, you know. But there are girls now that come and go into colleges and universities.

The 50 year anniversary of Vatican II is coming up and I would like to know how you would assess the impact of Vatican II on the church of Cameroon?

Oh! Vatican II was a revolution for our local Church. Many things changed. I am a priest of Vatican II. I was ordained in 1966. I was a seminarian in Nigeria. I studied in Nigeria. Things changed after Vatican II; for example, the participation of the laity in the life of the Church. Before then the laity were only onlookers. In the English-speaking part of the country we had a bishop, a Dutch bishop, who was very dynamic and he took part in Vatican II. When he came he had the first congress, we call it a convention, [of] representatives of all the parishes in this diocese, and he explained what Vatican II meant, what it meant for the Church now and so on, and it was with him that we started parish councils. He started parish councils. Where every three years there was this convention to evaluate and to make a program. And in now in quite a number of parishes the priest works with the laity, and a priest who does not work with the laity today is not a good pastor I think. Now in almost all our parishes we have two councils: the financial council and the pastoral council. And the laity of course they are in the majority of seats on those councils and we listen to them.

Is the Church in Cameroon very clerical?

It was clerical. That is in the sense that the priest decided everything. We cannot say today that it is so clerical. Why? Because they decide with the laity. [In] this diocese almost every precedent of the economic council of the parish is proposed by the laity. They all follow the directives, and the policy of the diocese. There are far many more lay Christians who know how to run financial institutions, than priests or bishops. Yes, they are professionals. During the missionary era there were no professionals. Like people building all these churches now, some of them are lay people because they are engineers. At the time the missionaries came here there were no engineers. So today, after Vatican II, the laity is very involved in the life of the Church.

Seeing as though we are talking about the laity, I wanted to ask you about the election of the bishops. Currently the elections of the bishops are finalised by Rome as a result of the Nuncio's list of suggestions generally speaking. But do you think nominations for bishop should perhaps be elected by the laity within each diocese?

Well what is the situation now? The situation now is this. Every conference in the world every three years sends its list of names of priests who can become bishops tomorrow. Then Rome looks at the lists of priests that we have been sending them every three years and they select always three names, and then they begin an inquiry – that is to say a questionnaire is sent to bishops, to some priests, and to the lay people.

Is that everywhere or just in Cameroon?

In Cameroon. Sometimes I sense that a bishop may not have been appointed because of intermission of a lay man or lay woman. I know one case where that happened. It is not just like democracy or anything, but today the bishops are consulted, the priests are consulted, and the lay people are consulted too. And if they send you the questionnaire the last question is always whether you know somebody who knows the candidate. And if you know somebody who knows the candidate then you write to the Nuncio with the person's address so that the questionnaire can also be sent to him or her.

Yes, today is not just only the bishops, no. It is not like the formal process in the history of the Church where it was a popular vote [inside the Church]. Now they consult quite a number of lay people.

Do you think that it happens in other countries in West Africa too?

I think so ... I was as cardinal a member of the study of documents concerning their election of the bishops in Rome. So what happens is that the documents are collected when they send the questionnaire to Cameroon. You have to send it back between it and without discussing it with anybody, and you must only say what you know yourself about the candidate. No inquiry. Just what you think of now. They only want to know your own opinion. There are cases where I have to say that I don't know the person, full stop. Usually when the Nuncio has collected all those replies to the questionnaire then he sends them to Rome. And the cardinals, for example who are in mission territory (our congregation is Propaganda Fide that is the congregation for the evangelisation of peoples) then that cardinal studies the three cases and then a meeting is formed for two cardinals to say yes. And then the cardinal who had studied it in detail gives his preferences [for] who [should be] first, second and third. Then the cardinals who are there are to study and give their opinion. And then they re-arrange and [it is] all sent again to the Holy Father. It is he who decides. There are many people involved.

Do you think there should be similar consultation with the election of a pope? Do you think perhaps the heads of Bishops Conferences around the world should be involved in electing the pope? (Pope Paul VI, for example, seriously thought of adding at least some of the presidents of the Bishops' Conferences to the Conclave that elects the pope). And do you think that that would have been a good idea in terms of achieving better representation for the global south within the Vatican?

Frankly I do not see its importance. I took part in the election of Benedict. And do you know how it came to be that only cardinals take part? The Pope doesn't have to have been a cardinal. You can elect a layman. Wherever he is in the world we can ring him and ask him, "Do you accept? To be the bishop of Rome?" [laughter] And if he says, "Yes", then they ordain him a priest, and then a bishop of Rome.

So that's the law of the Church. But the Canon Law does not say that the pope has to have been a cardinal. No it doesn't say that. And that is why formerly the pope was elected by the parish priests of the diocese of Rome. Yes. And that is why every cardinal has a parish in Rome, to fulfil the legal requirements.

Once you have become a cardinal you have a parish in Rome you are a sort of canonical parish priest but they say parish priest, effectively parish priest there. That's why every cardinal has to be a priest of the see of the dioceses of Rome. And the head of the parish should legitimately take part in the election of the pope because he was already elected by parish priests. Because he is first and foremost the bishop of Rome, before being head of the Church.

Do you think the global south is adequately represented in the Vatican?

Today, yes.

Today far more than formerly when it was just Italians there. Today, today you have us there, the Africans who are heading the congregations. Cardinal Arinze for example, he is now in retirement, there are those like him who are heading what you can call the civil society ministries, the services now are more international than formerly, far more.

Somebody said, some of the cardinals I have interviewed said that there haven't been as many cardinals appointed in Africa because the Church in some parts hasn't reached a certain level of sophistication in those parts, I think Cardinal Turkson said that and Cardinal Agré.

Oh [well], I agree there with him. We are a very young Church. There are many countries in Europe that have no cardinals and they are millennium churches. And by the way, you know, I accept that Christ did not institute the [cardinalate]. This is an ecclesial institution because a lay person can be a cardinal, a priest can be a cardinal without being a bishop, cardinals as well and bishops. There are cases where there isn't time for a priest to be appointed a bishop first, but in my case I was appointed cardinal when I was already archbishop. There are cases in recent times. I remember one cardinal said that he didn't want to become a bishop. And the Pope granted him [that right].

Why would he not want to be a bishop?

I don't know. He wanted to just be a figurehead. But he had no diocese, it was just a title.

You have been described as being outspoken in politics and critical of government decision making. Would you agree with that description?

Well, I express my opinion. I think I have been outspoken on certain issues.

What are the issues you feel most passionate about?

Political, socio-economic [issues], during my time as president of a Church conference of Cameroon I produced a document in 1990 on the economic crisis in Cameroon. From that time onwards they thought I was very outspoken – they thought I was the one who spearheaded the bishops. I proposed to the bishops, and they accepted, that we produce a document on economics.[158]

Did it have an impact?

Yes I think so.

Did it cause change in the government?

---

158 It has often be suggested that Tumi would be an excellent choice for president. Ongey, Grace. "Cardinal Tumi has never been interested becoming President of Cameroon, Archbishop Emeritus reaffirms." *L'Effort Camerounais,* August 2009, accessed 8 October 2012.

[Well] you know I think the people were waiting to hear what the bishops would say. They know that the bishops' conference is the only institution that can speak without fear. People here are afraid to say what they think.

What are they afraid of?
That they could be eliminated.

Really?
Yes, yes. There have been cases. They could be eliminated. There [have been] cases in the last 40 years about 300 priests have been assassinated in Africa.

Priests
Yes. Priests.

For speaking out?
For speaking out.

Against corruption?
Against evil practices, corruption and all of those. For myself, no, I say what I think.

Have you ever been afraid for your life?
No. No, I have not been afraid no ... but wherever I am preaching there are security people there. I am worried that where I am preaching the people I am preaching to are scared. They think that I do not like the president. I like him. Only if I see him, I tell him what I think. I tell him, "I am your senior brother." As his senior brother he has to listen. [laughs]

My real problems with the government started when I was first a priest.

How did that start up? Can you tell me about it?

Yes when I was the founding rector of the men's seminary in Barmenda, the archbishop told me to found a movement, an ecumenical movement, of those lay people who have done some post-secondary education to try to analyse how the gospel can influence our society. And no sooner had we started that group, than the bishops of Boya and Barmenda produced a letter on corruption in 1975. So we took it up [clicks his fingers] and shattered the government [laughs]. I was the president and the governor of Barmenda, who in the meantime became my good friend, called us to his office. We were with him for three hours. He told us that he had an order from [Leonda] to arrest us. He told [Leonda] that he doesn't think that it was subversion. That is the Anglo-Saxon style. So I was the one who told the governor, *"You do not criticise somebody you don't love! When you criticise it is because you want a person to change for the good!"* That was the time it started. And Ahidjo had a style of doing things. He wanted to disband our group. One of us was appointed a [government] minister so that way closed him up. He changed his language.

Was it a bishop who was appointed minister?

No, no, he was a Protestant. He died lately. And a security man came to me and told me that I would be the next person to live in the north-west. I told him that the government has no power over me. My bishop cannot transfer me away from Barmenda without my consent. If he is negotiating with other bishops sometimes, I must agree. Two weeks later I was appointed bishop in the north. [Laughs] So he said, "See I told you!" And I took my car and I went down to Leonda to see the Nuncio to ask him just one question: "Had the government anything to do with my appointment as bishop?" The Nuncio said, "Not at all." Because, you see, they have no agreement with the government. The agreement in Cameroon is that when they appoint a priest a bishop the government is informed, as the president of the country is informed, two days before it is published in Rome. And in my case, the Nuncio sent the information to the Ministry of International Relations and due to their slowness the president did not get the information – though he heard my appointment over the radio. He was not happy about it.

I bet. But it was too late.

So that's how my problems started. I go to the Yagoua.[159] They wanted to force some Christians and Protestants to become Muslims and I wrote a strong pastoral letter against that. The governor came and then he had to see me in Yagoua.

In the meantime I was transferred from Yagoua to Gawa. They were forcing Christians to become Muslims and so I wrote. So that is why they say that I was causing problems.

What about social issues. You have also being very involved in social issues, social justice issues?

Oh yes, social justice issues. In Cameroon every diocese has a Justice and Peace Committee.

Did you set that up?

Yes.

You created that?

In large part, yes. In Cameroon every diocese has a Justice and Peace Committee. I set it up and that's the thing they are saying. People were being maltreated and so we set up our Justice and Peace Committee, which met together to discuss instances of abuse. So I would write a letter to the governor and I would tell them that if they do not check out what is going on and deal with it appropriately then I will publish the letter.

---

159 Yagoua is in the extreme north of the country.

So then they checked it?

Yes. So the general was moved from here. Yes, so that's what happened.

And that system is still functioning? People can still come to that committee and say there is a problem and receive support?

Yes, exactly.

And do they come?

They do.

And they get help?

They do. And quite a number of the members of the committee are lawyers.

Yes Christians and lay people and they provide the legal representation.

Is there ethnic conflict in Cameroon?

This is a difficult question to answer.

Sorry

Yes I think [that] I already said there are tribal differences. People love the area from where they come to an exaggerated degree, and the tendency is to exclude those who are not from that area. But in our schools children are not aware of that. They have [intersecting] friendships, Especially now there are mixed marriages.

Mixed in terms of mixed ethnic groups?

Inter-tribal marriages. There are also mixed marriages between Christians. But inter-tribal marriage is very easy. Take my sisters, they are not married in my tribe. They were married to people who were not from my tribe. Their children are also my nieces. One day they will go to university to study together and then they will decide. My sister told us that she is only looking for advice. Her decision is her own. So that is what my junior sister told my parents and I told my parents she is right. So I presided over the marriage.

Yes. So it is with the youth. A Bassa girl killed herself because her parents did not want her to marry a boy who was not Bassa.[160] She over-reacted, she killed herself. She loved the boy so much.

Are the clergy divided on ethnic lines at all?
No. They do not show it. Take for example many countries where they appoint the bishop. A bishop ordained just a few months ago comes from one of the tribes. He was welcomed. But what has happened in the peoples' heart, don't ask me. That I don't know. There was celebration, and, by the way, many of us bishops in Cameroon are not in our diocese of origin. The archbishop here is from Yagoua. Ours is from Kumbu. The archbishop from Yaoundé is here. Very few are from their diocese of origin.

I wondered if religions like Catholicism can link people across tribal lines and across borders to ease some of the conflict that occurs in Africa. I wondered if the Church was aiming finding a communion in believers trying to bring people together.
In Cameroon we have about 240 tribes and yes it is.

Is it working? Is it possible?
I think it is possible because the faithful do not mind where a priest comes from on the condition that he does his work well. Nobody cares from where you come from if you are a person who works well as a priest or as a bishop. But if you do not do your work they begin to look at the small differences. But the priest who does his own work well is welcome.

---

160 Bassa, also spelled Basa or Basaa are a Bantu ethnic group in Cameroon.

Do priests in Cameroon rely on the input of women a great deal?

Women dominate in the Church! [laughs] The biggest association in this diocese is the association of women. It is, ah, called the Catholic Women's' Association, this is internationally recognised, yes.

So it is quite a powerful body.

And they are thoroughly active in the Church.

Can they influence decision making?

It depends on what [it's about]. What is the policy of the bishop and what is his council's general policy. But when it comes to the execution of that policy, the Catholic Women's Association (I was their chaplain when I was a priest) play a large part in their decision. But the decision can only be at the parish level of which they are member. There are cases here where women are presidents of the parish council. And that happens yes. Women are presidents of the parish council.

Is there a resistance to democracy both inside and outside the Church in Cameroon?

I think the Church is more democratic than society itself. Because, like I say, at the parish councils everything is decided by election, separate ballot, you know. When I was the archbishop here I had to make sure every tribal group was represented. I said, "Right, [we need] someone from this tribe; we [must] elect somebody otherwise the same people would be there all the time." So we give them three years. And you are able to vote only once. And then the people, they elect another person they like. Some people are so influential they like power. They would remain there till the end of the world!

Yes and they will fight to the death! So we had to regularise it to make sure that there were some regular rules to be followed.

Is there a resistance to democracy outside of the Church in society here?

In society and many who are in power don't like to give it up because power in Africa is money. They wield the money of the state. You know, in Cameroon we are fighting corruption, you know, embezzlement – there are some ministers who are now in prison. One minister was sentenced yesterday to 25 years imprisonment. Yes, yesterday, 25 years in prison and he was a general of the president. They gave him $30 million to buy a presidential plane, but he didn't buy the plane and the money is no longer there.

So the lawyers are still able to prosecute him? The lawyers are not controlled by the president?

I think the lawyers have assisted in the trial and I admire the way they went about it. There was a friend of mine, another minister who is now in prison. When he was on trial I went there, and they said that I support criminals, that I don't really care. Actually I went there and I was admiring the judges, you know, because when they ask the criminal a question they gave him time to consult his lawyers. So he said, "Okay, I will not answer that question. I will consult my lawyers." I was very impressed. And they went slowly, you know? There was no pressure. I left there admiring the judges on the bench who took part in that procedure.

So they are not sort of the lap dogs of those in power?

No.

And there is hope for the democracy?

Of course! I believe that the separation of power system is not here yet – the judiciary, the legislature, and administration. There is a way to go. So we cannot say that ... for example in 1992 the opposition won the election, but the party in power corrupted the results by force.

The person in power was an Anglophone and the Francophone did not want him in power.

In some discussions I have had it has been said that the problem with the Church in Africa is the imparting of the faith to social life. But in Cameroon the social life is problematic. What do you think?

Well there are problems that are related to human nature. Where a man is to be found you will find those problems. You know the basic principle in human life, [the] basic ethical principle, is that good must be done, evil must be avoided. That's for every culture. There is no culture that says evil must be done and good avoided. So it is good must be done and evil avoided. And the Christian religion comes and helps us, and I think that God saw that without revelation we can't go far. That's why he added revelation to human procedure.

I think the problem is that we are living in mixed society, religiously mixed. There are still pagans with us, there are still Muslims, Catholics, Christians, Protestants, new sects, and new religions that have come here and which promise heaven on earth, everything good, as if they were God. But that doesn't cover the crisis, a poverty crisis in our countries in Africa; [there is a] poverty crisis and people are looking for cheaper ways of getting out of [it]. So this religion promised them if you go and worship with us you will get so much and so on ... and that is what creates a certain, in my judgment, in my observation, certain confusion. So often I go on a pastoral visit and I am asked the question: what should one do with so many religions? So I answer them simply: to know the right religion you must know its founder. We hold strongly that Catholicism was the only Church founded by Christ. We know the historical origin of other churches, we know that Christ founded the Christian Church so you can't compare it with a Church founded by me! If it were a human institution it would have disappeared a long time ago. For all the new institutions or new religions of the time have disappeared except the Church, which continues because Christ who founded it says "I am with you always till the end of time". They were persecuting the apostles ... If what they are doing is from God, we will find ourselves fighting against God. If it is not from God it will disappear. The Church continues here today. Not because of us but because its founder is still with us; and he is God. You know there are moral problems, which are linked, but that's why I tell my Conference in Europe when I am there I say, "No your pastoral problems are exactly similar to ours." I do not see the difference. Divorce is there and it is here. Abortion is there, and here. There is nothing in Europe that is not found here. This is as far as Christianity is concerned.

The same problems as in the West. Except that you have this intense poverty ...?

Yes even the West there are poor people. Christ has the poor you will always have with you. In America I learn that about 40,000 people go to bed without eating. And there it is even worse! You know I have just come from the village; everybody in the village has his compound. When people have something to chew and a place to lie down [they will be alright], but I do not go into a village and see somebody without a house! By the way in my village everybody has a house and a compound where a person can plant potatoes and beans and so on and that's "living" in the farm life.

9 i. CONGO

The Democratic Republic of Congo is the second largest country in Africa. It is located in central Africa. It borders the Central African Republic and South Sudan to the north; Uganda, Rwanda, and Burundi in the east; Zambia and Angola to the south; the Republic of the Congo, the Angolan exclave of Cabinda, and the Atlantic Ocean to the west; and is separated from Tanzania by Lake Tanganyika in the east. The national language is officially French, though people also speak Lingala (a lingua franca trade language), Kingwana (a dialect of Kiswahili or Swahili), Kikongo, Tshiluba. The country has a population of 75 million people, and an unemployment rate of 50 per cent. There are over 200 African ethnic groups in Congo the majority of which are Bantu; the four largest tribes – Mongo, Luba, Kongo (all Bantu), and the Mangbetu-Azande (Hamitic) make up about 45 per cent of the population.

Fifty per cent of the population are Roman Catholic, 20 per cent are Protestant, 10 per cent are Kimbanguist,[161] 10 per cent are Muslim, and the rest hold indigenous beliefs or are members of syncretic sects. Most people live an average of approximately 56 years. On average women have five children (28.2 per cent of children under five years of age were underweight in 2007). Approximately 67 per cent of the population are literate (more men than women). Children will spend about eight years at school. 77,000 adults (3.4 per cent of people over the age of fifteen years) are living with HIV, and 7,900 children. There are 51,000 AIDS orphans. National GDP sits at 15.6 billion USD

---

[161] Kimbanguism is known officially as: "the church of Christ on Earth by the prophet Simon Kimbangu".

(2011) and the country has a population density of 29 people per square kilometre.[162]

Prior to colonisation by King Leopold and then the Belgian government (beginning in the 1870s), Congo was run by the Kingdom of Luba, a conglomerate of a number of previously distinct and wealthy kingdoms that had developed and implemented iron and copper technology and traded in Ivory across a relatively vast trading route. While the Kingdom had developed a strong central government by the 16th century (based on chiefdoms), the eastern region had been extensively disrupted by the Arab slave trade. Unlike other missionaries that took root in Africa in the 19th century, the Congolese Catholic Church is seen to have begun in the 1500s when the Kingdom was still comfortably in control. Requests from the then King lead to about 200 years of interaction between the King and his people, Jesuits (1619) and then Capuchins (1645),[163] and a laity that essentially took responsibility for maintaining the faith (and interpreting it with indigenous variables) once the missionaries had gone by the early 1800s.

Belgian exploration had taken over in 1870 and continued until the 1920s. King Leopold of Belgium made the country his own property in 1895, and installed a vicious regime that focussed on the construction of railways and national infrastructure at the expense of the local population. Half of the African population of the Congo is said to have died during that time. Severe brutality was used to ensure the production of rubber for the emerging motor vehicle and tire industry. Many Congolese lost hands and limbs as punishment for low productivity.[164] From 1908 and until 1960 the country became a colony of Belgium. The governing of the colony improved considerably and

---

162 See footnote 38.
163 The Capuchin mission's history is exhaustively studied and chronicled in *Graziano Saccardo [da Leguzzano] Congo e Angola con la storia del missione cappuccino* (3 vols., Venice, 1982-84).
164 Boahen, Op. Cit., p. 60.

much social progress was made though the white rulers maintained a racist and discriminatory approach to the indigenous population.

The nationalist movement, which grew under Patrice Lumumba, was realised in 1960 with the election of the Mouvement National Congolais (MNC), of Lumumba as Prime Minister and of Joseph Kasavubu as president. Lumumba's attraction of Communist support saw him assassinated and replaced by the anti-Communist government lead by Mobutu (president from 1971-1997). Once in power Mobutu renamed the country Zaire, installed a one-party regime, declared himself head of state, and ruled with impunity. His government was guilty of corruption, severe human rights violations, political repression, and a cult of personality.[165] Demands for reform began to hit home in the late 1980s at which time Mobuto installed the Third Republic as supposed evidence of his intention to reform the constitution. Conflict eventually forced him to flee the country in 1997, after which time the nation called itself the Democratic Republic of Congo. Laurent Kabila (assassinated in 2001) declared first himself president, and then later his son Joseph Kabila was elected president via multi-party elections.

1996 and 1998 saw the explosion of two wars in DRC, the first on the tail of the civil war in Rwanda and its accompanying genocide, and the second dubbed Africa's world war because it involved nine nations. Both involved a complex interplay between politics in Congo and in Rwanda (across the border), and ongoing competition for the vast resources of the Congo area. Both resulted in some of the most violent atrocities ever reported. The prevalence of rape and sexual violence was the worst in the world. In 2009, 45,000 people died every month. To date, ongoing conflict has killed as many as 5.4 million people. Forty-seven per cent of those deaths were of children under the age of five. Ninety per cent of the dead were not killed in combat

---

165 Mobutu demanded every Congolese banknote be printed with his image, hanging of his portrait in all public buildings, most businesses, and on billboards. It was common for ordinary people to wear his likeness on their clothing.

but from living in refugee situations that were prone to outbreaks of disease due to inadequate sanitation.

Laurent Cardinal Monsengwo Pasinya was born on 7 October 1939 in Mongobele, in the diocese of Inongo. He is the Archbishop of Kinshasa and de facto primate of the Democratic Republic of the Congo since his appointment by Pope Benedict XVI in 2007. He was ordained to the priesthood in 1963. He studied at the Pontifical Urbaniana University and the Pontifical Biblical Institute in Jerusalem, and was awarded a doctorate in biblical studies. He served as a faculty member at the Theological Faculty of Kinshasa, and as secretary-general of the Congolese Episcopal Conference between 1976 and 1980. Monsengwo Pasinya was appointed titular bishop of Acque Nuove di Proconsulare and Auxiliary Bishop of Kisangani in 1980. He served as president of the Congolese Episcopal Conference in 1980 and 1992, and he was appointed metropolitan archbishop of Kisangani in 1988.

When Mobutu Sese Seko lost his grip on power in the mid-1990s, Monsengwo Pasinya was appointed as president of the Sovereign National Conference (1991), president of the High Council of the Republic (1992) and then speaker of the Transitional Parliament (1994). He is currently co-president of Pax Christi International (2007) and was transferred to the metropolitan see of Kinshasa (2007). He was made cardinal-priest of Santa Maria Regina Pacis in Ostia mare in 2010, and in the same year, a member of the Congregation for Catholic Education. In 2011 he was appointed a member of the Pontifical Council for Culture, and of the Pontifical Council for Social Communications, and in 2012 of the Congregation for the Evangelisation of Peoples.

Just before publication of this book in 2013, the newly appointed Pope Francis chose Cardinal Monsengwo as the representative from Africa on his council of eight cardinals to act as his advisors in the government of the Catholic Church and the reform of the Roman Curia. I met Cardinal Monsengwo in Rome in October, 2012.

ii. Justice

"If you want to build a ship, don't drum up people together to collect wood and don't assign them tasks and work, but rather teach them to long for the endless immensity of the sea"[166]

On to Rome, and to the steps of St Peter's again, and then later the next day into the heart of the eternal city ... I took some time to look over the square with my back to the basilica this time. The ancient Egyptian obelisk marks the circus of Nero, once a haphazard mess of human misery encircled by opulence. These days it is beautiful. My meeting with Monsengwo had been arranged for Rome on the basis that he was at the Synod of Bishops on the New Evangelisation (the site of Turkson's blunder). The red hats were flat out, debating issues surrounding the decline of the Church in the West. I was flat out trying to get there and home again in a weekend.

Trying to recover from jet lag, I sat and drank coffee with journalists to watch bishops emerge from the Curia offices at the end of a heavy day of talks. Eager for a by-line, my journalist friends pounced on them as they emerged. They massaged their egos with attentive and impassive faces while memorising a sentence or two for their international Catholic periodicals. Coming back to our table all back-slapping and laughing they scribbled everything down in dog-eared journals, recounting each word gathered over and over, forming them into newsworthy sentences. "Did he really say that?" "Did you ask him ...?" I sat and marvelled at the Hollywood atmosphere. There was a buzz as celebrity bishops hurried past our table, red hats snug atop bald heads, brief cases conspicuously mundane beside the skirts of their theatrical soutanes. There was a presupposition of importance

---

[166] Antoine de Saint-Exupery (1900-1944), French aristocrat, writer, poet, and pioneering aviator.

in their determined haste, the length of their stride, the jerking of arms and fingers that reinforced hurried instructions to short-stepped and black-clad minions (skipping up the rear) who carried books and paperwork on both forearms. Here, red-clad cardinals took the lead in a cast of would-be thousands. Accompanied by the slightly off-key harmonies of pilgrimage choirs who had gathered in the early evening in St Peter's square, they made guest appearances, sweeping their way across the Vatican stage with elegance and precision and, disappearing into the wings and out of sight just as quickly as they emerged, leaving us with a fading shadow of red, a fleeting breeze from their hand-stitched robes, and an evening of street lamps that popped on in the twilight.

Everyone who visits the Vatican must wonder where the princes go. We see the large grey buildings that flank St Peter's and imagine priests in there. The lucky ones might catch the parting curtain and a papal wave on a Sunday, though there are no further indications as to the internal aesthetics. The grey walls and the huge wooden or iron clad doors with great blackened rivets for decoration hold back information about the present, just as much as they hint at the medieval hierarchy of the Vatican's past. Swiss guards stand seriously at entrances, adding to the royal gala with their jester attire, scarlet, yellow and blue, and a sword or halberd thrown in for exaggeration over their bloomers. Tourists photograph them, for the colour contrasts mostly, and wonder at their responsibilities. The bored and blandly coloured armoured guards, who patrol the square, search bags and observe the queues of tourists, seem to make them obsolete. And yet without the jesters the stage might disappoint us. Their regal velvets hint at the mysteries they conceal like the curtain in a theatre, and we wait, sipping cappuccino, for the show to begin. Sometimes the lead actors move amongst the crowd. Some made their way to a private atrium inside St Peter's while I was there and I craned my neck for a view. Cardinal Sarah passed me quickly while I stood beside the

Baldachin; he was small beside the tall European cardinals with him, earnest in his intellectual and spiritual preoccupations, perhaps blissfully unaware of the attention his party was attracting as they swept through. I tried to wave discreetly. I wanted to call out to him to reassure myself of the connection we had shared but he was duty bound, purposeful, removed and disconnected from the throng of sinners who stood with me. Together with his colleagues he carved a path through the tourists towards his end goal and disappeared as the group closed together again behind them.

Later that day I saw Cardinal Arinze too. It was the end of the day's Synod deliberations and together with a group of bishops he was walking up and into the space behind the Swiss guards to where I stood, having emerged from making arrangements for my meeting with Monsengwo that night. I was with my friend (a Jesuit theologian) and we approached him together, me with my hand outstretched to take his while reminding him of who I was, of our meetings earlier that year. He acknowledged our connection but seemed wary, perhaps confused, and he gave me his hand cautiously. I think I was once again a picture out of focus, a woman in jeans emerging from the sanctum, my self-confidence somehow irreverent, the assumption of friendship too confronting to accept in the context of the Synod and the acolytes who were with him.

When I went to meet Monsengwo I walked up beside St Peter's, past the Swiss guards and under the arched walkway that joins the great Basilica to the Vatican offices on either side. Through it and beyond a car park flanks more buildings that rise straight up into the air. They block the sunlight and cool the air. Huge cobbled stones give passing car tires an earthy rumble. The stones stretch out grey and desolate until they met the building's edge (no plants, no feminine ornamentation or artistic expression on the walls). They are softened only by wheels and the shoes that have marched across them all these years. Mercedes, Volvos, BMWs, tall grey walls and thick wooden doors: an ordinary and desolate space that reveals nothing but the public severity of Vatican (and a very masculine) seniority.

Behind the doors cool white marble flows down stairs, across floors, and into hallways like milk. Plants crop up in highly polished, creamy urns, at the base of great columns of stone and beside Italian leather sofas and parquet coffee tables that seem to bob up and down, floating, in the marble surrounds. One modern renovation merges with the next through green-tinged glass in that space, emphasising the softness of the aged elements of the building (the roman courtyard, the statues) with the shine on architectural fittings and sharp design that made undecipherable whispers rebound, and footsteps chill with the kind of echoed determination that announces the arrival of royalty.

Monsengwo is a giant on the African Catholic stage. "He stands head and shoulders above the rest," I was told. Taking that step into politics that others like Tumi or Wamala had declined, he accepted the role of "president" of his country's transitional government and guided the country out of the horrors of the Mobutu regime. His role in political situations is said to have held up his appointment as cardinal under Pope John Paul II, but saw him appointed nevertheless by Benedict in 2007. Today he continues to take a political stand against ongoing atrocity at home. Recently, he called for civil disobedience to protest corruption in the last election in true Gandhi style, and together with presidents of the Bishops' Conferences of Africa and bishop presidents of National Caritas in Africa (from 34 different countries) implored leaders of the EU, the AU, the UN, the DRC, and the world's multinational corporations to turn their attention to the plight of Congo's poor and the need for dialogue, demanding they do something to bring the perpetrators of violence to justice and end the ongoing human tragedy that Congo has become.

Some describe the violence in Congo as the biggest slaughter of people since World War II, yet the country is not at the forefront of media attention. The United Nations Security Council has been unable to stop it. And the economic and political interests that are fuelling the ongoing conflict and killings in the DRC's eastern provinces are largely unknown. While the genocide in Rwanda was given vast international media coverage, the genocide in the Congo is hardly reported in the West. On 13 November 2008 the Congo's Catholic Bishops publicly "denounced the silent genocide that is happening in the East of the country", Monsengwo told Gerard O'Connell,[167] "It is surprising to see the media coverage which has been given, and rightly so, to the genocide in Rwanda, even if the genocide of the Hutu is deliberately kept off the news." "But", he added, "it should be recognised that Rwanda carried out big lobbying on the genocide, and is more effective than the Congo in that." Given what is happening, it is still "... incomprehensible that they do not talk about the massacre of the Congolese people, which has now risen to five million people killed."

An investigative journalist from Cameroon (Charles Onana) writes that Tutsi killers are at the centre of the Congolese tragedy.[168] While presenting themselves as victims of Rwandan genocide, they murdered two African heads of state (1994) and killed thousands of innocent Rwandans as well as Canadian, French and Spanish witnesses. They invaded the Congo in 1997, exterminated thousands of Hutu refugees from Rwanda, raped women, killed innocent civilians, and were involved in President Kabila's assassination, Onana says. They continue to loot the Congo's mineral resources that they now sell in

---

167 Renowned journalist Gerard O'Connell (Vatican analyst and correspondent for various Catholic news outlets in the English-speaking world) loaned me an interview based on a discussion recorded between himself and Cardinal Monsengwo from which the quotations of Monsengwo in these pages are drawn. An edited version of the same work was first published as: "Minerals of blood", in *Justice (on Social Issues: A Catholic perspective)*, a monthly January/February 2010, pp. 42-44.

168 O'Connell also refers to Charles Onana's book, *Ces Tueurs Tutsi au Coeur de la Tragédie Congolaise (These killers Tutsi at the heart of the Congolese Tragedy)*, Duboiris Edition, Paris, 2009.

Kigali, the Rwandan capital, and the USA, UK, France, Belgium and multinational corporations continue to support them.[169]

As archbishop of Kisangani in the eastern Congo from 1988 to 2007, Monsengwo survived the shelling of his residence by Rwandan forces in August 2000. Today he is Archbishop of Kinshasa, the capital city, in the west of the country. He told O'Connell that the conflict in Eastern Congo has political and economic causes: The conflict relates to "the transfer to the Congo of the ethnic conflicts of neighbouring countries, so much so that only those provinces in the East are at war while the rest of the country, that is to say some 350 tribes are at peace", and "a certain will to balkanise the country, which we are following from close up." Ethnic conflicts from Rwanda and Uganda have been transposed to Congo. Furthermore, various actors have tried to break up the mineral-rich territory into small, even hostile units, so as to gain control of its resources.

There also exists a "... will to exploit the minerals of the Congo in the midst of the disorder: colombo-tantalite (coltan), gold, petroleum, diamonds and, now it seems, uranium," he said. The conflict is for the most part related to the struggle for control of the artisanal informal mines in North and South Kivu which access the region's natural resources: coltan or tantalum (used in cell phones and laptops), gold and cassiterite (tin ore, also used in computers) and other precious minerals. The USA (1998-2001) and then China (2002-) were the world's leading importers of coltan, while cassiterite is currently one of the Congolese metals most sought after by electronic and computer firms. Highly coveted 'blood' minerals find their way into international markets illegally, a recent UN report and O'Connell noted. On 4 March 2009, Monsengwo told *L'Osservatore Romano*, the Vatican daily, that

---

169 For a preview of Onana's book go to "CHARLES ONANA: BREAKING THE SILENCE ON THE CONGO" by Congoindependant, 23 April 2009 (http://hungryoftruth.blogspot.com.au/2009/04/charles-onana-breaking-silence-on-rd.html), published 25 April 2009 and accessed 9 July 2013.

the Congo "has vast deposits of uranium that can also be used to make an atomic bomb," and said, "... if this natural wealth is not managed wisely, it could lead to a proliferation of atomic weapons in the world ... When one knows the usefulness of these metals in world trade, one can guess the appetite of the Big Powers and the multinationals", the Archbishop told O'Connell.

I had wanted to ask Monsengwo about his role in creating the nation after the Mobutu regime. His decision to enter politics (even if only temporarily) made him different from the other cardinals and I wanted to know what made him take that step, and how his country and the Church were approaching the challenges now faced by the poor. But he wasn't keen to talk to me. Waiting for him in a side room, empty but for a couch, he came to me briefly but then left again. When he arrived he was all business. Suited (good quality Italian wool), a clerical collar and exaggerated and gold rimmed cat's eye glasses – a throwback to the 1950s that tickled me – he was brusque and hurried like Turkson, the enormous demands on his time distracting the focus I wanted on me. There were no revelations. In fact there was barely any conversation. Talking to me was something that he needed to avoid at all costs. My ability to misrepresent what he said was problematic for a man with a wager on his head and we had no trusting rapport. Monsengwo was polite. He made an effort simply because I had flown a long way but he would not record anything with me, much less in English (not his first language). He would email some answers, he told me, but in French, and I believe he would have done so had armed conflict not broken out in Syria and he not been whisked away as head of a special Vatican envoy to lead and mediate dialogue that could possibly lead to peace. I took strength from the existence of generous reporters like O'Connell who had offered his own interview if Monsengwo did not send the promised replies, and swallowed my disappointment.

I was struck by his bold masculinity when we left that small room, the way that he owned the space around him, filled it with magnetism.

He is not a very tall man, but I felt dwarfed by his charisma nevertheless and in the brief moment that we shared he could have been anything: He was Pele.[170] He was Willie Mays.[171] He was Australia's own Polly Farmer.[172] Captain of Team Cardinal, the talented and indigenous African All-Stars, Monsengwo was kicking goals, redefining the code, and dominating the game. Was this too much? It did not feel like it at the time. I was speaking to him in the very heart of the eternal city, in a space where the architecture alone spoke a language of power and influence, a space in which he had no hesitation openly criticising his highly influential and high profile European colleagues for their lack of focus on Africa's poor. In a matter of days he would be named one of an elite few in Pope Benedict's special envoy to Syria, and with the election of Pope Francis he would be chosen as the African representative on a council of eight advisors in the government of the Catholic Church and the reform of the Roman Curia.

Floating out across the marble and towards the stairs and the door above them we were met by three young priests who bowed deeply, and kissed his ring before acknowledging me. To my surprise he introduced them, the first two by name and then the third; "This is the fat one", he said. The young man giggled. (I felt uncomfortable!) Clearly embarrassed at being admonished by the cardinal (and before a woman), he trailed the foursome as they began to move away. As I walked back up the milky staircase towards the door I turned to look back at them briefly. Monsengwo was in front, gesticulating as he talked loudly. Unrestrained despite the hard surfaces, the echoing walls; he was leader of the pack (his companions were laughing), and from that angle, yes, he was very much one of the Vatican's boys.

---

170 Edson Arantes do Nascimento (1940-) otherwise known as "Pele" played soccer for Brazil and is today regarded by many as the best football (soccer) player of all time.
171 Willie Howard Mays Jr (1931-) played baseball for the New York and San Fransisco Giants and the New York Mets, and is today considered one of the best baseball players of all time.
172 Graham Vivian "Polly" Farmer (1935-) was an indigenous Australian Rules footballer and coach, and is today a recognised legend of the game.

Conclusion

... You'll say I walked across Africa with my wrists unshackled, and now I am one more soul walking free in a white skin, wearing some thread of stolen goods: cotton, diamonds, freedom at the very least, prosperity. Some of us know how we came by our fortune, and some of us don't, but we wear it all the same. There's only one question worth asking now: How do we aim to live with it? ...[173]

Each of the men interviewed for this book represents a different country, and within that country a different ethnic group; in that they are divided. Africa is as diverse as it is large. To imagine these men as all representing "one Africa" is naïve. What they represent instead is a single approach to human suffering and human struggle that derives from Catholic doctrine and is empowered by enviable strength. That approach is built upon a single set of very simple rules about how we should all get along.

The cardinals are joined by their application of those rules to a number of equally challenging circumstances that in the modern climate are quintessentially African. Some of those circumstances reflect the same level of injustice apportioned during Europe's last "scramble" for Africa in the late 1800s. These days it is the financial behemoths who take up arms in pursuit of the wealth found in the vast and valuable resource deposits found across the African continent.[174] Competition for that wealth has led to war, human misery, and death on a large scale and is often backed either inadvertently or deliberately by international muscle flexed beyond Africa's shores.

---
173 Barbara Kingsolver (1998), *The Poisonwood Bible*, Faber and Faber, London.
174 Patrick Radden Keefe, "Buried Secrets: How an Israeli Billionaire wrestled control of one of Africa's biggest prizes." (http://www.newyorker.com/reporting/2013/07/08/130708fa_fact_keefe), accessed June 2013.

Other circumstances arise from of the failures of various African independence movements to establish unified and modern societies after the end of old colonial regimes. Modern and heroic governments quickly descended into murderous dictatorships that flaunted (and in many cases continue to flaunt) new-found wealth and power at the expense of the common interests of the entirety of each nation's needy. Past injustices and European discriminatory practices ensured that ties to the few valuable aspects of European leadership (education, health, and infrastructure) were generally severed. Fledgling nations were cast adrift in a modern space. Defining which direction to take has been difficult in climates where so many different interests simultaneously compete for the future, and cling to identities of the past. Doing so has led to further conflict, poverty, and the spread of disease.

At the most basic level survival itself is a challenge. Religious enlightenment provides the hope, forgiveness, courage, optimism, and resilience that make life and living possible in such difficult circumstances. Apart from anything else, it is free. Wealth and power tempt even the most genuinely intended. Only those with ethical scaffolding that can lift them above and beyond the scramble below can maintain a clear view of the direction in which they need to head. Strength and wisdom in such powerful hands potentially create bridges to the benefits of the modern world.

Coming together from variously divergent pasts the cardinals stand together on that scaffolding. They alone understand the extent of their challenges at home and together share an experience of a myriad of those challenges. All have devoted many years, often under severe duress, to assisting their people, their communities, and their countries. All have taken brave stands to keep their governments honest, and to provide a voice to the oppressed at home despite the dangers. Some have often watched colleagues die at the hands of corrupt regimes. Some have risked their lives in attempts to establish international peace and some have lost loved ones in the battle. They all continue to work tirelessly for charity efforts around the world as well as in Africa, establishing and supporting educational opportunities for the young, providing medical support in many ways, reaffirming cultural values and cultural identities, and bolstering social cohesion where it has been undermined by social disarray. All are joined in a mutual recognition of women as central to the health of society and many have made important steps towards promoting women to the most senior positions available to women in the Catholic Church, often despite criticism from male colleagues. All have been recognised for their efforts to support peace and reconciliation, for their focus and for their enormous abilities, through their promotions to some of the most senior positions the Catholic Church can offer. They have been made leaders on international bodies that share ideas and problems in times of armed conflict, and they have been created not only cardinals but also put in charge of entire segments of the Roman Curia.

It is clear that the success of their efforts at the most senior levels of national and international decision making sets them apart. Their accomplishments are quantifiable in terms of modern and rational indicators, just as they have been recognised within the ancient traditions that define the hierarchy of the Church. Their ascension to seniority is typical of any career hierarchy, but their work as leaders of a powerful organisation that holds sway over the hearts and private choices of millions of people makes maintaining the balance between the privileges of their seniority and its responsibilities all the more urgent. Abusing the privileges of leadership would be as devastating as the successful expression of their responsibilities would be vast. In these men the balance is tipped markedly and admirably towards the latter. Their ability to negotiate past, present, and future challenges, whilst nurturing entire populations at the most fundamental level, is testament to a singular special status as spiritual leaders.

Indeed they are beloved. They preach the gospel with the simplicity of shepherds but with the power of some of history's greatest minds;

yet they remain humble, quiet, and undemanding. They draw people together across ethnic, cultural, national, and racial lines purely for the purposes of human betterment. And they availed themselves to me without hesitation and despite the demands of their work, reaching out and touching me at a most personal level. Whether or not we choose to see their work as the work of God, it goes without saying that their seniority within the Church was not a barrier to interaction but one point of contact between their world and mine. A bridge was created that had not existed before.

It has been no small surprise to me, to find myself seeking the approval of men whose religious leanings I once judged archaic. The abuse of children at the hands of some priests in Australia has sullied my view, along with blatant expressions of wealth in the name of the Church over centuries. More devastating have been those movements conducted in the name of God and responsible for so much death and human suffering; from the Jews of Masada in the first century, through to the war in Syria today. I remain conflicted over the stand the Church has taken in a number of arenas. As an international organisation I think its public face has been and continues to be out of touch with modern challenges on a number of levels.

Nevertheless, despite having judged the Church as an irrelevant anachronism as a result of my upbringing I have witnessed first hand the success the Church has had in solving conflicts, healing division and fighting for social justice where "modern" attempts have failed. My expectations of arrogance and lives of privilege were dispelled by my experience of the cardinals as people. The risks they took, and the personal sacrifices they make give the Church relevance in Africa that it lacks in the Western world, where aspirations for the perfection of the divine have been replaced with civilisation as an end point in itself. Ignorant of religious doctrine, indeed of history itself, we confuse the impressively complicated and intricate scaffoldings of civilisation as evidence of our triumph over God, as proof that we no longer need the guidance of religious doctrine or even, for that matter, the past. Self-contained, perfect, and complete we think ourselves separate from the Christian heritage and belief systems that continue to underlay our Western sense of being. (It is impossible, even for self-proclaimed atheists, not to absorb them by a process of osmosis.) Being unaware that while civilisation is durable it is ultimately temporary, forgetting that we must compare and contrast ourselves not to bygone civilisations (that we often judge using our own relative values) but to an ideal. It is a common mistake, made so easily by those of us in the West who have immortalised the individual. Wealth and social stability, self-sufficiency and progress, have turned us inward. We make decisions on the basis of singular desires and without a view to the community that will support us when our luck runs out. In celebrating our individual magnificence, we fail to grow.

Many mortals have attempted to define the ideal. Before the Bible there was Virgil's *Aeneid*, before that was Homer's *Iliad* and *Odyssey*. As books they have been required reading across generations because their fables and their heroes have provided insights into our own humanity and how best to negotiate it. It is understandable that their messages are today less accessible in view of language alone, though that does not make them any less relevant to modern contexts. The merits of ancient Greek and Roman philosophy may be beyond the reach of most, but the virtues of Christianity are still within our grasp, brought into a modern space and interpreted for the world through the decrees of the Second Vatican Council which was called into being by *il Papa Buono*, the Good Pope, John XXIII. Faith, hope, and love, prudence, justice, temperance, and courage continue to be taught, sought, embraced and nurtured by a long and ever growing procession of multi-cultural Christians who have found strength and direction within them. Modern civilisations are triumphantly complicated. Perhaps it's not such a bad idea to get back to some of the basics.

At the very end of my travels for this book I found myself perched on the walls of the old city of Bergamo, overlooking the province, with its length and breadth taking in an expanse of valleys and thin backdrop of mountains. The Good Pope came from Bergamo province. He was one of fourteen children, the son of sharecroppers, a man of the people with a passion for equality inside and outside of the Church. I had not known that the Pope came from Bergamo until I arrived there for a brief holiday with my husband. It was a strange coincidence perhaps, but one amongst many that I am now prepared to embrace. Discovering the limitations in my thinking has been a grand adventure and a privilege. I have travelled into my own heart of darkness and back out into the light of Africa, trying to prove my worth as a writer and as a woman, but learning that the only thing that really matters is love. I still do not regard myself as well versed in Christian doctrine, but knowing that love is central perhaps means that I am off to a good start. I think it was Aristotle who suggested that if you really want to understand something you should begin by coming to terms with its best qualities. On that note, I suggest that if you want to get to know Christianity, you should probably begin in Africa.

Appendix

1. Bishops of Africa
Call for the cessation of the war and the respect of the territorial integrity of the DR Congo

Kinshasa, 22 November 2012[175]

1. We, Presidents of the Bishops' Conferences of Africa and Bishop Presidents of National Caritas in Africa, coming from thirty four countries of the continent, gathered in a Conference on the identity and mission of Caritas in Kinshasa from November 20th to 22nd, 2012, express deep concern and solidarity with the Congolese people. We are outraged and shocked by the escalating armed violence in eastern Democratic Republic of Congo which is causing again a major human tragedy.

2. Thousands of men, women and children, the victims of this war which is imposed on them, are displaced and abandoned in destitution in Goma and its surroundings. They are exposed to the bad weather, hunger, rape and all kinds of abuses, including recruiting of children into the army. This constitutes an offence to their dignity as human beings and children of God.

3. We are convinced that the time is no longer for war or conquest, but rather to promote cooperation between peoples and that the territorial integrity of the Democratic Republic of Congo must be protected and respected by all. We are aware of the contribution of the exploitation of natural resources to this situation, and we therefore urge a fair, just and transparent exploitation of natural resources and distribution of the proceeds of such an activity to benefit all.

---

175 (http://www.cafod.org.uk/Media/Files/Resources/Press-releases-and-news/Declaration-of-African-Catholic-Bishops-on-Eastern-Congo-Crisis), accessed 7 June 2013.

In communion with the Bishops of the Congo who have frequently taken position on this situation, we launch a pressing appeal to the UN, the AU, the EU, the DRC Government and the governments of the other countries involved in some way in this war as well as to multinational companies in the extractive sector. May they, once and for all, address the causes of this recurrent violence through promoting dialogue in an honest and transparent manner so as to find, urgently, a fair and concerted solution, able to put an end to the suffering of the civilian populations of the Eastern DRC; thus avoiding plunging them into despair and violence. The perpetrators of such violence and destruction should be brought to justice.

In the face of the aggravation of the suffering afflicting these brothers and sisters, and faithful to the mission of Christian charity and solidarity, we ask our Caritas network, other charitable organisations of our respective Churches and humanitarian agencies to double their efforts to come to their help.

We implore the Almighty God, the Lord of Peace, to inspire Peace to those who wage war, plan and program it, and to let grow in the hearts of the people who live in the Great Lakes Region brotherhood and mutual respect.

May Mary, Our Lady of Africa and Our Lady of Peace, intercede for us.

Signed in Kinshasa, on November 22, 2012.

2. Gerard O'Connell with Cardinal Arinze[176]

(Rome, 2013)

The Nigerian Cardinal, Francis Arinze, who once headed the Vatican offices for dialogue with the other religions, and for Divine Worship, was present in the Hall of the Consistory (Sala del Consistoro) when Pope Benedict made his historic announcement on 11 February. In this interview with Gerard O'Connell, he talks about his own reaction and that of the other cardinals to that news.

You were one of some 40 cardinals present when the Pope read his letter of resignation on 11 February. Can you describe what happened?

It was like thunder, the announcement came without advance warning. It came at the end of the ceremony for voting for canonization. We were expecting to receive the Holy Father's blessing, but he told us to sit down as he had something important to say. Then he began reading a text in Latin.

When he had read a few sentences I began to suspect where he was going, because he started by telling us that after having repeatedly examined his conscience before God, he had come to the certainty that due to advanced age he no longer had the strength of mind and body to answer the demands of the Petrine Ministry. Especially in the last few months, he said his strengths had deteriorated to such an extent that he recognised he was no longer able to adequately fulfill the papal ministry.

Once he said that it was clear to everyone that he was going to resign. He announced that he would no longer continue as bishop of

---

176 "Cardinal Arinze praises Pope's courageous decision to resign", first published Vatican Insider, 23 February 2013. (http://vaticaninsider.lastampa.it/en/news/detail/articolo/22607//pag/1/), accessed 12 June 2013.

Rome and Successor of St Peter from eight o'clock in the evening of February 28.

What was the reaction of the cardinals when he finished reading?
Silence! We cardinals looked at each other. We didn't have words to say. We were still digesting the import of what he had said when, as if to save us from that embarrassing moment, Cardinal Angelo Sodano, the Dean of the College of Cardinals, stood up and spoke. Obviously, he had been tipped off in advance because he had written what he was going to say.

He expressed the incredulity of all present, and the sense of feeling lost. He said the Holy Father's words conveyed yet again his great love for the Church. He summed up the feelings of everyone when he said, "We are closer than ever to you in these days" and "will remain close to you."

After Cardinal Sodano's speech, the Holy Father imparted his blessing and left. What happened then?
After Pope Benedict left the hall with his assistants, all the cardinals stayed on. Nobody told us to stay, we just stayed. We gathered in little groups, each one asking the other, "What do you make of all this?" How? When? We were there for quite some time. Then we began to walk away, slowly, each one reflecting, not saying much.

I was still trying to digest the meaning of all that as I went down in the lift to the Belvedere, and then walked back to my residence. It was clear to me that the Pope had taken that decision over a long period, he hadn't rushed it. He's not a person who rushes things. It was also clear that he took a courageous decision, because something like this has not happened in the Church for about 600 years. It was clear too that he loves the Church. He didn't put himself at the centre; he was only concerned with what is good for the Church. That was his only preoccupation; he was not concerned about his personal convenience, nor the honor or praise that he gets as pope.

So I said to myself, the Pope is teaching us all something very important by this act. One of the titles of the Pope is "Servant of the servants of God". We come and go. Any of us can go, only Christ does not go. Without Christ the Church loses its foundation, its direction, its harmony. Popes come and go, bishops come and go, and so do politicians. The Pope is teaching us all that the most important consideration for anyone in public office is not 'Do I like this seat?' No! The most important consideration is this: Does the community I serve profit by my service?

Were you shocked at his announcement?

Yes. I was shocked, and surprised. But very soon with shock came a type of calm because of his love for the Church and because of the good effects his action can have. So I was not so shocked that I went away with low spirits. No! I didn't go away confused or depressed. I was reassured by his courage and by the knowledge that the Church lives because Christ lives, and I was therefore strengthened in my faith.

In the Credo we confess our faith in the Father, Son and Holy Spirit, but also in the One, Holy, Catholic and Apostolic Church. For some people there's no problem in believing in God, but they are shaken by the Church when they see the elements in the Church: the Divine elements, sure, but the human elements that can fall short. If you can have faith in the Church all the time, whether you like the bishop or not, whether you like the parish priest or not, but if you love the Church and have enough faith in Christ – this is what is important in our Catholic faith. The Pope by his decision is teaching us all that.

Do you think his resignation changes the papacy in some way?

It doesn't change the nature of the papacy, but it can help us in reflecting on the faith, and how we look at the pope. It can also help any of us who is in a position of authority to ask ourselves some questions, because sometimes an objective assessment could lead a person in a position of authority to conclude that it may be better that somebody else should take up this office and that I should step aside for the sake of the community which I serve. That is the lesson the Pope is teaching us.

The Anglican Archbishop Rowan Williams said that Pope Benedict has demystified the papacy by his decision to resign.

He's right. You know there's always a danger of personality cult, because some people believe that the person who is in authority now is the best person ever in that position. They think there's nothing to be changed in anything this person in authority decides, even though some decisions may be administrative not dogmatic, and there can be different opinions. So I think each of us should be humble, beginning with the person in the authority, and extending also to those who have to obey authority.

Do you think there are too many expectations of the Pope today, in terms of audiences, travel and so on?

I think the Pope must be allowed a little more time to breathe. He must be allowed a little more time to do his thinking and reflection. We must not expect him to meet all the groups that think the Pope should meet them. I don't deny the comfort people get in meeting the Pope but we have only one Pope at a time and there are some two billion Catholics in the world.

On the other hand, I think it is very good that the Pope travels. When he travels, as Paul VI, John Paul II and Benedict XVI did, he strengthens the local Church and gives the Church visibility in the world. If the Pope is able to travel, I would be in favour of him continuing to do so. But every Pope cannot be as physically strong as John Paul II, so there must be allowance for different styles, different approaches, and we mustn't force every pope to do exactly what his predecessor did.

What is the legacy that Benedict XVI leaves the Church?

Pope Benedict will be remembered for his teaching, both what he has said and what he wrote. His talks at the Wednesday audiences alone are a gold mine, so too are his homilies, and his biography of Jesus. The future generations may even appreciate him more, as his teachings become better known. His liturgical celebrations too are a lesson for us all.

Is there something else that stands out?

His love for the Church, in which he does want himself to be prominent, but only Christ. He reminds us of that central truth that Christ is at the centre; and that we preach not ourselves, but Christ and Him crucified.

3. Gerard O'Connell with Cardinal Turkson
(Rome, 2010)

Cardinal Turkson, why do think the Pope chose you to head of the Pontifical Council for Justice and Peace?
I don't know! I didn't have any indication whatsoever from the Holy Father as to why he chose me. I suppose it could be for the fact that there was no African cardinal or archbishop heading an office in the Roman Curia and maybe he chose me to fill that gap, but all this is conjecture.

For my part, I see this as part of a package which I accepted in deciding to go for the priesthood. When one accepts to be ordained a priest, one accepts in principle everything that belongs to this order of the priesthood, including becoming a bishop, a cardinal, being invited to serve the Church in any capacity.

In that sense I'm not bothered by what virtues or what qualities the Pope saw in me to appoint me to this position. I like to consider it as an invitation to serve the Church, just as I have been doing up to now as archbishop in the diocese of Cape Coast, Ghana, and as consultor to various Vatican offices.

What are your priorities as you take up this important post?
Stepping into this office I recognise that this is part of the ministry of the Holy Father. The Roman Curia is there to help the pope exercise leadership in the Church. Seeing in it that light I recognise that I cannot come to this work with my own agenda, I need to discover what the Holy Father intends for this office.

So when I got here, some four weeks ago, the first thing I tried to do was to seek an audience with the Holy Father, which I am still waiting for. I'd like to confer with him, to see whether he has got any particular vision or direction which he wants us to follow in this office. After that audience I will sit with my team here and try to unpack what it is the Holy Father is telling us.

Additionally, I think he has already given us something that the whole world is now buying into: the encyclical, *Caritas in Veritate*, and his Message for the World Day of Peace (1 January 2010). There's a lot of work for our office in those texts.

Furthermore as a council we'd like to study the last synod on Africa, and have the different officials look at it from their various areas of competences: human rights, the environment, armaments and so on, and explore what the encyclical has to say about each issue. We'd like to publish our findings in small pamphlets that could serve as study guides to help people delve deeper into the encyclical.

What do you see as the main challenges facing the Church today in the areas of social justice and peace?
It's difficult to respond because you put the two terms together: justice and peace.

Looked at it from where I come from, I think the relations between the southern and the northern parts of the hemisphere require a lot of attention to justice concerns, whether in business, investment, mining or other areas. The contracts fashioned between investors, entrepreneurs and businesses from the north and people in the south need to be inspired by justice and ethics, and concern for the well-being of people in the southern hemisphere. The same is true of aid-packages from the North to the South.

I think also of concerns for justice in relation to mining communities in the South. Today there is a lot of surface mining which leave behind gaping craters; they deprive people of the lands on which they were farming and create these craters and then say it is not cost effective to fill them in. That's just not fair!

Likewise, one could mention the impact of lumbering in various places, and the failure to carry out re-forestation.

Another great concern relates to the whole area of employment. One sees it, for example, when Europeans come to the South, but also here in Europe where one can rightly ask whether people receive just wages, whether there is downright exploitation in the workplace, and whether businesses are not being moved to other parts of the world and people here are left jobless. Greater concern for justice here would benefit everyone.

A second major area of concern relates the immigration from the South to the North. This could benefit from greater respect for justice. The demographic texture of many countries in the North lead people there to treat the arrival of newcomers with a certain amount of apprehension, and this has begun to affect a lot of legislation and raise concerns for justice.

Overall as I look across the world, I think it would be most important if the machinery that is responsible for situations of injustice and oppression were dismantled. I think that would be a more radical way of dealing with the various situations in the so-called poorer countries. Exploitation has a face. It is people who exploit; it's not just faceless machinery that exploits us. This is true also when we refer to globalisation; we have to look for the faces behind all the dazzling figures.

If all Christians understood that working for justice is an integral part of preaching and witnessing to the Gospel then probably some of the situations of injustice worldwide would be dismantled. Of course oppression in the world is not always caused by Christians, but if a lot of the Christians were moved by a real sense of conversion, which is an experience of God's love, and if they realised that they are called to witness to that love to other people then a lot of things could change in our world.

What about challenges in the area of peace?

I think the separation of peace from justice is for me a little bit false because for me where true justice prevails peace will automatically come in its stead. So in Africa we have learned to talk about peace as the fruit of justice, but where justice is absent or put to flight it is difficult to experience peaceful conditions of existence.

Peace and justice go very closely together. Where there is no justice it is very difficult to have peaceful conditions prevail. This is true for the North-South situations that I mentioned earlier, but it is equally true for South-South situations.

In the countries of the South one can talk about the relations between the political leaders and the people, and various instances of injustice. When political leadership is not just, is not fair and does not respect the rights of the people again there is no peace.

We talked much about the need for good leadership at the African synod. We need such leadership to change a lot of things on the African continent. In the synod's Message we challenged the political leaders in Africa to shape up or to shape out.

It is a fact that quite a few of the problems in some African countries have to do with political leadership. Either it exploits ethnicity, exploits religious differences and divergences, or just outright pitches on peoples' democratic rights and so on. So there's a lot that we can do together in this area.

In a recent interview with my friend John L. Allen of **National Catholic Reporter** *you said that when it comes to a black pope, "a lot of people say it doesn't matter, but the truth is that it would matter a lot" and, you added, "but I wouldn't want to be that first black pope. I think he'll have a rough time". What exactly do you mean?*

If you want me to put it in other words then the truth is that unfortunately – and I say this without any sense of bitterness, anger or anything

– the truth is that our world is still too colour sensitive. You cannot wish it away. It's not a criticism against anybody. It's something one sees, and it shows through, and the fact is that it would affect a lot of relationships, and a lot of ways of relating to people and all that would make the work (of a black pope) more difficult.

If you become pope then you are expected to exercise leadership for the universal Church, but with a tendency today to look at who, rather than at the issues, this would not be the best that you would wish for the Church.

But then who am I to determine what is good for the Church? If however it should happen by God's design that a black man becomes pope, then, of course, all of us would accept His will.

Cathedral of Saints Peter and Paul, Duoala, Cameroon

4. Brief biographical notes on Cardinal Polycarp Penzo, Archbishop of Dae-es-Salaam, Tanzania

Polycarp Pengo was born on 5 August 1944, the sixth of nine children – five boys and four girls, to first generation Christian parents in Mwazye, diocese of Sumbanga, Tanzania. In early life, he felt the vocation to the priesthood, and was ordained on 27 December 1970. Later, he studied for his doctoral thesis in theology in Rome, under the world-famous German moral theologian, Father Bernard Haring. Named bishop of Nachingewa, November 1983, he was promoted to co-adjutor to the archbishop of Dar-Es-Salaam, July 1990 and took charge of the diocese in 1992. Pope John Paul II created him cardinal in February 1998. He is a member of the Congregations for the Doctrine of the Faith and the Evangelisation of Peoples, and is also a member of the Pontifical Council for Inter-religious Dialogue.

This interview between Cardinal Pengo and Gerard O'Connell took place at the Headquarters of the Salvatorian Order in Rome, 20 October 2003, when over one hundred cardinals were in the eternal city to celebrate the silver jubilee of the election of Pope John Paul II.

Gerard O'Connell with Cardinal Polycarp Pengo of Tanzania

(Rome, 2003)

Your Eminence, I would like to begin by asking you what you consider the two or three major challenges facing the Church to-day?

I think one of the major problems, if I look at it from the background of my country and African countries in particular, would be the question of Islamic fundamentalism.

Islamic fundamentalism is really a big problem for the Church in the future. After we were liberated from Communism, I think this is the major problem facing the Church at this particular moment. And from the way the Church in Europe and North America, say in the

West, is looking at this problem, I don't think they realise the danger as much as we do, we who live in societies and communities that are very much involved with Islamic fundamentalism.

What's the breakdown in Tanzania?

Well, the Muslims always want to count much more than what they actually are but, generally, we count as follows in a total population of seven million people: Christians, that means Catholics and Protestants together, of all denominations, would count for 32-35%. The Muslims would like to think that they are 45% or more, but actually they are not more than 30%. So, Christians together outnumber the Muslims. The rest would be mainly the traditional religions, even though we also have some Hindus and followers of other Eastern religions, but they are a small minority.

But it all depends on the regions: on the coast and on the islands of Zanzibar, the Muslims are, of course, the vast majority; on the islands they are about 90%, if not more. But on the coasts, now that the Christians are coming more to the coasts of the mainland, they would now count for 40% or even 50%. As for the situation inside the country, there the Christians and the traditional religions are by far the majority.

So you see Islamic fundamentalism as the main challenge, and you think the Western churches really don't understand the seriousness of this. How is this?

I said that precisely because when you come to countries like Italy or France– traditionally Catholic countries, you see the way the Muslims are attacking, almost taking control of the situation; it indicates very much that the West doesn't realise what we are getting into.

The Muslims everywhere always come slowly, but then in the end they take control. And you can see what happens. Like in the USA, one can say whatever one wants, but behind it there was the question of Islamic fundamentalism on 11 September 2001; there is no doubt about it. And also the troubles we're getting into here in Europe, they are very much connected with that.

Now, by saying this, I am not condemning Islam as such, I'm just speaking about Islamic fundamentalism. That's the main challenge, and the main problem we have to face, and to try and find a solution to it.

You see this as a challenge for the next pontificate. I presume, therefore, that you will be discussing this issue before you enter the conclave – whenever that will be – to elect the next pope?

At least such a thing would be in my mind, yes!

What other major issue would there be, what other major challenge do you see facing the Church now?

The other issue is the question of secularisation. In our countries we are very much concerned about the continuation of the Catholic faith, but when you come to the West and try to tell them that we need help, maybe also of a financial kind, or whatever, they take the Church the way it is here. They look at their churches on Sundays, they are almost half empty, and there is no active life concerning the liturgy and so on, and they can hardly believe that our churches are too few and too small.

When we tell them we need money to build churches, and even seminaries to train future priests, they think it is a waste of money because in Europe and the United States the churches are not frequented enough and they think the same is bound to come to Africa and the Third World, and even to Latin America. Now that's a pessimistic attitude, and I don't think we're allowed to have it as Christians.

You mean this pessimistic attitude comes from secularisation?

That's right, as Christians we really cannot have this pessimistic attitude, and particularly as Catholics we must learn from the present pope; his idea was that there is a future for us, there is a future for us Catholics, and that future depends very much on what we do today. For this, I think that Pope John Paul II has really contributed a lot in our countries, because we are facing other problems too. I mentioned the lack of finances, but we also have problems like AIDS and many other problems too. But the message the Pope has told us is, "Do not be afraid! Do not be afraid, God is with us, Emmanuel, God is with us and because of that we continue – one could say, we almost continue – hoping against hope. But we continue hoping, and that keep us going. But, if we come to have this pessimistic attitude, then I would say we are fighting a losing battle, and then in the end everything will collapse. God's ways are many, of course, but we should also contribute something to the future if we want to ensure that our faith continues.

Secularisation is the second challenge that you see, is there a third?
The other challenge, the third challenge, would be this lack of balance between "the haves" and "the have nots." One would say that it is particularly between the North and the South. The financial situation of the world today is very much against the developing nations, and we know very well that a situation like that cannot continue. It cannot continue for ever. There will come a time when the bomb will blow up, and then there's a big threat to the peace and prosperity of the whole world. Why is that a concern for the whole Church? Well, it's obvious that when there's no peace, and when there's no equality in the distribution of the world's goods, then it's definitely a concern for us.

It's not that the Church wants to have a lot of money, but we want that there be peace so that people can progress and develop calmly, and in that way they will realise more easily that there is a God, who takes care of them. But if people are dying of hunger, if people have no houses to live in, then it's difficult to convince them that there's a God who loves them.

So this question of dire poverty, the utter poverty that is facing these developing countries is, or should be a concern for us as well.

You see this in Tanzania?
Yes, very much so. Yes!

You have already mentioned three major challenges facing the Church at this time. Do you see yet another, a fourth major problem or challenge at this time?
The final one that I would speak about is the lack of respect for life. In our countries – let me speak about Tanzania, we are faced with the problem of AIDS: people are dying and, of course, we try to find help to solve their problems – help from the West, but what we get are things like condoms, which we know very well is not helping, in fact it is making the situation even worse. When it comes to medication, we see that the question of money comes prior to the concern for life, saving life. In that way people, because of their poverty, despair of live, and those who have given them hope to live are the ones who are discouraging, and suggesting means which are not very encouraging.

This is a problem in developing countries, but the same problem is very much also in the North where you have the question of euthanasia and the question of abortion, and the way governments are supporting these questions, one realises that we are facing a very delicate, and a very horrifying situation.

That people can decide on abortion, which means putting the life of the unborn, of the innocent people at the mercy of those who already have life – the mother, the doctor and so on. Also the question of euthanasia: a person who has grown older seems to lose relevance, or because he is sick he loses meaning. This is not very encouraging for the future.

In any case, the coming pontificate will have to really struggle with this question of respect for human life. Of course, Pope John Paul

II has very much spoken about these questions, but it seems we are not having a solution, so that the pontiff that comes after him must continue on this line and must never give up. If he gives up, then there will be no voice which speaks of respect for human life.

That would be my fourth point.

These are really big issues because they touch all aspect of life. But what comes through all your answers is the very positive attitude with which you approach these questions: an attitude that shows you have a lot of faith, a lot of trust in God.

That's right.

I'm sure you must see some terrible situations, and yet you never despair.

No. In fact, I think because I have been very much influenced by Pope John Paul II, despair doesn't come into my mind. I face lots of problems; even if I were to speak of the situation in the archdiocese of Dar-Es-Salaam, there are problems, but I must say I have learned, you might say inherited from this pope, this optimistic, this strong faith that God will always be the winner, because God is there.

We face these problems, and this often reminds me of Our Lord himself on the cross; it seems that's the end of everything. But because we have faith, we know that he rose again, and we also, as St Paul says, "since Christ died and is risen, we will also rise, but how and when exactly, that of course is a matter of time, but we will have to pass through the cross and we are actually passing through this event of the cross".

When you look inside the Church, do you see situations that need addressing at this present time?

Yes. Inside the Church we have this question of the lack of vocations to the priesthood and the religious life, particularly in the North.

But even in our countries, where we have lots of vocations to the priesthood and the religious life, we are threatened by the fact that we do not have sufficient (number of) good formators for those vocations, and so a good number of priests are not qualified enough to face the actual challenges of life today, because they are not formed. And it's not their fault, because we do not have enough formators who are qualified enough.

So this question of the formation of formators is one of the big questions inside the Church today. You see when you have questions like we had in the Church in the USA in recent times – the question of child abuse, paedophilia and so on, it all goes back to the fact that the formators were not serious enough in giving formation, and perhaps they were already themselves deformed, and so perhaps they couldn't give the proper formation. We are now facing this.

In Africa and in Tanzania we may not face the question of paedophilia and sex abuse of the young because these are not the tendencies here, but we have the question of promiscuity, which is bound also to create problems in the future. We do not, in general, go for homosexuality, even though in Africa the problem is coming up, because you cannot isolate people.

For us, however, the major problem is promiscuity, a lack of faithfulness, even among priests. They do not go for little children, or boys, but they go for women, and it is rather sad to realise that among those people who are dying of AIDS, we have religious and we have priests who are dying of AIDS. So if priests come to that, which is going to encourage others to live a chaste life, so as to come out of this problem.

So, you can see that inside the Church itself we have a lot of things to mend, in order to create hope for the world of tomorrow.

Recently I interviewed the new archbishop of Manila, Gaudencio Rosales, and we spoke about their problems of sexual abuse of

minors by clergy in the Philippines, and how one might explain the fact that such problems have emerged in many countries from the USA and Canada to Ireland, the UK, Germany, Poland, Australia and so on. He recalled how this was the sixth crisis of this nature in the history of the Church, all linked to the misbehaviour of the clergy and, like you, he insisted very much on the importance of formators and putting the focus on spiritual renewal. I pointed out how in the last five conclaves, from 1939-78, when the cardinals came to elect a pope, three of the five popes chosen were actually men who, for one reason or another, had not been through the traditional seminary system – Pius XII, Paul VI and John Paul II. I asked him if God were not saying something to the Church today by this very fact. He admitted the possibility. I'd like to know your view?

I think so also. But maybe what God is trying to tell us is not that the seminary system is outdated, maybe not that. Perhaps he is trying to tell us that maybe we should work more on this if we want to get the real good results. Another thing, not one of the three popes you mentioned has ever said that the seminary system is outdated. None of them said so. In fact all three have very much insisted on serious formation, and they have done so because they believe if God has taken them from a system different to that of the seminary, the seminary is still good and valuable and what must be done is to improve it.

Or alternatively there could be alternative ways to prepare people for the priesthood?

That also.

Is there another issue that you see within the Church which needs to be addressed at the present time?

No, at the moment I'd prefer just to stay with that one.

At some time in the future you're going to find yourself entering the conclave to elect the next pope. What kind of characteristics will you be looking for in the candidate to be pope, what qualities will you be seeking?

I think I would be looking for a man of faith. Yes, exactly the kind of person that John Paul II is, a man of faith, because these challenges we've spoken of are not things that can end tomorrow, or the day after tomorrow, they are bound to continue, and without faith one is bound to lose sight of the goal and then one can make decisions that are detrimental to the life of the Church.

So he must be a real Peter, a rock on which the Church is founded, and this can only be done by a person of strong faith. Strong faith!

So that's the number 1 characteristic?

Yes, number 1, and it must also be a person who because of his faith is not swung by the winds of the world today. For in being swung by the winds of the world, there's the danger of following only the Western world.

But there's also the danger of being so involved in the problems of the Third World that you do not see the balance in between. So, I think, it must be a person who is realistic and can charge that here there is justice that must be followed. It's not simply because it is a question of the Third World that one goes supporting, because supporting the Third World in that way we have had lots of deplorable conditions, particularly among the leaders – presidents and leaders of the countries, so if you went supporting those you'd create a mess.

So it must be a man of clear discernment, who can say here there's something, whether it be from the West, or whether it be from the South or the North: when it is wrong, it is wrong, it is wrong.

Too often I have seen in the Church, particularly in our countries in the South, people tend to blame every bad thing on the North, as if the countries of the South are dirt poor also because the North has done this and this and this. But there are lots of mistakes and blame which should be put on the people themselves, and only when you put those two things together can you come out with a real judgement which is balance.

So the pontiff who is to come, because of this struggle between North and South, must not be swung by either the North nor the South, he must be somebody who is more balanced.

He must be a man of faith, who doesn't sway with the winds.

Yes, and then not swaying with the winds refers also to problems within the Church. Today, there are inside the Church many people arguing concerning the value of priestly celibacy, for example. Many people are thinking that the marriage of the clergy would solve the problems among the priests, but I don't think that would be the solution, because if you take the problems of paedophilia or promiscuity or whatever, it's not as if it is just found among priests, it's found in other sectors of society too but, because its found among priests it is trumpeted up and it would seem that only priests are committing these things.

But some would argue that you are here dealing with the two different questions: one, whether to allow priests to marry in an effort to overcome these problems; the other question, whether to return to the practice of the early Church and allow both married and celibate men to become priests.

It's true that these are different issues, but because of the present situation of the world, where hedonism and easy life seem to predominate, I would want the coming pope to continue insisting on priestly celibacy so that there is a voice which tells the world that where you are heading is not in this direction.

You see is as a counter-witness.

Yes, a counter-witness.

Apart from those you already mentioned, are there any other qualities or characteristics that you would be looking for in a candidate to be the next pope?

No, at the moment I cannot say,

How much is nationality a question?

That has not come to my mind before, but I think I can say something about it. My feeling is that after we have had a pope from outside Rome and Italy for a long period, I think the natural reaction of the Italians would be to have an Italian.

Is that right? No, I don't think it is right. But maybe it would be necessary to give the people who are around the pope a kind of break in this struggle. (??) I hope you understand what I am trying to say.

I've spoken to many cardinals over the past few years, and most think that nationality is no longer an issue. They said that up to the election of John Paul II it was an obstacle, but they no longer see it as such because they see that a non-Italian has brought a lot of riches to the whole Church and so on. Some told me that we've had nationalism in history and tribalism too, even in the Church; we've had situations where a man cannot be appointed bishop because he is of one particular tribe and so is not accepted by another. They said we can't have this kind of thinking at the centre anymore, we have to look at who the man is, what kind of character he is, what his vision is, rather than what is his nationality.

Yes, that is true, even though, I think, we have not yet completely overcome this feeling, and maybe by going too strongly against those feelings we maybe overdoing it. That is why I say we may need to play it, and have a break.

Most of the foreign cardinals I have spoken to share the ideas you mentioned: they want a man of faith, a really spiritual man, and a person who is not swayed by the winds of the world. They also look for a man of vision, and one who speaks a number of languages. They point to the fact that John Paul II spoke Italian and other languages, and actually visited more parishes in the Rome dioceses than any recent pope – over 300 parishes. As far as I can work out, most of the foreign cardinals – at least those whom I have spoken to, and a minority of the Italians say that nationality is no longer a real concern, they are more interested in finding a person with characteristics such as those I mentioned, and they say if we find these in an Italian, that's good, if we find them in an African, an Asian or Latin American then we'll go for that one. They note that in the UN, UNESCO, FAO, WHO and other international bodies, people of different nationalities with the appropriate skills hold the top jobs and do well, and they feel this can be true for the Church too.

I think that's the right attitude, and I wish it were as common among the cardinals as it would seem to be. But I am not sure that it's widespread.

Well I know that some Italian cardinals would like to have the papacy back, that's clear.

It's clear.

You've met the present pope many times, what personal memory of him stands out in your mind? You mentioned earlier how his words "Do not be afraid" have meant so much to you, but I'm sure you have some personal memories.

My personal memory: to me this pope has been everything. I was ordained priest during Paul VI's reign, in 1971. After that I became rector of the major seminary during the pontificate of John Paul II, and he's the one who appointed me bishop and created me cardinal. I don't know, I don't think he had any kind of favour for me, but given all this it's natural for me to have a particular attitude and liking towards him.

Beyond that, as I said, he has really taught me what it means to be a man of faith. Apart from what he has meant for anybody else, he has really played a great role in my life, and in my ministry wherever I went.

You mean he has been your formator?

Yes. Maybe I'd call him my rector. He has really been my formator, and I will remember him for the rest of my life; very positively and appreciating a lot the formation he has given me.

What stands out from the many personal meetings you've had with him?

The first time – if you forget the time he made me a bishop, when we were 20 in St Peter's – when he came to visit Tanzania, in Dar-Es-Salaam, in 1990, he arrived on 1 September and on 2 September, I was then coadjutor bishop to Cardinal Rugambwa, so I had to introduce the clergy and religious to the Holy Father because he wanted to speak to them. And so I had to give a short message, and when he started to reply, he said "I thank the bishop for the words he has just addressed to me" and then he repeated my name, "Polycarp" three times, and said, "Polycarp is a great name", and then he stopped at that.

That evening, we had supper in the cardinal's residence and I was supposed to be with the other guests, while the cardinal was with the pope. But then, when they entered the room, the Holy Father said, "We are not going to sit at the table unless the archbishop is here with us!" What message he had heard about the whole situation, I do not know, but people came running for me, and so I had to go and be at the table with him. That showed me, that besides being an archbishop and so on, the Pope had some kind of special eye.

And noticed you.

He noticed me So I was not very much surprised later when he made me a cardinal. It seems that there's something personal, something personal. Normally, at least so far as things have been turning out in Africa, a new cardinal is not chosen before the death of the previous one. But for me it happened that the previous one – Cardinal Rugambwa – died only 40 days before my nomination as cardinal.

So you must have been on the Pope's mind and list already?
Yes, he must have thought of it, and must have decided to make me a cardinal even when the old cardinal was still alive. It may be that I am reading too much into events but, of course, they are personal events and they mean a lot to me, even if the objective truth may not be there.

You've actually met the Pope many times?
Oh yes, many times, besides when we had ad limina visits; many times when I came to Rome for meetings of the councils and all that, and he invites us for lunch or for supper. There have been many times, but I cannot count them all.

Do you keep a diary of all this?
I didn't think of keeping a diary of this, and now I'm regretting that I haven't done so.

What has it meant to you to be a cardinal?
Well at first I was frightened about the whole idea, but then I said, after all God must be wanting something from me. And for me, a cardinal, according to the colour of the vestments, it means, it implies the idea of martyrdom.

Maybe, if I'm not too long, I'd like to give you the story of how I wanted to become a priest.

My name is Polycarp, and Polycarp was a bishop and martyr. As a child I was always going to tell my mother, "Mammy, I want to become a bishop and martyr because my name is Polycarp". My mother said, "Look here, you cannot become a bishop unless you are a priest". I said, "No, I don't want to become a priest. Polycarp was not a priest, he was a bishop and martyr, and that's my name".

Then, of course, gradually I came to realise what it means and because of that I entered the seminary, as a child of course, with the idea of becoming a bishop and martyr.

How old were you then?
I was eight or nine.

This was a junior seminary?
Even before. But when I went to seminary, and was more grown up, I came to understand what it means to be a bishop and maybe to be a martyr and that frightened me, and I said, "No, I'd be happy to become a priest. That's enough!" Then the events kept on coming up and so I was made a bishop and then I was given this red garment of martyrdom.

I'm not really like St Ignatius who was longing for martyrdom, I'm really scared about it, but it tells me that I must work unreservedly for the good of the Church, no matter what the demands, no matter what the condition of my life. Should it mean dying, well I am not praying for it, but I don't think I would have the choice of saying 'no', if I had to face it, since it would seem to realise that childish longing when I didn't realise what I was saying.

Did you tell the Pope this?
No, I didn't have the time to do so. I'd be shy to tell him this (laughs).

Have you many brothers and sisters?
We were born five brothers and four sisters, and I'm number six. I'm

the third of the brothers. At the moment, all my brothers have died, the younger ones and the elder ones, and two of my sisters have died. So there are only two sisters left, and now we are three left in the family, and my mother is still alive, she's 87 and can still move around. I can realise what she went through losing all the children.

Were your parents Christian?

Yes, both of them; my father and mother were both baptised already as infants. After their parents, they would be the first generation of Christians. My grandparents, of course, were from the traditional religions and they were converted by the missionaries who came to our country. (The White Fathers worked in my area, while the Holy Ghost Fathers worked in other parts of the country).

So you have a lot of nephews and nieces?

Yes, a lot of them. I can't count them (laughs), but one thing I'm happy about my family is that they realise what it means for me to become a priest and a bishop, differently from many of my fellow priests and even bishops. In my country, when you become a priest, and more so when you become a bishop, the family turns around you and they expect you to support them and kind of elevate them materially. But I am glad that this is not a problem for me, maybe because I was very clear from the very beginning. As a seminarian, I told them, "I'm going and you count me dead as a member of your family" and so I have not been bothered by that problem, even today.

You studied here in Rome, and specialised in moral theology.

That's right.

You studied under Fr Bernard Haring, the famous moral theologian?

Bernard Haring was the principal moderator of my thesis.

What was the subject of your thesis?

The thesis was on Christian morality and the Ujama society of Tanzania.

You mean the system under President Julius Nyerere?

Yes, Ujama, African socialism under Nyerere.

I interviewed Haring shortly before his death, but I would like to know what are your memories of this man?

I've very pleasant memories of him. He's another person who had a kind of liking towards me. In fact, I also visited him exactly two weeks before he died. I went to the place where he was staying in his community at Gars am Inn (???), in Southern Germany. At that time the superior of the community had told him, "No more visitors for you because your condition is not good enough to allow for visits". But then when I sent a message, three days before arriving there, the Superior told him. "An African cardinal wants to come to see you", and he said, "For him, even if I'm dying, I'll walk down and meet him, and, if you permit him, I'll allow him in my bedroom if I cannot walk down to meet him".

Actually, when I went there, he came down walking and gave us coffee. He couldn't eat much. He took a piece of cake, tried to eat it and I said, "No, it's giving you trouble". He said, "Yes". I said, "Now if you don't mind, I'll take a little of my piece and I'll take yours also" and I said, "So sit down." He was very glad about this.

So we talked for more than an hour, until the Superior, who was a bit worried, came and said, "Are you not feeling tired?", and he said, "No, don't worry, when I'm tired I will know and I will tell him to go". In fact, after an hour and 20 minutes he said, "Well I'll have to say bye, bye!"

Today, as you look back, is there one memory that stands out that you could share?

Some people believe that Bernard Haring was someone who stuck to his ideas and who would like to impose those ideas on all of his students. But knowing him from close up, and having worked with him, I realised that he's a person who can take the situation of having a difference of ideas.

We were talking one day with him about the question of polygamy in Africa, and he was speaking very much in favour even of baptising polygamists, but I told him, "Father, I'm sorry but I must disagree with you on this point, because I come from the background of this polygamous life. Even though my father was not a polygamist, and my grandfather was not, but I have relatives close enough to know what is going on". I said, "I would be very hesitant to baptise a situation of hatred and antagonism such as is found in polygamous families that I know, where you find the woman who is faced with the situation when her husband has another wife and says, 'OK, because I'm a woman, I have no voice'. But then the hatred that arises between that woman and the new one, and particularly between the children coming from these two women, even though they have the same father, it's not something you can say is a normal way of life. You'd really have to say, it must come to an end. I know the situation from inside this and I cannot simply go on and baptise a situation like than".

I was very impressed at the way he took all this, because he had written, even articles, trying to speak in favour of this baptism. That is one of my memories of Bernard Haring.

Bibliography

Achampong, Peter, *Christian Values in Adinkra Symbols*. self-published, no date.

Achebe, C. (1994) *Things Fall Apart*, 50th Anniversary edition. Anchor Books, U.S.A.

Achebe, N. (2011), *The Female King of Colonial Nigeria, Ahebi Ugbabe*, Indiana University Press, Indiana.

Akindes, Francis, Research Report no. 128. "The Roots of the Military-Political Crises in Cote d'Ivoire", Nordisk Afrikainstitutet, Uppsala, 2004.

Allen, Christopher. "Keeping it together", *The Australian*, July 14-15, 2012, pp. 11-12.

Allen, John L. Jr. (2009) *The Future Church, How Ten Trends are Revolutionizing the Catholic Church*. Image, New York.

Armand B. Depeyla, "Ange Kessi ordonne l'audition du cardinal Agre: Enquete sur l'assassinat du Gal Guei Robert", *La Nouvelle, 16 September, 2012*, pp. 1-4.

Ayitte, G.B.N., (1992). *Africa Betrayed*. St. Martin's Press, New York.

Bediako, K., (1995) *Christianity in Africa*. Maryknoll: Orbis Books.

Boahen, A. Abu (1987), *African Perspectives on Colonialism*. Johns Hopkins University Press, Maryland

Clements, S. 'The Catholic Church in Kenya: a Centre of Hope', *Pro Mundi Vita*, African Dossier 22 (July 1982), p. 6.

Ferguson, Niall. (2011) *Civilization The Six Killer Apps of Western Power*. Penguin Books, London.

Godobodo-Madikizela, P. (2003) *A Human Being Died That Night*. Mariner Books, Boston, New York.

Hastings, Adrian (1994) *The Church in Africa, 1450-1950*. Clarendon Press, Oxford.

Heyward, L. and Thornton J. (2007) *Central Africans, Atlantic Creoles, and the Foundation of America*, Cambridge University Press, New York.

Hill, Jonathon (2012) *Nigeria Since Independence*. Palgrave McMillan, New York

Hinchliff, P. "Africa" (chapter 13). In McManners, J. (ed.) (1990). *The Oxford Illustrated History of Christianity*. Oxford University Press, Oxford,

Isichei, E. (1995) *A History of Christianity in Africa, From Antiquity to the Present*. Society for Promoting Christian Knowledge, London.

Jackson, Robert H. & Rosberg, Carl G. (1982) *Personal Rule in Black Africa: prince, autocrat, prophet, tyrant*. University of California Press, Berkeley/ Los Angeles London.

Kalu, O. U. (2007) *African Christianity An African Story*. Africa World Press, Inc. Trenton, N.J., and Asmara, Eritrea.

Kertzer, David I. (1998) *The Kidnapping of Edgardo Mortara*. Vintage Books, New York, p. 130.

Kington, Tom "Holy See rebukes anti-Islam video", *The Age*. Thursday October 18, 2012, p. 14

Kobusingye, O. (2010) *The Correct Line? Uganda under Museveni*. AuthorHouse U.K. Ltd., Keynes.

Daniel A. Madigan, "Muslim-Christian Dialogue in Difficult Times". In Heft, James L., *Catholicism and Interreligious Dialogue*. Oxford University Press, 2012, pp. 57-87.

M.D. Markowitz (1973), *Cross and Sword: The Political Role of Christian Missions in the Belgian Congo 1908-1960*. Hoover Institution Press, Stanford.

John Mbiti, quoted in Kalu, Ogbu U.(ed.) (2007) *African Christianity, An African Story*. Africa World Press, Inc., p. 7.

Mbiti, J.S., "Christianity and Traditional Religions In Africa". In *International Rev. of Missions*, 59, 236, 1970:430-441.

Mickens, Robert. "Power behind the papal throne", *The Tablet*, 15 December, 2012.

Morris, J. (1978) *Farewell the Trumpets*. Faber and Faber, U.K.

Mudimbe, V.Y. (1988) *The Invention of Africa, Gnosis, Philosophy, and the Order of Knowledge*. Indiana University Press, Bloomington Indiana.

O'Connell, G. (2006) *God's Invisible Hand, The Life and Work of Francis Arinze, an Interview with Gerard O'Connell.* Ignatius Press, San Francisco.

Ogbu Kalu, (2008). *African Pentecostalism: an introduction.* Oxford University Press, Cape Town,

Ogbu Kalu, "Introduction: The Shape and Flow of African Church Historiography". In Kalu, O. (2007) *African Christianity, an African Story.* Africa World Press, Eritrea.

Oliver R. (1952) *The Missionary Factor in East Africa.* Longmans Green, London.

Oliver R. (1956) *How Christian is Africa?* Highway Press, London.

Osaghae, E. E. (1998) *Crippled Giant, Nigeria since Independence.* Indiana University Press, Bloomington Indiana.

Pakenham, T. (1991) *The Scramble for Africa.* Abacus, Great Britain.

Peel, M. (2012) *A Swamp Full of Dollars, Pipelines and Paramilitaries at Nigeria's Frontier.* Lawrence Hill Books, United Kingdom.

Perry/Obo, Alex, "The Warlord vs. the Hipsters. How a group of American filmmakers and 100 special-operations troops are pursuing Africa's most-wanted war criminal." *Time.* March 26, 2012, pp. 18-23.

Seftel, A. (2010). *Uganda, The Bloodstained Pearl of Africa and its struggle for Peace – From the pages of Drum.* Fountain Publishers, Kampala Uganda.

Takwa Z. Suifon, WARN Policy Brief, "Crisis in Cote D'Ivoire", July 27, 2004, West Africa Network for Peacebuilding.

Tchimbo, Raymond-Marie (1987). *Noviciat d'un évêque: huit ans et huit mois de captivité sous Sékou Touré*, Fayard.

Uganda Joint Christian Council Parliamentary Bulletin. May-August, 2011.

Uzukwu, E. E. (1996) *A Listening Church, Autonomy and Communion in African Churches.* Wipf and Stock, Eugene, Oregon.

Wilson, Peter. "Video hits Africa's papal push", *The Weekend Australian.* October 20-21, 2012, p. 13

Woolf, Stuart (1979) *A History of Italy 1700-1866: The Social Constraints of Political Change.*

Sources for further study

The Capuchin mission's history is exhaustively studied and chronicled in Graziano Saccardo [da Leguzzano] *Congo e Angola con la storia del missione cappuccino* (3 vols., Venice, 1982-84).

Sources with website access (ordered by access date)

2010

"Apartheid Lessons for Australia", *The Archdiocese of Canberra News and Events*, 22 November 2010, (http://www.cg.catholic.org.au/new/view_article.cfm?id=397), accessed 24 November 2010.

"Feature Interview: Cardinal Wilfred Napier ofm, ABC *Sunday Nights Home*, 18/09/2005, (http://www/abc/net.au/sundaynights/stories/s1461934.htm), accessed 24 November 2010.

"Pope signals shift on condom use by HIV infected", *Total Catholic*, Sunday 21 November 2010 (http://www.totalcatholic.som/tc/index.php?/201011211491/news/pope-signals-shift-o), accessed 24 November 2010.

"... what the cardinals believe ... Interview with Cardinal Napier", (http://www.cardinalrating.com/cardinal_66_article_442.htm), accessed 24 November 2010.

(http://en.wikipedia.org/wiki/Cape_Province), accessed 24 November, 2010.

"Religion and Apartheid", (http://countrystudies.us/south-africa/53.htm), accessed 24 November 2010.

"SA Church map", (http://www.sacbc.org.za/Site/index.php?option=com_wrapper&Itemid=209), accessed 24 November 2010.

2011

"St Gregory's College Notables", (http://gregs7479.5u.com/notables/okogie_profile.htm), accessed February 2011.

"Anthony Olubunmi Okogie", (http://en.wikipedia.org/wiki/Anthony_Olubunmi_Okogie), accessed November 2011.

"Anthony Olubunmi *Cardinal* Okogie Archbishop of Lagos", (http://www.catholic-hierarchy.org/bishop/bokogie.html), accessed November 2011.

"Cardinal Okogie", (http://www.catholicnewsagency.com/resourcephp?n=216), accessed November 2011.

"Okogie", (http://www.mercyjohnson.com/tag/anthony-cardinal-okogie), accessed November 2011.

Michael Jegede, "Garlands for a spiritual leader", *Daily Independent* (Lagos), 22 June 2011 (http://allafrica.com/stories/201106241032.html), Accessed November 2011.

"We Need a Revolution – Catholic Archbishop of Lagos Comments", (http://www.mercyjohnson.com/we-need-a-revolution-catholic-archbishop-of-lagos), accessed November 2011.

2012

"Why bombings will continue", December 28, 2011, (http://babajideallibalogun74.blogspot.com.au/2011/12/cardinal-okogie.html), accessed February 2012.

"Timeline of Important Events in Ghana's History", (http://www.ghanaweb.com/GhanaHomePage/history/timeline.php), accessed 20 February, 2012.

"Sub-Saharan Africa HIV and AIDS statistics", (http://www.avert.org/africa-hiv-aids-statistics.htm), accessed 13 March 2012.

(http://www.catholic-pages.com/hierarchy/cardinals_bio.asp?ref=82)

(http://www.catholic-pages.com/hierarchy/cardinals_bio.asp?ref=)

"Alexandre José Maria dos Santos", *religion wiki,* (http://religion.wikia.com/wiki/Alexandre_Jos%C3%A9_Maria_dos_Santos), accessed March 2012.

Dinis S. Sengulane and Jamie Pedro Gonçalves, "A calling for peace: Christian leaders and the quest for reconciliation in Mozambique", 1998, (http://www.c-r.org/our-work/accord/mozambique/calling-for-peace.php), accessed 13 March 2012

"Aro Confederacy", (http://en.wikipedia.org/wiki/Aro_confederacy) accessed 13 March, 2012.

"Sub-Saharan Africa", (http://en.wikipedia.org/wiki/Sub-Saharan_Africa), accessed 13 March 2012.

"Igbo Women's War", (http://en.wikipedia.org/w/index.php?title=Igbo_Women%27s_War&printable=yes), accessed 13 March 2012.

"Igbo people", (http://en.wikipedia.org/w/index.php?title=Igbo people&printable=yes), accessed 13 March 2012.

"Nigerian Civil War", (http://en.wikipedia.org/w/index.php?title=NIgerian_Civil_War&printable=yes), accessed 13 March 2012.

Tom Cooper, "Civil War in Nigeria (Biafra), 1967-1970", November 13,2003, *acig.org*, (http://www.acig.org/artman/publish/printer_351.shtml), accessed 13 March 2012.

"History of West Africa", (http://en.wikipedia.org/w/index.php?title=IHistory_of_WEst_Africa&printable=yes), accessed 13 March 2012

"Cardinals created by John Paul II (1988)", (http://www.gcatholic.com/hierarchy/data/cardJP2-4.htm), accessed 13 March 2012.

"Mozambique fears growth of Islam", *Mail and Guardian,* 5 July 1996, (http://mg.co.za/article/1996-07-05-mozambique-fears-growth-of-islam), accessed 13 March 2012.

John L. Allen Jr, "A papal contender grabs the spotlight", *National Catholic Reporter*, October 28, 2011, (http://ncronline.org/blogs/all-things-catholic/papal-contneder-grabs-spotlight), accessed 13 March, 2012.

"Alexandre Jose Maria Cardinal do Santos, O.F.M.", *Catholic Hierarchy*, (http://www.catholic-hierarchy.org/bishop/bsanajm.html), accessed 13 March 2012.

Mozambique News Agency AIM Reports, no. 311, 3 January 2006, (http://www.poptel.org.uk/mozambique-news/newsletter/aim311.html) accessed, 13 March, 2012.

Mozambique News Agency AIM Reports, no. 400, 27 April 2010, (http://www.poptel.org.uk/mozambique-news/newsletter/aim400.html), accessed 13 March 2012

"High Commision of the Republic of Mozambique to the United Kingdom of Great Britain and Northern Ireland", news 28 May 2010 (http://www.

mozambiquehighcommission.org.uk/?s=10&grupa=1&id=329&new=ok), accessed 13 March, 2012.

"Ending Insurgencies, building peace", *'Just World News' with Helena Cobban*, February 2, 2006, (http://justworldnews.org/archives/001707.html), accessed 13 March, 2012

Luis Benjamin Serapiao, "The Catholic Church and conflict resolution in Mozambique's post-colonial conflict, 1977-1992", *Journal of Church and State*, Spring, 2004, (http://findarticles.com/p/articles/mi_hb3244/is_2_46/ai_n29105402/pg_9/), accessed 19 March 2012.

(http://www.freebase.com/view/en/zavala_mozambique), accessed April 2012.

"Gonçalves", (http://www.hds.harvard.edu/cswr/resources/lectures/goncalves.html), accessed April 2012.

(http://www.state.gov/r/pa/ei/bgn/7035.htm), accessed April 2012

(http://en.wikipedia.org/wiki/Overseas_Province_of_Mozambique), accessed April 2012.

(http://www.infoplease.com/ipa/A0107804.html), accessed April 2012.

(http://encyclopedia.farlex.com/Mozambique), accessed April 2012.

(http://en.wikipedia.org/wiki/Peter_Turkson), accessed April 2012.

Peter Godwin, "Making Mugabe Laugh", *New York Times,* 18 April 2011, (http://www.nytimes.com/2011/04/19/opinion/19godwin.html?_r=1&ref=ivorycoast), accessed April 2012.

(http://en.wikipedia.org/wiki/Francis_Arinze), accessed 22 May 2012.

"Kivu conflict", (http://en.wikipedia.org/wiki/Kivu_conflict), accessed 22 May 2013.

"Education in Ghana", *Great Start Ghana,* (http://www.greatstartghana.org), accessed 27 July 2012.

"Education in Ghana", (http://ghanaweb.com.GhanaHomePage/education/, accessed 27 July, 2012.

"Ivory Coast", November 30 2011, *New York Times*, (http://topics.nytimes.com), accessed 24 July 2012.

Embassy of the United States Abidjan, Cote d'Ivoire, "National Daily Press

Review Archive", December 29, 2006, (http://abidjan.usembassy.gov), accessed 24 July 2012.

Notisia Katoliko Korsou, "Pope Benedict sees changing hearts as ultimate challenge for African Church", 5 October 2009, (http://notisiakatoliko-korsou.clogspot.com.au), accessed 24 July 2012.

"Ghana's 1st Cardinal-designate marvels at God's timetable", 28 September 2003, ZENIT The World seen from Rome, (http://www.zenit.org), accessed 24 July 2012.

"Cape Coast rejoice with Cardinal Turkson", *Modern Ghana*, (http://www.modernghana.com), accessed 24 July 2012.

Robert Mickens, "The Rising Star of Justice and Peace", (http://jaazsw.org), accessed 24 July 2012.

"Prayers can't bring peace unless Ghanaians desire same", *Joy Online*, (http://politics.myjoyonline.com), accessed 24 July 2012.

Mark Oppenheimer, "A strongman found support in prominent conservative Christians in the U.S.", *New York Times*, 12 April 2011, (http://www.nytimes.com), accessed 24 July 2012.

"Nigeria", (https://www.cia.gov/library/publicawtions/the-world-factbook/geos.ni.html), accessed 1 August 2012

"French undermine Ivory Coast, cardinal charges", *Catholic Culture,* 24 November 2004, Trinity Communications 2012, (http://www.catholicculture.org), accessed 1 August 2012.

"The social credit lessons are based on the social doctrine of the Church: we must take action to settle the problem of poverty", "The time for economic liberation has come: encouraging words of Cardinal Agre at our Congress and the Synod", (http://michalejournal.org), accessed 1 August 2012.

"A mission has been confided to me: to be an apostly for the Pilgrims of St. Michael", (http://michalejournal.org), accessed 1 August 2012.

"Cardinal Bernard Agre", *Catholic African World,* (http://www.catholicafricanworld.org), accessed 1 August 2012.

"Ivorian Cardinal appeals to French to restore calm", 20 November 2004, *The Tablet,* (http://m.thetablet.co.uk/article/1982), accessed 1 August 2012.

"Ivory Coast Prelate raps French", *Catholic Culture*, 22 November 2004, (http://www.catholiculture.org), accessed 1 August 2012.

"Ghana", (https://www.cia.gov/library/publications/the-world-factbook/geos.ni.html, accessed 1 August 2012.

"South Africa", (https://www.cia.gov/library/publications/the-world-factbook/geos.ni.html), accessed 1 August 2012.

"Mozambique", (https://www.cia.gov/library/publications/the-world-factbook/geos.ni.html), accessed 1 August 2012.

"Cote D'Ivoire", (https://www.cia.gov/library/publications/the-world-factbook/geos.ni.html), accessed 1 August 2012.

"Uganda", (https://www.cia.gov/library/publications/the-world-factbook/geos.ni.html), accessed 1 August 2012.

Papa Cy, "Ghana Catholic Bishop's Conference Engages the Electoral Commission (EC), 20 March 2012, *Ghana Catholic Bishops Conference,* (http://cbcgha.org), accessed 2 August 2012.

"Consolidated Appeal for Cote d'Ivoire 2012", 25 January 2012, *OCHA*, (http://unocha.org/cap/appeals/consolidated-appeal-c%C3%B4te-divoire-2012-english-version), accessed 3 August 2012.

"Guide to the conflict and peace building in Ivory Coast", *Insight on Conflict,* (http://www.insightonconflict.org), accessed 3 August 2012.

"Global Christianity, A Report on the Size and Distribution of the World's Christian Population", December 19, 2011, (http://www.pewforum.org/Christian/Global-Christianty-exec.aspx), accessed 4 August 2012.

"Cameroon", (https://www.cia.gov/library/publications/the-world-factbook/geos.ni.html), accessed 5 August 2012.

"Celebrating women in leadership", *Lokoleyacongo*, 22 August 2012, pp. 1-7, accessed 18 October 2012.

Ongey, Grace. "Cardinal Tumi has never been interested becoming President of Cameroon, Archbishop Emeritus reaffirms." *L'Effort Camerounais,* August 2009, accessed 8 October 2012.

"What makes Kinshasa Tick." *Lokoleyacongo*. 24 June 2012, pp. 7-14, accessed 18 October 2012.

"The Congo's Vision Loss", *Lokoleyacongo*, 14 May 2012, pp. 14-16 accessed 18 October 2012.

"Is the world ready for a democratic republic of Congo?" *Lokoleyacongo*, 14 May 2012, accessed 18 October 2012.

Cardinal Monsengwo Pasinya, "Declaration of Cardinal L. Monsengwo Pasinya on Presidential Elections in DRC", *Africa Faith and Justice Network*, 13 December 2011 (http://www.afjn.org/focus-campaigns/promote-peace-d-r-congo/29-news/1021-declaration), accessed 18 October 2012.

Jukali Kambale, "Cardinal Monsengwo's controversial post-poll statement", 14 December 2011, *Africa Review*, (http://www.africareview.com), accessed 18 October 2012.

"Synod of Bishops-Day Nine", October 17, 2012. (http://incaelo.wordpress.com), accessed 18 October 2012.

"Synod of Bishops – Day Six", October 15, 2012, (http://incaelo.wordpress.com), accessed 18 October 2012.

"Guiding the Synod – the presidents-delegate", June 30, 2012, (http://incaelo.wordpress.com), accessed 18 October 2012

Nieves San Martin, "Church in Congo Begins Non-Violence Program", *EWTN News*, 18 January 2012, (http://www.ewtn.com/vnews/getstory.asp?number=117431), accessed 18 October 2012.

"Call for the cessation of the war and the respect of the territorial integrity of the DR Congo", 22 November 2012 (http://www.cafod.org.uk/content/view/line/7521), accessed 23 November 2012.

(http://en.wikipedia.org/wiki/Laurent_Monsengwo_Pasinya), accessed November 2012.

"A discussion with Archbishop John Onaiyekan of Abuja", *Berkeley Centre for Religion, Peace and World Affairs*, (http://berkleycentre.georgetown.edu/intervews), accessed 23 November 2012.

"African Church Leaders outraged by escalating violence in DR Congo", *ICN Independent Catholic News*, 22 November, 2012 (http://www.indcatholicnews.com/news.php?viewStory=21483), accessed 23 November 2012.

2013

Nussbaum, Martha (1998), C. *Sex and Social Justice*. Oxford University Press. p. 122, (http://books.google.com.au/books?id=7zoaKIolT9oC&pg=PA119&redir_esc=y#v=onepage&q&f=false), accessed 16 May 2013.

"Rawlings: The Legacy", *BBC News,* 1 December 2000. (http://news.bbc.co.uk/2/hi/africa/1050310.stm), accessed 20 May 2013.

Irving Hexam, "Religious Extremism in Sub-Saharan Africa", March 2002, (http://www.refworld.org/pdfid/3daec69d4.pdf), accessed 20 May 2013.

Roger Boyles, "One warlord down, plenty more where he came from", *The Australian,* 16 March 2012, (http://theaustralian.newspaperdirect.com/epaper/viewer.aspx), accessed 22 May 2013.

"Catholic Clergy calling for Mass Civil Disobedience in Congo", *Lokoleyacongo*, 4 February 2012, accessed 22 May 2013.

Iraê Baptista Lundin, "The peace process and the construction of reconciliation post conflict – the experience of Mozambique", Presented in Barcelona under the International Seminar "Experiences of Penal Alternatives in Peace Processes" – Barcelona 27-28 February 2004 (http://escolapau.uab.cat/img/programas/procesos/seminario/semi008.pdf), accessed 22 May 2013.

"Martin Luther King on Our March to Freedom". *Lokoleyacongo*, 6 May 2012, accessed 22 May 2013.

"The real results of the Congo Election", *Lokoleyacongo*, 22 February 2012, accessed 22 May 2013

"Guilio Andreotti", *The Economist,* (http://www.economist.com/news/obituary/21577350-giulio-andreotti-many-times-prime-minister-italy-died-may-6th-aged-94-giulio-andreotti), accessed 23 May 2013.

(http://www.indexmundi.com/facts/south-africa/population-density), accessed 25 May 2013.

(http://www.tradingeconomics.com/nigeria/population-density-people-per-sq-km-wb-data.html), accessed 25 May 2013.

Kathleen Hunter, "Cardinal Turkson wouldn't be the first African Pope", *Polymic – Culture,* (http://www.policymic.com/articles/29018/cardinal-peter-turkson-wouldn-t-be-the-first-african-pope), accessed 11 June, 2013.

(http://www.mevlana.net/), accessed 11 June 2013.

(http://www.bu.edu/afam/faculty/john-thornton/john-thorntons-african-texts/), accessed 13 June 2013.

Patrick Radden Keefe, "Buried Secrets: How an Israeli Billionarie wrestled control of one of Africa's biggest prizes." (http://www.newyorker.com/reporting/2013/07/08/130708fa_fact_keefe), accessed June 2013.

Acknowledgements

A book like this doesn't happen without support. Finding, tracking and making contact with the cardinals was one thing, securing interviews was another. A letter of introduction from the Archbishop of Melbourne, Dr Denis Hart, was fundamental to the success I had in securing interviews, as was the collegiality that exists between members of the Society of Jesus (the Jesuits) across the world. Those connections began with Gerald O'Collins, former professor at the Pontifical Gregorian University, uncle to my husband and friend to all. The admiration that some of his past African students continue to have for him made them willing to assist me in this endeavour. I will remain ever indebted to Gerald and to his friends, particularly Ezequiel Gwembe (in Mozambique) and Paul Bere (in Ivory Coast) and to two others, Gerard O'Connell and Robert Mickens, both journalists and renowned writers, who were very kind to me in Rome. Furthermore, for the transcription of the interviews I must thank Laura Astasiadis who made time in her outrageous schedule to type up interviews; for on-going enthusiasm, encouragement, interest and support I must thank my father Barry Ninham who has made the subjects covered here a life-long passion and ignited the same interests in me; my mother-in-law Moira Peters for her eternal optimism, my friends and special mentors Professor John Molony and Dr John Slaughter for reading my work and for their faith; my children for the love that keeps me going every day, and my brothers for their unstinting humanity. In the end this book is dedicated to my husband Jim, whom I think I have learned to love better since I started writing it.

INDEX

Adamawa Empire, 269

African Bishops' Synod (Rome), 107, 130, 188,

African National Congress (ANC), 34,

African Prisons' Project, 104, 120

African traditional religion, 81, 87, 95-6, 239, 240

Africanisation, 65, 125, 132, 134

Afrikaners, 42

Agrè, Bernard Cardinal, 213-4, 218-9, 221, 226, 241-2, 259-268

Ahoua, Bishop Raymond, 214, 215-233

Amin, (Idi Amin Dada), 24, 103, 106, 111, 115, 120, 122, 128

Amissah, John Kodwo, 191

Andreotti, Guilio, 144, 157

Anglican 324, 87, 124, 130, 141, 142, 156, 324

Annan, Kofi Atta, 186, 206

Antonelli, Ennio Cardinal, 196

Apartheid, 33-5, 37, 39, 41-2, 48, 51, 53, 55, 57, 67, 126, 145

Arinze, Francis Cardinal, 7, 20, 24, 61, 62, 63-100, 111, 112, 114, 206, 226, 239, 240, 266, 290, 307, 321

"Back to Africa" Movement, 181

Baker, Samuel, 101, 102

Baldachino, 64

Bantu, 133, 296, 301

BBC, 142, 156, 182

Bernini, Gian Lorenzo, 64

Bishops' Conference, South African 35; Nigerian 79; Mozambique 155; Ghana Catholic 182; Italian 204; Ivorian 219, 248; Cameroon 289; 292; DRC Congo 308, 319

Blacks, 33-4, 37, 43-4, 55, 207

Boers, 14, 33

Buddhists, 81

Bush, US President George W., 144, 257

CAFDIL, 186, 207

Camp Boiro, 167

Canon Law, 12, 46-7, 82, 259, 290

Capuchins, 11, 14, 302

Caritas Internationalis, 91

Caritas Mozambique, 138, 155

Caritas National in Africa, 308, 319, 320

catechist, 12, 22, 23, 125-6, 149, 169, 173, 176, 199, 200, 227, 236, 237, 239

Catholic Women's League, 56

Catholic Women's Organisation, 97

Cesari, Giuseppe, 64

Chissano, Mozambican President, 136, 137, 139, 143, 144, 155, 157, 161

Christ, 173, 237-9, 248, 261, 277, 282, 284, 291, 299-300, 301, 323, 325, 336

Christ the King Cathedral, 116

Comboni Fathers, 124

Congregation for Catholic Education, 182, 304

Congregation for Divine Worship and Discipline of the Sacraments, 82

Congregation for the Evangelisation of Peoples (*Cor Unum*), 167

Constitution of the Church, 24

Corsa, 43

crucifix, 114, 227

Da Fonseca, Artur, 142

De Gaulle, Charles, 166,

Decree on Missionary Activity (*Ad Gentes*), 24

Dhlakama, Alfonso, 143

Dominicans, 126-7

Dos Santos, Alexandre Josè Marion Cardinal, ch. 4

Du Bois, W.E.B., 181

Dutch East India Company, 32

Elmina Castle, 187

Eucharist, 175, 182

evangelisation, 11, 12, 20, 35, 83, 126, 134, 168, 174, 182, 188, 196, 280, 289, 304-5, 331,151, 167

Fantis, 21

Francis, Pope, 312

Francis, St, 51, 52, 58

Franciscans, 45, 47, 51-3, 58, 127, 141, 148-9, 151, 185, 191-2

Freedom Charter, 34

FRELIMO, 136, 141, 144, 157-59, 160, 162

Gantin, Bernardin Cardinal, 206

Garvey, Marcus, 181

Gbagbo, Ivory Coast President Laurent, 213, 219, 224, 233, 246, 247

Goldberg, Denis, 34

Gonçalves, Archbishop Jamie Pedro, 134, 136, 137, 138, 141-5, 156, 158-164

Gospel, 14, 20, 23, 26, 65, 91, 121, 124, 125, 169, 172-4, 176, 189, 190, 225, 241, 248, 275, 293, 315, 328

Grant, James, 101, 102, 111

Heaven, 64, 65, 80, 175, 238, 299

Hindus, 81, 332

HIV, 24, 31, 59, 71-2, 101, 103, 115, 120, 121, 133, 179, 211, 269, 301, 352

Holy Ghost Fathers, 265, 279-80, 346

Holy See, 134, 148, 150

Holy Trinity, 112

Houphouët-Boigny, Ivory Coast President Fèlix, 212-3, 224, 260

Hurley, Archbishop, 58

Ibos, 59

IMBESA (Regional Conference for Southern Africa), 48, 49

Islam, 16, 17, 76, 95, 96, 102, 133, 166, 224, 286, 331, 332, 333

Islamic State, 166

Jesuit, 11, 14, 22, 149, 151, 154, 219, 224, 226, 272, 275-6, 280, 302, 307, 361

Jews, 81, 92, 146, 157, 263, 316
Joseph of Cluny, St, 150

Kasavubu, Joseph, 303
Kathrada, Ahmend, 34
King, Martin Luther, 9, 181
Kingdom of Luba, 302
Kiplagat, Bethuel, 142
Kiwanuka, Bishop Joseph, 24, 114-5
Koney, Joseph, 111, 115

Lefebvre, Archbishop Marcel, 265
Leopold, King of Belgium, 302
Lincoln, Abraham, 9
Livingstone, David, 13, 102, 111, 180
Lord's Resistance Army, 24, 103, 111
Lumumba, Patrice, 303

Mahama, John Dramani, 181
Malinke Empire, 166
Mandela, Nelson, 34, 56
Marian Fathers, 279-80, 286
Martino, Renato Cardinal, 196
Marxist, 135
McCann, Owen Cardinal, 49
Meraud, Pierre, 14
Michelangelo, 63, 64, 77, 232
Mill Hill Fathers, 124
Mills, John Atta, 181
Milner, Alfred, 33
Ministry After Custody, 120
missionaries, 32, 67, 87, 94, 124, 125, 126, 135, 141, 148-52, 154, 169, 171-2

MNC National, 303
Mobuto, King Sese Seko Kuku Ngbendu wa Za Banga, 303
Monsengwo Pasinya, Laurent Cardinal, Ch. 9
Mormon, 68
Moses, 93
Mugabe, Zimbabwean President Robert, 38, 157
Museveni, Yoweri, 103, 115, 120, 122
Muslim, 10, 17, 31, 59, 60, 81, 96, 101, 109, 124, 165, 170, 171, 175-6, 179, 188-9, 211, 222, 223, 240, 244-6, 264, 269, 279, 286, 294, 299, 301, 332
Mutesa, King Walugembe Mukaabya, 102, 103

Napier, Wilfred Fox Cardinal, Ch. 1
Napoleon Bonaparte, 59
Nascimento, Alexandre do Cardinal, 7, 71, 106, 312
National Socialist Party (NAZI), 34, 55
Nigerian Civil War (War in Biafra), 24, 60, 70, 74-5, 91
Nkrumah, Kwame, 180-2, 213
Nyado, Steven, 49

Obama, US President Barack, 186, 206, 244
Obote, Ugandan President Apolo Milton, 24, 103, 111, 113, 115, 120, 122, 128
Okello, Tito, 103
Okogie, Anthony Olubunmi Cardinal, 7
Organisation of African Unity (OAU), 181

Ouellet, Marc Cardinal, 196
Outtara, Ivory Coast President Laurence, 218-9, 224

paedophilia, 72, 74, 337, 340
Pan Africanism, 22, 182, 213
Patrick Fathers, 283
Pengo, Polycarp Cardinal, 228, 331
Pentecostal, 124
Pieta (Michelangelo), 63, 77, 231
Polygamy,17, 18, 221-243, 255, 348
Pontifical Biblical Institute (Rome), 182, 304
Pontifical Commission for the Cultural Heritage of the Church, 182
Pontifical Committee for International Eucharistic Congresses, 182
Pontifical Council for Culture, 98, 304
Pontifical Council for Family, 98
Pontifical Council for Inter-religious Dialogue, 331
Pontifical Council for Justice and Peace, 73, 168, 182, 184, 191, 326
Pontifical Council for Promoting Christian Unity, 182
Pontifical Council for the Pastoral Care of Health Care Workers, 35
Pontifical Urban University, 61, 167
Pope Benedict XVI, 62, 265, 304
Pope Gregory XVI, 13
Pope John Paul II (Karol Wojtyla), 49, 62, 78, 114-5, 129, 143, 156, 182, 184, 265, 308, 331, 334, 336
Pope Urban VIII, 64
PR Sapo, 56
Propaganda Fide, 11, 83, 172, 289

Protestant, 87, 101, 128, 156, 279, 293, 294, 299, 301, 332
Protestant Consuelo Cristao de Moçambique (Christian Council of Mozambique), 156

Rawlings, Jerry, 181, 182
RENAMO, 136, 142-144, 155-163
Rhodes, Cecil, 14, 37, 86
Rigali, Justin Cardinal, 196
Roman Curia, 66, 71, 72, 77
Roosevelt, US President Franklin, 9

San Egidio, 144, 161, 162
Sarah, Robert Cardinal, ch. 5
SECAM (Symposium of Episcopal Conferences of Africa and Madagascar), 80
Second Vatican Council (Vatican II), 13, 15, 17, 23, 24, 45, 46, 62, 70, 73, 74, 75, 77, 89, 99, 100, 127, 128, 129, 130, 134, 141, 144, 152, 153, 225, 226, 240, 241, 265, 278, 287, 288
Second World War, 23, 111, 212, 279
Sengulane, Bishop Dinis,134, 143, 156
Sisulu, Walter, 34
Slave Trade (non-specific), 15, 29, 32, 180; trans-Atlantic, 12, 13, 134, 180, 187; Arab, 14, 302; British, 32, 59, 134; Portugese, 11, 12, 14, 133
Speke, John Hanning, 101-2, 111
St Anthony's-on-Hudson, 182, 185, 191
St Joseph's Cathedral (Cape Coast), 187
St Joseph's Cathedral (Bamfoussam), 277

INDEX

367

St Patrick's Cathedral (Melbourne), 35, 38
St Peter's (Rome), 24, 63, 64, 73, 74, 305-7, 343
St Pius X, Society of, 265
Stanley, Henry Morton, 101, 102, 111, 180
Stanley, John, 102
Streicher, Henri, 13
Studium Biblicum Franciscanum of Jerusalem, 167
Swahilis, 133
syncretism, 221, 224, 225, 237-8, 239, 284

Tansi, Cyprian Michael, 24, 61, 65, 69-70, 77, 80, 83
Tchidimbo, Archbishop Raymond Marie, 171
Togoland Trust Territory, 179
Tourè, Ahmed Sèkou, 166, 171
Tourè, Samory, 166, 167, 179
Trappists of Marianhill, 32

Tumi, Christian Wiyghan Cardinal, Ch. 8, 308
Turkson, Peter Kodwo Appiah Cardinal, 73, Ch. 6, 290, 305, 311, 326

UNESCO, 214-5, 342

Van Sambeek, Jan, 13
Vilanculo, Artur Lambo, 142

Wamala, Emmanuel Cardinal, 24, 71, 76, Ch.3
Wassoulou Empire, 166
White Fathers, 24, 116, 124-5, 346

Xavarians, 280
Xhosa, 32

Yago, Bernard Cardinal, 260
Yoruba, 22, 59

Zulu, 32

www.ingramcontent.com/pod-product-compliance
Lightning Source LLC
Chambersburg PA
CBHW052048230426
43671CB00011B/1836